The New Political Economy of Land Reform in South Africa

Adeoye O. Akinola · Irrshad Kaseeram ·
Nokukhanya N. Jili
Editors

The New Political Economy of Land Reform in South Africa

palgrave
macmillan

Editors
Adeoye O. Akinola
University of Zululand
KwaDlangezwa, South Africa

Irrshad Kaseeram
University of Zululand
KwaDlangezwa, South Africa

Nokukhanya N. Jili
University of Zululand
KwaDlangezwa, South Africa

ISBN 978-3-030-51128-9 ISBN 978-3-030-51129-6 (eBook)
https://doi.org/10.1007/978-3-030-51129-6

This Palgrave Macmillan imprint is published by the registered company Springer Nature Switzerland AG
The registered company address is: Gewerbestrasse 11, 6330 Cham, Switzerland

Contents

List of Contributors

Adeoye O. Akinola University of Zululand, KwaDlangezwa, South Africa

Modupe A. Daramola University of KwaZulu-Natal, Pietermaritzburg, South Africa

Desan Iyer University of Zululand, KwaDlangezwa, South Africa

Nokukhanya N. Jili University of Zululand, KwaDlangezwa, South Africa

Irrshad Kaseeram University of Zululand, KwaDlangezwa, South Africa

Sultan Khan University of KwaZulu-Natal, Durban, South Africa

Tumo Maloka University of Limpopo, Limpopo, South Africa

Mfundo M. Masuku University of Mpumalanga, Mbombela, South Africa

Victor H. Mlambo University of Zululand, KwaDlangezwa, KwaZulu-Natal, South Africa

Luyanda Mtshali University of Zululand, Kwadlangezwa, South Africa

Mandla Mubecua University of Zululand, KwaDlangezwa, KwaZulu-Natal, South Africa

Oluwole Olutola University of Johannesburg, Johannesburg, South Africa

Lizelle Ramaccio Calvino University of Zululand, KwaDlangezwa, South Africa

Stella Chewe Sabi University of Zululand, KwaDlangezwa, South Africa

Mzingaye Brilliant Xaba Postdoctoral Research Fellow - SARChI Research Chair in the Sociology of Land, Environment and Sustainable Development, Department of Sociology and Social Anthropology, Stellenbosch University, Cape Town, South Africa

Listen Yingi University of Limpopo, Mankweng, South Africa

List of Figures

CHAPTER 1

Expropriation and the Discontent of Land Reform in South Africa: An Introduction

Adeoye O. Akinola, Irrshad Kaseeram, and Nokukhanya N. Jili

This book presents an opportunity to contribute to the intellectual exposition on land and to reconceptualize land and land policy in the 'new' South Africa (i.e. a democratic country after the end of apartheid). This becomes pertinent due to the failure of existing policy, which accounts for South Africa's efforts to 're-package' land reform, under the populist's tag, land expropriation without compensation (LEWC). Pessimists still struggle to grasp why it took the government about 25 years to accept the failure of the market-driven reform programmes, particularly its incapacity to redress historical land dispossession and

A. O. Akinola (✉) · I. Kaseeram · N. N. Jili
University of Zululand, KwaDlangezwa, South Africa
e-mail: AkinolaA@unizulu.ac.za; aoakinola@uj.ac.za

I. Kaseeram
e-mail: KaseeramI@unizulu.ac.za

N. N. Jili
e-mail: JiliN@unizulu.ac.za

A. O. Akinola et al. (eds.), *The New Political Economy of Land Reform in South Africa*,
https://doi.org/10.1007/978-3-030-51129-6_1

the attendant structural violence that characterized post-apartheid South Africa. Furthermore, land policy has faced the challenge of outlining long-term planning scenarios or effective implementation strategies because of the complicity of the issue and government's lacklustre attitude towards land reform. The pressures of democratization and globalization impede effective policy in the land sector, which is founded on land restitution, redistribution and a tenure system.

As stipulated in the 1997 White Paper on Land Reform, land restitution targets the return of the land (or otherwise compensating victims of land seizures) lost since the June 1913 Land Act due to racially discriminatory laws. Land redistribution makes provision for previously disadvantaged, poor and underprivileged people to buy land with the help of a Settlement/Land Acquisition Grant, and land tenure reform 'aims to bring all people occupying land under a unitary, legally validated system of landholding' (Department of Land Affairs, 1997: 7). Building on the 1997 White Paper on Land Reform, the government in 2014 formed the current land policy on four pillars: restitution of land rights; redistribution of land; land tenure reform; and development of the land (Department of Rural Development and Land Reform, 2014). However, it has been accepted unanimously that the government's performance in these four elements remains very low and certainly fell short of public expectation.

At the advent of majority rule in 1994, black South Africans were restricted to only 13% of the national land, which constituted the former Bantustan land (Ciskei, Gazankulu, Kangwane, KwaNdebele, KwaZulu, Lebowa, Qwaqwa, Transkei, Venda and Bophuthatswana) (Department of Rural Development and Land Reform, 2013: 8). Decades after majority rule, this skewed land arrangement still holds sway. In 2018, the land audit reveals that,

> Whites own 26 663 144 ha or 72% of the total 37 031 283 ha farms and agricultural holdings by individual landowners; followed by Coloured at 5 371 383 ha or 15%, Indians at 2 031 790 ha or 5%, Africans at 1 314 873 ha or 4%, other at 1 271 562 ha or 3%, and co-owners at 425 537 ha or 1%. (Department of Rural Development and Land Reform, 2018: 2)

Indeed, rethinking the existing land policy is a matter of necessity and not of choice. However, land reform must represent a radical and rapid break from the past without significantly disrupting agricultural production and food security. The state must mobilize resources to reverse both the human and material conditions of those displaced by previous land policies (Department of Rural Development and Land Reform, 2014: 1).

As enshrined in the 2011 Green Paper on Land Reform, 'national sovereignty is defined in terms of land. Even without it being enshrined in the country's supreme law, the Constitution, land is a national asset' (Department of Rural Development and Land Reform, 2011: 1). The policy document conceives social cohesion as a direct function of land use, access and ownership.

While the struggle against apartheid was not rooted in land issues, Kariuki (2009) maintains that the land issue was a major instrument of mass mobilization against foreign domination and support for the attainment of democracy in 1994. Failure of many African states, like South Africa, to address the land and development nexus accounts for the national struggles for access to land that have been experienced on the continent in the mid-2000s (Moyo, 2007). More than a decade after Moyo's presentation, the South African states have been unable to resolve the land question by redressing land inequality, occasioned by the history of dispossession during colonialism and apartheid.

While South Africa adopted a liberal democratic constitution after apartheid, the seeming radicalization of its constitutional provisions has failed to significantly address unequal access to land and disempowerment of black people. The Department of Rural Development and Land Reform (2014: 2) reiterates the fact that,

> Colonialism and Apartheid brutalized African people, turning them hostage to perennial hunger and want, and related diseases and social strives and disorders. Thus, rural development, agrarian change and land reform must be a catalyst in the ANC-led government's mission to reverse this situation.

This has not been the case, but instead, land conflict continues, illegal occupation and land/farm evictions persist, while the majority of blacks remain very poor and vulnerable.

Furthermore, the land reform, funded on a neoliberal policy framework, tagged 'willing buyer, willing seller' approach, marginalizes both the rural and urban poor (Moyo, 2007). The willing buyer, willing seller approach has faced budget restraints, which has manifold manifestations: internal allocation of budget for competing priorities in the land and agricultural sector; involvement of different professional players (land valuers, lawyers or land practitioners, officials of several government agencies, private service providers); and rising cost of land, since the policy was launched (Kepe & Hall, 2016: 41).

South Africa is becoming cognizance of the place of small-scale farming as opposed to the general privilege accorded large commercial farmers, before, during and after apartheid. The 'over-emphasized' commercial farmers have enjoyed 'historical privileges (in terms of credit, services, electricity, irrigation and marketing infrastructure)' (Moyo, 2007: 6), whereas the small-scale farming sector has been characterized by under-development and farm struggles. This contradiction engenders farm conflicts and attacks, leading to loss of lives and property. There is a growing advocacy that 'farm attacks and farm murders should be treated as a separate crime category; be regarded as a priority crime; and need a particular solution' (Burger, 2018: 2). While there is generally an upward trend in violent crimes in the country, the recurring brutality against white farmers and resultant racialization of farm murders require an urgent solution (Burger, 2018).

In many African countries, large parcels of lands are controlled by the government, but the large hectares of land controlled by white South Africans, amidst prevailing land hunger by black people, is of great concern. One of the land audits of the South African government reveals that 14% of the entire land is state owned, 79% privately owned and 7% unaccounted for (Department of Rural Development and Land Reform, 2013: 9). Many farms that are also managed by the government are becoming nonviable. The reluctance of the state to cede part of its land and farms for redistribution, which has been received with mixed feelings, constituted one of the strongest arguments employed by the antagonists of the proposed LEWC under the South African President Cyril Ramaphosa's administration. The opposition party, the Democratic Alliance (DA), categorized the current land reform struggles as 'a lost opportunity to empower a growing pool of South Africans for economic participation' (DA, 2013). While there is a genuine need to revisit the existing land reform, the proposed LEWC may not be the most appropriate policy option required to achieve an effective land reform programme.

Structure of Book

This book draws from the standpoint of critical epistemology to interrogate the existing land reform programmes and engage the proposed policy choice of LEWC. The book adopts divergent research methodology (qualitative and quantitative founded on survey, focus group study and unstructured interviews) to properly locate the unresolved land question in scholarship exposition. The book, subjected to peer-reviews, is divided into fourteen chapters.

In this **Chapter**, *Expropriation and Discontent of Land Reform in South Africa: An Introduction*, the authors, Adeoye O. Akinola, Irrshad Kaseeram and Nokukhanya N. Jili, draw from the chapter synopses and provide the background to the book. It locates the book in context and explores the decisive factors responsible for the contradictions inherent in a post-apartheid land reform scheme. The chapter connects with the history of land dispossession in the apartheid regime to locate the choice of LEWC.

Chapter 2, *Expropriation as an Effective Tool for Land Reform,* by Desan Iyer and Lizelle Ramaccio Calvino, provides a brief overview of the pre-democracy policies that may have contributed towards the injustice of land dispossession in South Africa, as well as assesses whether, and to what extent, the post-democracy land reform policies have redressed historical inequality. The chapter analyses the current legislative framework and possible land expropriation, and the probable inconsistencies of the Constitution and the Expropriation Act 63 of 1975 and considers whether Section 25 of the Constitution requires amendment or whether land can be expropriated without compensation within the current South African legislative framework.

In **Chapter** 3, *Globalization of South African Land Reform Scheme: An Interrogation*, Adeoye O. Akinola and Irrshad Kaseeram relate land policy to the history of foreign domination and dependency. The authors hold that land issues shape the interaction between the Global North and South, through the history of imperialism, colonialism and apartheid. Through historical conversations, the chapter examines the trajectories of land reforms and evaluates the nation's performance in the land reform scheme. The chapter finds that the reality of land reform in Africa has not achieved equity to redress historical injustices, but rather it has been driven by a neoliberal order at the expense of the rural poor.

In **Chapter** 4, Mandla Mubecua and Halalisani V. Mlambo present the title, *Expropriation of Land without Compensation in South Africa: A Strategy for Alleviating or Worsening Poverty?* Through historical analysis, the authors expose the prevailing land inequality, which is associated with the increasing poverty and unemployment rates of the black population. The chapter engages the land reform schemes and the proposed expropriation without compensation option in relation to poverty alleviation, and concludes that the failed land reform has given rise to the rhetoric of expropriating land without compensation.

Chapter 5, *South African Land Question and the Dilemma of 'Expropriation Without Compensation: A Critical Examination*, by Mzingaye B. Xaba, assesses land reform programmes, engages the motivations for the advocacy for LEWC and explores the legal and political implications of the proposed policy shift. The authors hold that the cross section of the stakeholders identifies the 'willing buyer, willing seller' approach as the main challenge, and thus, pressures within the ANC, the Economic Freedom Fighters (EFF), Democracy Alliance (DA) and some land-based civil society groups, popularized the LEWC conversation. Due to political mobilization and legitimacy, the ANC embraced the proposed LEWC as the best policy instrument to effectively address the land issues.

In **Chapter** 6, *Land Expropriation, Food Security and Local Economic Development (LED) in South Africa,* Nokukhaya Jili and Mandla M. Masuku advocate that access to land for many rural communities constitutes life and the core mechanism for addressing poverty, hunger and advancing inclusive development. Government's failures to achieve these led to the advocacy for LEWC as the more effective policy, which presents an ideal opportunity to redress historical injustice and enhance economic development and food security. Thus, the chapter explores the prospects of LEWC for enhancing food security and local economic development in the country. The chapter argues for a robust policy of land expropriation, which is an essential mechanism for redressing policy failures in the land sector.

Chapter 7, *South Africa and the Quest for Land Reform: Implications for Integrative Food Security, and Nation-Building*, by Stella Sabi, maintains that the persistent skewed land arrangement impedes agricultural productivity and food security, and thus, household food insecurity is one of the key indicators of chronic poverty in the country. Through desktop research, this chapter deepens an understanding about South African land reform strategies, assesses their implication for integrative food security and nation-building, and explores how post-apartheid South Africa manages to strike a balance between land redistribution, integrative food security and national building.

In **Chapter** 8, Motivations for Land Reform in Contemporary South Africa: The case of Balobedu in Tzaneen, Province of Limpopo, Listen Yingi defines South Africa by the entrenched inequalities which stretch from social to economic spheres of which land access is the most apparent. Drawing lessons from Zimbabwe, Yingi adopts the Afrocentric perspective to engage LEWC and unravel the scepticism around the proposed policy. Contrary to the antagonists of the populist agenda, this radical approach may reverse land-related inequality and resolve a major national question.

Subsequently, in **Chapter** 9, *Small-Scale Farming, Fourth Industrial Revolution and the Quest for Agriculture Development*, Luyanda Mtshali and Adeoye O. Akinola engage the globalization and the development of commercial farming, which provides the foundation for exploring the gains of the Fourth Industrial Revolution (4IR) in South Africa's agricultural sector. The use of a cyber-physical system and infrared receiver will increase farm productivity. Thus, the chapter assesses the impact of 4IR on small-scale farmers and concludes that 4IR, if fully operational, will strengthen large commercial farming, while small-scale farming will be underdeveloped.

In **Chapter** 10, *Rural Land Reform and Local Economic Development through Agri-parks—A Case Study of Harry Gwala Municipality in KwaZulu-Natal*, Sultan Khan acknowledges the contribution of agriculture to development but notes that the rural economy is depleted, underdeveloped and caught in a vicious cycle of poverty. He delves into the reality of land inequality and embraces the Agri-park concept as a platform to stimulate local economic development. Using the Harry Gwala District Municipality as a case study, the chapter explores the prospects and challenges encountered in the application of the Agri-park concept.

Chapter 11, *Balancing Land Restitution and Public Interest in South African Socio-economic Development: A Critical Appraisal of the Restitution of Land Rights Act*, by Tumo Maloka, engages the Restitution of Land Rights Act 22 of 1994 and Section 34 of the Restitution Act, which focuses on competing claims from several traditional communities for the restitution of their rights, often over the same piece of land, situated within the environs of peri-urban and urban municipalities. The chapter locates the extent to which public interest considerations operate to bar the actual restoration of land has become a thorny issue in land reform. This was achieved through sustained appraisal in the light of a trilogy of cases.

In **Chapter** 12, *Climate Change and Land Issues in South Africa: A Convergence*, Olutola Oluwole examines the intersections between climate change and land-based resources (two critical challenges), and assesses its impact on land issues in South Africa. The author is sceptical about the place of climate-development nexus in the proposed LEWC discourse. While climate change is still treated as a sub-component of the environment, through political, ecological and theoretical exposition, this chapter brings into context the linkage between the two concepts.

Chapter 13, *Urbanization, Poverty and the Paradox of Land Reform in South Africa*, by Adeoye O. Akinola, links the development of cities to the consequences of civilization in Africa. Apartheid policies broadened the gap between cities and rural areas, which engendered the impoverishment of 13 million black South Africans through land dispossessions and restriction to the impoverished hinterland. Thus, this chapter explores how land reform impacts on rural-urban migration and the convergence between poverty and urbanization. Contradictions generated in urban centres are linked to the unresolved land question. In conclusion, an equitable land reform scheme is an essential corollary for combating poverty and rural-urban migration.

In **Chapter** 14, *Land Reform and the Quest for Women's Land Rights in South Africa: A Case of KwaZulu-Natal Province*, Modupe Daramola notes the complexity of the reform agenda and maintains that the absence of effective land management and gender construction in land allocations have deepened land inequality. This has restricted women's capacity building, engendered land unproductivity and aggravated poverty in South African households, particular that of black people. Through interviews and a focus group study, she assesses the effectiveness of the state's legal framework on women's land rights, explores the place of women's rights in the land reform scheme and reconciles women's land rights with the reality of land reform in the province of KwaZulu-Natal.

References

Burger, J. (2018). Violent crime on farms and smallholdings in South Africa. *Institute for Security Studies Policy Brief, 115*, 1–11.

Democratic Alliance (DA). (2013). *Land reform policy*. Available https://cdn.da.org.za/wp-content/uploads/2018/02/14234228/Land-Reform1.pdf.

Department of Land Affairs. (1997). *Department of land affairs White Paper on land policy, 1997*. Pretoria: Department of Land Affairs.

Department of Rural Development and Land Reform. (2011). *Green Paper on land reform, 2011.* Available https://www.gov.za/sites/default/files/gcis_document/201409/landreformgreenpaper.pdf.

Department of Rural Development and Land Reform. (2013). *Land audit*. Available http://www.ruraldevelopment.gov.za/phocadownload/Cadastral-Survey-management/Booklet/land%20audit%20booklet.pdf.

Department of Rural Development and Land Reform. (2014). *Final policy proposals on "strengthening the relative rights of people working the land"*. Available http://www.ruraldevelopment.gov.za/publications/land-reform-indaba-2015/file/3397-final-policy-proposals-on-strengthening-the-relative-rights-of-people-working-the-land.

Department of Rural Development and Land Reform. (2018). *Land audit report 2017: Phase II: Private land ownership by race, gender and nationality*. Available http://www.ruraldevelopment.gov.za/publications/land-audit-report/file/6126.

Kariuki, S. (2009). Agrarian reform, rural development and governance in Africa: A case of Eastern and Southern Africa. *Policy brief 59*. Rosebank: Centre for Policy Studies.

Kepe, T., & Hall, R. (2016). *Land redistribution in South Africa*. Commissioned Report for High Level Panel on the Assessment of Key Legislation and the Acceleration of Fundamental Change, an Initiative of the Parliament of South Africa.

Moyo, S. (2007). Land in the political economy of African development: Alternative strategies for reform. *Africa Development, 32*(4), 1–34.

CHAPTER 2

Expropriation as an Effective Tool for Land Reform: A Legislative Perspective

Desan Iyer and Lizelle Ramaccio Calvino

Introduction

Land reform was introduced in an effort to restore inequalities in land ownership and access. Internationally, some of the most extensive land reforms took place after World War II in South East Asia, the 1960s and 1970s in Latin America and currently persisting in Africa. Although land reform is not inimitable to South Africa, the racially based disposition of land ownership throughout South African history makes it an emotive and complex topic. The colonisation of South Africa, the imposition of the apartheid regime and the adoption of legislation and policies that resulted in racial domination contributed towards the perpetuation of the unjust land dispossession. Accordingly, as a result of many South Africans being disposed of their land, whilst were denied the right to be land owners outside demarcated reserves, the majority of South Africa's agrarian land was owned by the white minority.

D. Iyer · L. Ramaccio Calvino (✉)
University of Zululand, KwaDlangezwa, South Africa
e-mail: CalvinoL@unizulu.ac.za

A. O. Akinola et al. (eds.), *The New Political Economy of Land Reform in South Africa*,
https://doi.org/10.1007/978-3-030-51129-6_2

Afrikaner and black land ownership in terms of South African history, as well as the past political and racially motivated land occupancy patterns in favour of whites, has resulted in an increasing demand for radical economic transformation and the equitable distribution of land. This position is proliferated by the recent announcement by the South African government to amend the Constitution of the Republic of South Africa (1996) (hereinafter referred to the Constitution) to enable government a more radical land reform process by expropriating land without compensation (Committee Report on Amending Section 25 of the Constitution, 2019).

It is against this backdrop that this chapter provides a brief overview of the pre-democracy policies that may have contributed towards the injustice of land dispossession in South Africa, as well as assess whether, and to what extent, the post-democracy land reform policies have redressed historical inequality. This chapter analyses the current legislative framework regulating land reform and in particular the expropriation of land. Inconsistencies that may exist between the Constitution and the Expropriation Act 63 of 1975 will be analysed. The chapter will firstly consider whether Section 25 of the Constitution requires amendment or whether land can be expropriated without compensation within the current South African legislative framework.

Secondly, the study evaluates the effectiveness of expropriation without compensation as a mean to eradicate the injustices of the past, whilst underpinning constitutional values *inter alia* to "Heal the divisions of the past and establish a society based on democratic values, social justice and fundamental human rights" (Preamble to the Constitution). For purposes of analysis and consideration, a qualitative approach has been applied. Primary sources, such as legislation and case law, as well as secondary sources, including journals, text books and articles, have been consulted to provide a synthesis of the relevant literature relating to land reform in South Africa.

Historical and Legislative Overview: Pre-democracy

As far back as 1655, South Africa experienced land ownership conflicts in the Cape between the Dutch settlers and the Khoi-Khoi people (Lewin, 1944: 99). History furthermore reveals how the San people were almost exterminated by the white colonialists and how African tribes resigned their land either by force or by being coaxed into selling their land (Davenport & Hunt, 1974). Although the colonisation of South Africa led to the indigenous inhabitants being deprived of their land, racial segregation by way of state policy and various pieces of legislation exacerbated the injustice of land dispossession that eventually led to the need for land reform once apartheid ended (Murray & Williams, 1994).

One of the first pieces of legislation that resulted in the systematic limitation of South Africans of colour land ownership and occupancy was the Glen Grey Act that was passed in 1894. The act provided for the division of all unalienated land into locations, whilst limiting the number of non-whites who qualified to own land within the said locations (Flemmer, 1976). Despite the restrictions through the Glen Grey Act 25 of 1894, the government introduced further stringent land ownership provisions in terms of the Natives Land Act in 1913.

Natives Land Act of 1913

With the adoption of the Natives Land 27 of 1913 (hereinafter referred to as the Natives Land Act) non-white land ownership and rights became even more restrictive. Section 1(1) of the Native Land Act provided that

> Except with the approval of the Governor-General-
>
> (a) a native shall not enter into any agreement/or transaction for the purchase, hire, or other acquisition from a person other than a native, of any such land or of any right thereto, interest therein, or servitude thereover and
> (b) a person other than a native shall not enter into any agreement or transaction for the purchase, hire or any other acquisition from a native of any such land or of any right thereto, interest therein, or servitude thereover.

In terms of Section 10 of the Natives Land Act, "natives" were defined as "any person, male or female, who is a member or an aboriginal race or tribe of Africa". In essence, the Natives Land Act prohibited non-white South African from buying or hiring land located outside allocated "native regions", thereby resulting in a territorial segregation based on race (Flemmer, 1976).

The Natives Land Act therefore formalised limitations on non-white land ownership (Robinson, 1997). This resulted in more land being made available to white farmers (Wickins, 1981). The provisions of the Natives Land Act also resulted in the confinement of black people to live within the allocated "native" regions, which was mostly barren land that was not conducive for agricultural purposes (Davenport, 1985). As a result of the aforesaid, the majority of black farmers became impoverished, and they grew more dependent on employment from white farmers (Davenport, 1985).

The initial percentage of South African land allocated to "natives" in terms of the Natives Land Act was 7%, which percentage was later increased to 13.5% in 1963, in terms of the Native Trust and Land Act 18 of 1936 (hereinafter referred to as the Native Trust and Land Act) (Rugege, 2004). This land allocation percentage remained unchanged until the beginning of the 1990s.

Native Trust and Land Act 18 of 1936

In terms of the Native Trust and Land Act, a state agency, the South African Native Trust, was established to administer the trust land. In terms of Section 10(2) of the Act, the Trust was mandated to purchase land within the "native" areas or release areas for the purposes of native settlement. Despite the total percentage of land allocation for "natives" being increased, the implementation of the Act also resulted in the abolition of individual land ownership by Africans. Therefore, the South African Development Trust become responsible for the acquisition of land in certain areas allocated for black settlement (Robinson, 1997).

Group Areas Act

In addition to limiting black land ownership and confining black people to "native areas", the Group Areas Act 41 of 1950 (hereinafter referred to as Group Areas Act) established group areas according to race. In terms of Section 3(1) of the Group Areas Act, a particular area of land was designated for the exclusive ownership of, and use by, a specific race group of people. The Group Areas Act, differentiated between the racial groups in the country: whites, coloured (mixed race) black people, Indians and Asians (Loveland, 1999). Accordingly, a person was only allowed to occupy or own premises or land that was located within his/her designated race group area. The act accordingly controlled the attainment of immovable property and the occupancy of land according to racial classification (Loveland, 1999). Black farmers who had title deeds to their land and accordingly escaped the provisions of the Natives Land Act could and were removed from their land in terms of the Group Areas Act.

The Group Areas Act was repealed and re-enacted as the Group Areas Act 36 of 1966. The promulgation of the Group Areas Act of 1966 reiterated the restriction of land ownership according to racial groups. Section 17(2) of the Group Areas Act of 1966 made the provision that a bona fide servant or visitor be allowed to reside in premises or occupy land in an area which they were disqualified from for a limited period of ninety days. The act furthermore provided the South African police the authority to enter and search premises without a warrant, as well as forcibly remove non-whites from valuable land in order for such land to become available for white settlements (Loveland, 1999). The impact of the aforesaid racially based land acts is evident from the number of three and a half million people, mostly black South Africans, being forcibly removed from their land during the period 1960 and 1983 (Robinson, 1997).

A New Dawn: Post-democracy

Abolition of Racially Based Land Measures Act

Up until 30 June 1991, non-white South Africans were precluded from land ownership outside scheduled areas (Klopper & Pienaar, 2014). With the promulgation of the Abolition of Racially Based Land Measures Act 108 of 1991 (hereinafter referred to as the "Abolition of Radically Based Land Measures Act") the Natives Land Act, and related legislation, were repealed and provisions were made in terms of Section 12 of the Abolition of Radically Based Land Measures Act to facilitate the transfer of the land owned by the South African Development Trust to state departments. In addition, the Group Areas Act of 1966 was abolished in terms of Section 48 of the Abolition of Racially Based Land Measures Act, thereby allowing South Africans, regardless of race, to own and occupy land anywhere in South Africa (Du Plessis, Olivier, & Pienaar, 1991).

Reconstruction and Development Programme

In 1994, the new democratically elected government, the African National Congress (hereinafter referred to as the "ANC"), implemented the Reconstruction and Development Programme (hereinafter referred to as the "RDP"), that provided a socio-economic framework to address *inter alia* inequalities caused by apartheid, especially the high poverty and unemployment rates in South Africa. In terms of the RDP, the ANC acknowledged that,

> No political democracy can survive and flourish if the majority of its people remain in poverty, without land, without their basic needs being met and without tangible prospects for a better life. Attacking poverty and deprivation is the first priority of the democratic Government. (RDP, 1994)

The ANC acknowledged that in alleviating poverty and correcting the injustices of the past, created by depriving and denying non-whites access to land, land reform would be of paramount importance (RDP, 1994). Accordingly, within a South African context, land reform can be defined as essential initiatives, entrenched in legislation, with the aim to extend access to land, progress security of tenure and restore rights to land (Pienaar, 2015).

One of the leading projects identified in terms of the RDP was land reform. The aim of the land reform pilot was "To develop and support integrated sustainable rural development and rural local government models through land restitution, redistribution, tenure reform and settlement support to kick-start a wider land reform process" (RDP, 1994). In addition to the land reform pilot, the ANC undertook to carry out land reform in terms of three main strategies, namely land redistribution, restitution and tenure reform (RDP, 1994).

Legislative Framework for Land Reform

Interim Constitution 200 of 1993

In drafting the Constitution of the Republic of South Africa, Act 200 of 1993 (hereinafter referred to as the "Interim Constitution"), the ANC and its allies argued for the inclusion of property rights, in terms of the Interim Constitution, to ensure that land owners would not be dispossessed of their land without compensation. The national government and its allies argued that by including property rights in terms of the Interim Constitution would not only hinder the execution of land reform but also "legitimize and entrench, as a human right, the consequences of generations of apartheid and dispossession" (Budlender, 2000). Although a property clause was ultimately included in the Interim Constitution, the provisions relating to land reform were not comprehensive. Section 28 of the Interim Constitution provided that:

> (1) Every person shall have the right to acquire and hold rights in property and, to the extent that the nature of the rights permits, to dispose of such rights.
> (2) No deprivation of any rights in property shall be permitted otherwise than in accordance with a law.
> (3) Where any rights in property are expropriated pursuant to a law referred to in subsection (2), such expropriation shall be permissible for public purposes only and shall be subject to the payment of agreed compensation or, failing agreement, to the payment of such compensation and within such period as may be determined by a court of law as just and equitable, taking into account all relevant factors, including, in the case of the determination of compensation, the use to which the property is being put, the history of its acquisition, its market value, the value of the investments in it by those affected and the interests of those affected.

It is evident that, as far as land reform is concerned, Section 28 of the Interim Constitution only provided for the right to the restitution of land rights for persons or communities dispossessed of such rights under apartheid's discriminatory laws.

The Constitution of the Republic of South Africa, 1996

A land reform programme was embedded in the Constitution. Any reformative measure must consequently be in accordance with the Constitution. The land reform programme therefore provides the "framework blueprint" for land reform in South Africa and must consequently be tested against the Constitution. Section 25 of the Constitution, also referred to as the property clause, provides that:

> (1) No one may be deprived of property except in terms of law of general application, and no law may permit arbitrary deprivation of property.

(2) Property may be expropriated only in terms of law of general application:
  (a) For a public purpose or in the public interest; and
  (b) Subject to compensation, the amount of which and the time and manner of payment of which have either been agreed to by those affected or decided or approved by a court.

Section 25(1) of the Constitution consequently seeks to protect the land owner's property rights, whilst Section 25(2) safeguards the interests of society by providing for the dispossession of property from the owner by the government, on the provisions that such dispossession of property is for a public purpose, or in the public interest, and that the owner be compensated for the property (Badenhorst, Mostert, & Pienaar, 2006). The Constitution therefore authorises expropriations in lieu of the government's obligation to redress the land injustices and inequalities of the past, plus the need to utilise such property for the benefit of the public at large (Van der Walt & Pienaar, 2009).

In terms of the Extension of Security of Tenure Act 62 of 1997 and the Provision of Certain Land for Settlement Act 126 of 1993, land may be expropriated for purposes of redistribution and tenure reform. The Minister of Public Works has the authority to expropriate property provided the organs of state require such land. Compliance with land procedure and processes in accordance with the regulatory framework is therefore imperative. The process of expropriation entails a decision made by the Provincial Director of the Office of the Department of Land Affairs, whereafter:

a. A notice of expropriation must contain "a clear and full description of the property" and
b. A clear date of the expropriation (Centre for Rural Legal Studies).

In the event of the procedural framework not being followed, the expropriation may be declared invalid, as held in the case of *Offit Enterprises (Pty) Ltd and Another v Coega Development Corporation (Pty) Ltd and Others* 2011 1 SA 293 (CC).

In this regard, the Promotion of Administrative Justice Act 3 of 2000 (hereinafter referred to as the "PAJA") provided a disgruntled landowner the opportunity to have the expropriation order reviewed or set aside. Section 14 of the Expropriation Act of 1965 furthermore provides that in the event of the government or the landowner not being able to agree on the amount of compensation, either party may refer the matter to the High Court.

Section 25(5) of the Constitution furthermore places an onus on the government's to "take reasonable legislative and other measures, within its available resources, to foster conditions which enable citizens to gain access to land on an equitable basis". Despite government's commitment to land reform, the process of land reform has been slow. Unresolved restitution claims, complex and expensive land claims, the lack of capacity in the Department of Land Affairs and Department of Agriculture, the inoccupation of agrarian land, a discrepancy between the Department's budget and the likely cost of meeting government's land reform goals (CDE Research Report, 2008) are but a few reasons for the delay in land reform.

In addition to the aforesaid restrains, the willing buyer–willing seller approach, that was supported in terms of the White Paper on Land Policy, has, according to the Committee on Rural Development and Land Reform, failed to achieve its aim of gaining land for land reform purposes (Committee on Rural Development and Land Reform, 2012). The lengthy time frame to acquire land and negotiate compensation, delays in the payment of compensation, as well as the reluctance of beneficiaries to negotiate are a few reasons for the dysfunctionality of the said land reform module (Du Plesis, 2014).

Discord Between the Expropriation Act and the Constitution

In addition to the lack of an integrated support system to regulate a confusive environment for managing the regulatory land reform framework, inconsistencies between the Expropriation Act of 1965 and the Constitution have contributed to the delay in finalising land claims as the compensation calculation is not clear.

Expropriations can be categorised as administrative expropriations and judicial expropriations (Marais & Maree, 2016). In terms of judicial expropriations, a court order will authorise the expropriation, whilst in the case of administrative expropriations, expropriation takes place by way of an administrative action that is generally regulated by an administrator, who acts in accord with the empowering statutes (Marais & Maree, 2016). In terms of South African land reform, the government is authorised by the Constitution to expropriate private property (Centre for Rural Legal Studies, 2003).

Despite the aforesaid, expropriations within a South African context are regulated by the Expropriation Act of 1965 which was later repealed by the Expropriation Act 63 of 1975 (hereinafter referred to as the "Expropriation Act") (Jacobs, 1982). The Expropriation Act accordingly forms the basis of expropriation law in South Africa.

In terms of Section 2(1) of the Expropriation Act, the Minister of Public Works has the authority to expropriate immovable and movable property for public purposes. Thus, public purposes include "any purpose connected with the administration of the provisions of any law by an organ of State" (Section 1 of the Expropriation Act).

In analysing the wording utilised in terms of Section 2(1) of the Expropriation Act, it appears as if the provision is in conflict with the Constitution, as the Expropriation Act provides for the expropriate of immovable property on behalf of a juristic body but not for the benefit of a private individual (Eisenberg, 1995). It is furthermore noteworthy that the Expropriation Act does not specifically make reference to "public interest" whilst the Constitution does. It can thus be inferred that the specific reference to "public interest" was included in the Constitution to enable expropriations for land reform purposes (Van der Walt, 2005). Despite the ambiguity in respect of the existing legislative framework regulating expropriation and the uncertainty regarding the interpretation of "public interests", the Constitution guarantees that, as a general rule, public consideration would outweigh individual property rights (Slade, 2014).

The calculation of the compensation must be decided by considering the factors listed in terms of Section 25(3) of the Constitution that provides that:

> The amount of the compensation and the time and manner of payment must be just and equitable, reflecting an equitable balance between the public interest and the interest of those affected, having regard to all relevant circumstances, including the following:
>
> (a) The current use of the property;
> (b) The history of the acquisition and use of the property;
> (c) The market value of the property;

(d) The extent of direct state investment and subsidy in the acquisition and beneficial capital improvement of the property; and
(e) The purpose of the expropriation the current use of the property.

Section 25(3) of the Constitution accordingly expressly insists, that in calculating the compensation, the calculation test must be just and equitable (*Du Toit v Minister of Transport* 2006 (1) SA 297 (CC)). The Expropriation Act, in turn, only requires that the market value and actual financial loss be considered when calculating the compensation.

Section 2(2) of the Expropriation Act, unlike the Constitution, does provide for reimbursement in the form of an addition to the fixed percentage of the compensation monies, referred to as solatium, which considers *inter alia* emotional distress and inconvenience. This discrepancy underpins the problem in calculating just and equitable compensation. From the factors mentioned, it is evident that one of the main restrictions in progressive land reform is the ambiguity that is created as a result of the differences between the Expropriation Act and the Constitution, as well as the delay and uncertainty with regard to the calculation and payment of the compensation.

In the case of *Haffajee NO and Others v Ethekwini Municipality and Others* 2011 6 SA 134 (CC) (hereinafter referred to as the "Haffajee case"), yet another question pertaining to compensation was addressed. In this case, the owner of the property frustrated the expropriation process by not being agreeable to the selling price of the property. The Constitutional Court had to consider whether the amount, time and manner of compensation may be determined after expropriation has taken place. The property in question belonged to the YGM Haffajee Family Trust and was designated by the Ethekwini Municipality for the implementation of a canalisation programme to reduce flooding in the Umgeni area. On the refusal of the compensation offer, the expropriation process was correctly executed. Ultimately, the Constitutional Court had to determine whether Section 25(2) (b) of the Constitution necessitated that the amount of compensation and the time and manner of payment should always be determined prior to expropriation (Haffajee case).

In considering the Haffajee case, the Constitutional Court applied the constitutional analysis of Section 25 of the Constitution, as addressed in the *First National Bank of South Africa Ltd t/a Wesbank v Minister of Finance* 2001 (3) SA 310 (C) case. The Court concluded that the property in dispute did comply with the provisions of Section 25(1) of the Constitution and that the expropriation was accordingly for a public purpose, or in the public interest, as provided for in terms of Section 25(2) (a) of the Constitution.

In considering whether the "determination of compensation is a prerequisite for expropriation", the Court gave consideration to the need for transformation and held that Section 25(2) (b) of the Constitution does not refer to the "determination of compensation as a condition precedent for expropriation". The Court furthermore held that a flexible approach should be applied to compensation for expropriation and that Section 26(3) and Section 34 of the Constitution provide sufficient safeguards to ensure proper relief (Haffajee case).

Accordingly, the Court held that determining compensation as a prerequisite for expropriation is not compatible with the Constitution and unduly burdens the government (Haffajee case). Consequently, compensation remains a requisite for expropriation but not a precondition. This case may set a precedent for future cases where the owner frustrates the expropriation process, which will ultimately result in the speeding up of the land reform process.

Therefore, it may be argued that the call for the amendment of Section 25 of the Constitution to provide for expropriation without compensation as a means to expedite land reform may have been impulsive.

Land Reform Elements and Strategies

In establishing an overall land reform policy, the White Paper on Land Policy 1997 was published (hereinafter referred to as the "White Paper") (De Villiers, 2003). The main purpose of the White Paper was to address the injustices of the past which were caused by racially based land dispossession, unequal land ownership and the need for the sustainable use of land (White Paper, 1997). As in the case of the RDP, the White Paper identified three land reform strategies in achieving equitable access to South Africa's natural resources, namely restitution, redistribution and tenure reform (Diagnostic Report on Land Reform in South Africa, 2016).

Land Redistribution

Land redistribution refers to the acquisition of land by the state for purposes of providing the poor access to land for residential and productive use, thereby offering them an opportunity to improve their quality of life (White Paper, 1997). Despite the Land Reform (Labour Tenants) Act 486 of 1996, which applies only to labour tenants, as well as the Extension of Security of Tenure Act 62 of 1997, which is aimed at providing security of tenure to occupiers living on other people's land in rural areas, there is no comprehensive law providing for mechanisms for the redistribution of land (Provision of Certain Land for Settlement Act 126, 1993).

Land redistribution is accordingly dealt with in terms of Section 25(2) of the Constitution, which provides that "The state must take reasonable legislative and other measures, within its available resources, to foster conditions which enable citizens to gain access to land on an equitable basis". Indeed, onus is placed on the government to ensure people have access to land. Although the Constitution does not expressly provide for the right to land, the Constitutional Court has interpreted it as such, as seen in the *Government of the Republic of South Africa and Others v Grootboom and Others* 2000 SA 46 (CC) (hereinafter referred to as the Grootboom case).

In this case, the court further held that "The state must also foster conditions that enable citizens to gain access to land on an equitable basis (Grootboom case). Those in need have a corresponding right to demand that this be done". Therefore, the state is obliged to give effect to socio-economic rights, although such rights are not absolute (Grootboom case). It was concluded that the government is only obliged to take "reasonable legislative and other measures" and is only obliged to act "within its available resources" to provide conducive conditions that would allow citizens access to land (Grootboom case).

In fostering conditions to enable access to land, the government does not participate in the purchase of land for redistribution but rather adheres to the principles guiding the approach of willing buyer, willing seller, by providing the resources to finance market-led redistribution transactions, whilst not become a landowner (Lahiff, 2007).

As stipulated in the White Paper, the redistribution of land has to ensure "viability and sustainability by giving attention to the economic and social viability of intended land use; fiscal sustainability by the local authority; environmental sustainability; proximity and access to markets and employment; availability of water and bulk infrastructure" (White Paper, 1997).

Despite the restrains discussed, the total number of hectares delivered by the land redistribution programme, between the period 1994 and 2015, amounts to five million hectares, averaging 238,000 hectares per year (Diagnostic Report on Land Reform in South Africa, 2016).

Restitution

The aim of restitution is "to restore land and provide other restitutionary remedies to people dispossessed by racially discriminatory legislation, in such a way as to provide support to the vital process of reconciliation, reconstruction and development" (White Paper, 1997). Restitution of land is addressed in terms of Section 25(4) of the Constitution, as well as the Restitution of Land Rights Act. Based on Section 25(4) of the Constitution, "public interest includes the nation's commitment to land reform and to bring about equitable access to all South Africa's natural resource".

In terms of the aforesaid, legislations' four elements for restitution are identified, namely the qualification criteria, forms of restitution, compensation and urban claims (White Paper, 1997). Section 25(7) of the Constitution furthermore provides that,

> persons or communities dispossessed of property after 19 June 1913 as a result of past racially discriminatory laws or practices is entitled, to the extent provided by an Act of Parliament, either to restitution of that property or to equitable redress.

The Restitution of Land Rights Act 22 of 1994 provides people who were dispossessed of their land after 19 June 1913 the right to claim restoration of those rights or equitable relief, such as alternative land or compensation. The act furthermore provides for a Commission on the Restitution of Land Rights (CRLR), as well as the Land Claims Court (LCC). A period of eighteen years was set out to complete all restitution claims (White Paper, 1997). Initially, a period of three years was allowed for claims to be lodged, which deadline was later extended to 31 December 1998. In addition, a period of five years was envisaged for settling the land claims and a further ten years for the implementation of court orders and settlement agreements (White Paper, 1997).

Despite numerous restitution claims being lodged, the lack of finance, infrastructure and institutional supports for emerging farmers and new land beneficiaries has resulted in unproductive use of agricultural land. In addition to the lack of post-settlement support, approximately three million hectares of land had been restored through restitution but not necessarily transferred into citizens' names (Diagnostic Report on Land Reform in South Africa, 2016). This has called into question the effectiveness of tenure reform.

Tenure Reform

People resident on communal land in the rural areas has no security of tenure on the land. In most cases, they are given the right to use or occupy the property based on customary law, and have no title deeds or any documents in support of such use. In terms of Section 25(6) of the Constitution,

> A person or community whose tenure of land is legally insecure as a result of past racially discriminatory laws or practices is entitled, to the extent provided by an Act of Parliament, either to tenure which is legally secure or to comparable redress.

In an attempt to ensure that the government allows South African citizens the right to gain access to land on an equitable basis, the Communal Land Rights Act 11 of 2004 (hereinafter referred to as the "Communal Land Rights Act") was enacted. Its objective was:

> To provide for legal security of tenure by transferring communal land, including KwaZulu-Natal Ingonyama land, to communities, or by awarding comparable redress; to provide for the conduct of a land rights enquiry to determine the transition from old order rights to new order rights; to provide for the democratic administration of communal land by communities; to provide for Land Rights Boards; to provide for the co-operative performance of municipal functions on communal land; to amend or repeal certain laws; and to provide for matters incidental thereto. (Communal Land Rights Act)

Unfortunately, as the provincial legislatures were not involved in passing the act, as well as the fact that the act denied security of tenure to black South Africans living in the former Bantustans, the Constitutional Court struck the Communal Land Rights Act down in 2010 (*Tongoane and Others v National Minister for Agriculture and Land Affairs and Others* (CCT100/09) 2010 ZACC 10; 2010 (6) SA 214 (CC); 2010 (8) BCLR 741 (CC) [11 May 2010]). Consequently, no current legislation offers redress to those rural people who are still without security of tenure of land due to apartheid and colonialism.

Barriers to Land Reform

Over the years, land reform has stagnated to a large degree, and many factors have contributed to the unresolved land question. Some of these include unresolved restitution claims; complex and expensive land claims; lack of capacity in the Department of Land Affairs and Department of Agriculture; productive land remaining unoccupied; lack of a proper audit on all state land and budgetary constraints, which have hampered land reform goals (CDE Research Report, 2008). To address the situation, there have been rising pressures on the government to adopt a more progressive approach to land reform by seeking additional funding, advocating new taxes on land, moving away from applicant-driven reform to direct state action and seeking legislative and policy reform (CDE Research Report, 2008). The Department of Land Affairs has also pushed for legislative reform over the years.

Whilst post-democracy, successive governments have raised expectations on land reform, government has failed to deliver in its key mandate of speeding up the land reform process more than twenty-five years after the attainment of majority rule (Klopper & Pienaar, 2014). The series of legislative reforms which have been attempted have also failed to yield significant positive results. Indeed, the Expropriation Bill has not come to fruition as a strong land reform legislative in line with the Constitution. The supposed leak of the draft Green Paper in 2010 has also not helped the reform process. Inconsistencies that exist between the Constitution and the Expropriation Act have not really been addressed, despite attempts to provide a clearer framework in the promulgation of the draft Expropriation Bill (Wentzel, 2005).

In spite of the 1997 White Paper on South African Land Policy supporting the willing buyer–willing seller principle, there appears to be general consensus that this approach has failed to achieve its objective of acquiring land for land reform purposes (Committee on Rural Development and Land Reform, 2012). The reasons given for its failure revolve around the drawn-out time frames around acquisition and the negotiation of compensation; the Department of Land Reform acting as agents and negotiators for beneficiaries; delays in payment, even after agreement had been reached, and officials failing to negotiate as a willing buyer would do so (Du Plesis, 2014).

At some stage, the Ministry contended that the expropriation process was being hindered by inflated property prices and the willing buyer and willing seller approach had to be abandoned for a method that uses expropriation as an alternative method of land acquisition (The Green Paper on Land Reform, 2011). The perpetual discord between the Expropriation Act and the Constitution, and the consequential uncertainty surrounding payment of compensation, has also been blamed for the sporadic pace of land reform.

Overcoming the Barriers to Land Reform

It was expected that the South African state would fast-track the appointment of a reliable and structured land valuator years back. The core function of the valuator would be to determine financial compensation in cases of land expropriation, set fair and consistent land values, create and maintain a proper database of information and provide property-related advice to government (Land Reform Policy Discussion Document, 2012).

However, the process eventually and belatedly commenced with the appointment of the country's first Valuer-General in May 2015, after the Property Valuation Act was signed into law. This office, which is answerable to the Minister of Rural Development and Land Reform, is seen as key to ensuring that government's land reform runs smoothly.

The responsibility to change the current land reform landscape is one that is accompanied with responsibility and due diligence, and any attempt by the land valuator's office to come up with prices that favour the government would be frowned upon and could frustrate the land reform process even further. In addition, the appointment of a Land Rights Management Board and Commission that could provide the required support structure and to ensure a conducive climate for managing the current regulatory property framework would provide the much-needed structure for progressive land reform.

The Land Reform Policy Discussion Document (2012) specifically mentioned that "land reform must represent a radical and rapid break from the past without significantly disrupting agricultural production and food security" and accordingly, there is an urgent need to enhance skills development, infrastructure development, service provision and credit access. The strengthening of the Land Bank, as well an attempt to finalise the Expropriation Bill to fall in line with the Constitution, has been bandied around for years and even mentioned in the Land Reform Policy Discussion Document (2012), but yet little has come from it to date.

In fact, in 2014, the Minister in the Presidency for Planning, Performance, Monitoring, Evaluation and Administration announced that Cabinet had approved the tabling to Parliament of the Expropriation Bill 2014. It was anticipated that the bill would consolidate the processes of expropriation across the various spheres of government. More importantly, it was going to address the discord between the Constitution and the current Expropriation Act by providing a consistent framework to incorporate expropriations with compensation in the public interest, thereby allowing government to achieve its commitment to land reform.

In addition, the bill was to cater for the payment of just and equitable compensation and the sharing of relevant information between the expropriating authorities and affected persons. From a procedural perspective, the bill was to provide for a proper notification process, as well as an objection and representation stage before the decision to expropriate. It seemed positive that the legislature tabled the bill to address the shortcomings of the Expropriation Act and bring it in line with the Constitution, which was crucial to expediting the land reform process. However, in 2019, the bill has been referred back to Parliament for reconsideration over issues pertaining to public participation and expropriation without compensation. Many believe that the sooner Parliament remedies the Expropriation Bill, the better the prospect of improving land reform and redistribution.

The words, "expropriation without compensation", have been discussed in many forums as being the impetus that is needed to accelerate the land reform. However, as many parties, including the ruling party, see the amendment of the Constitution as a must, others have argued against such a change, on the basis that the Constitution is not a barrier to change, but corruption, constrained budgets and the lack of will by the government are the real reasons behind the slow progress of land reform. For some, such debate has sparked anxiety, confusion and fear about the future and existing land rights. Recent developments suggested that "expropriation without compensation" could become a reality.

In 2018, the Joint Review Committee recommended that the Constitution be amended to allow for expropriation without compensation. An important point to note is that the Constitution has not been amended but a process has been put in place to commence such an action. In terms of the recommendation of the Joint Review Committee, the report will have to be tabled in both houses of Parliament, the National Assembly and the National Council of Provinces where it will be debated and put to vote.

The report can only be adopted by Parliament, with a two-thirds majority in the National Assembly, and supported by at least six out of the nine provinces in the National Council of Provinces. The process could take months, if not years, as it could be delayed if opposition parties oppose the amendment or the committees' process is reviewed. Even if the Constitution is amended, further legislation will have to be enacted to affect the constitutional amendment. The implementation of such changes will have to be clarified through court processes and state programmes (Hornby & Royston, 2017). President Ramaphosa has repeatedly stated that "expropriation without compensation" was necessary in order to address "ownership inequality" and "special equity" (SONA, 2018d). However, there has been a deep, racially polarised division on the issue of expropriation.

A cross-section of the white minority argues that their own hard-earned resources have been spent on their properties (mainly farms), whilst the majority of black people continue to complain about evictions, hardships and abuse on those same farms. Through these divisions, what has become clear is that land reform has failed the rural poor by providing little access to restituted property, productive resources and insecure tenure (Hornby & Royston, 2017). A constitutional amendment is likely to "clarify that land reform does not have to conform to a willing buyer-willing seller principle nor to market-related compensation" (Hornby & Royston, 2017).

In order for land reform to succeed, a progressive approach to expropriation must go beyond allocation of land to include to the provision of basic services, such as water and sanitation, and access to other services and clear tenure arrangements. The next few years will determine whether South Africans have risen above the politics of land.

Furthermore, legislative reform may take years and the government has to be proactive in addressing land reform. The landmark decision of the Haffajee case does allow the government, in the interim, to depart from the controversial willing buyer–willing seller approach and it is clear that it may expropriate property in instances where the seller has turned down a reasonable offer of compensation. However, it must be noted that where the determination of compensation takes place after expropriation, it must be done as soon as reasonably possible, in accordance with Section 25(3) of the Constitution.

The message from the Constitutional Court is that a landowner cannot frustrate the process of expropriation by refusing to accept a reasonable offer of compensation for the said property. The Constitutional Court has shown a willingness to ensure that the acceleration of the land reform process is prioritised, especially against the backdrop of redressing land inequalities and safeguarding the rights of landowners. The Constitutional Court has cleared the path for government to expedite the land reform process and it is suggested that similar cases be dealt with in the same manner.

Conclusion and Recommendations

There is no doubt that the current legislative framework regulating expropriations in South Africa is far from ideal. The discord between the Expropriation Act and the Constitution has been responsible for the slow progress made in rectifying the historical land issues. Rather than criticising land legislations, the government needs to take a closer look at the implementation of the legislations and query those state officials who are failing in their tasks of implementing such legislations (Van Dalsen, 2017). No doubt, an assessment of past mistakes is crucial to improving the management of the land reform process. The lack of infrastructure and the ineffective state structures to support the land reform strategies need to be re-evaluated. In the absence of a supportive structure, land reformation strategy will not succeed.

Government's early vision of land reform, as stipulated in the White Paper "to addressing dispossession and injustices, reducing poverty and assisting economic growth and providing sound land administration", can only be achieved if government provides the necessary support to utilise the land productively and in a sustainable manner. The roles of the organs of state must be clearly defined and understood, and realistic objectives must be set and achieved by all role-players.

A pre-colonial audit of land ownership has been spoken about in the past with little action to back it up, and it may be time to fast-track such an audit with the changing property landscape.

The Constitutional Court has, to some degree, provided a way forward in terms of accelerating the land reform process and deviating from the willing buyer, willing seller approach. It is surprising that cases against the willing buyer, willing seller approach have not come to the forefront. The decision can be used as a tool to address the unstable land reform issues, during the current period, when legislative change and an amendment to the Constitution appears to be considered for the future.

There is no doubt that government needs to strengthen and transform its land reform framework, without impeding economic development, food security and improved livelihoods. Expropriation is central to all the three pillars of land reform and must be used by government as the central means of undoing the social, economic and cultural effects of the previous property situation.

References

Badenhorst, P., Mostert, H., & Pienaar, J. (2006). *Silberberg and Schoeman's the law of property*. Durban: LexisNexis Butterworths.

Budlender, G. (2000). *Juta's new land law*. Cape Town: Juta.

Cape of Good Hope. (1894). *Glen Gray (Act 25 of 1894)*. Cape Town: Cape Times.

Centre for Rural Legal Studies. (2003). *Briefing paper: Expropriating land for re-distribution, unpublished research report*. Stellenbosch: CRLS.

Constitutional Court. (2000, 4 October). *Case SA46*, Johannesburg.

Constitutional Court. (2002, 16 May). *Case SA310*, Johannesburg.

Constitutional Court. (2006, 20 January). *Case SA297*, Johannesburg.

Constitution Court. (2010, 11 May). *Tongoane and others v National Minister for agriculture and land affairs and others* (CCT100/09) ZACC 10; 2010 (6) SA 214 (CC); 2010 (8) BCLR 741 (CC).

Constitutional Court. (2011a, 20 January). *Case SA293*, Johannesburg.

Constitutional Court. (2011b, 20 June). *Case SA134*, Johannesburg.

Davenport, T. (1985). Some reflections on the history of land tenure in South Africa, seen in the light of attempts by the State to impose political and economic control. *Acta Juridica*, pp. 53–76.

Davenport, T., & Hunt, K. (1974). *The right to the land document no. 17*. Cape Town: David Philip.
De Villiers, B. (2003). *Land reform: Issues and challenges*. Cape Town: Konrad Adenauer Foundation.
Department of Land Affairs. (1997). *White Paper on land policy*. Available www.ruraldevelopment.gov.za/.../White-Papers/whitepaperlandreform.pdf. Accessed December 2018.
Du Plesis, E. (2014). Silence is golden: The lack of direction on compensation for expropriation in the 2011 Green Paper on land reform. *Potchefstroomse Elektroniese Regsblad, 17*(2), 24.
Du Plessis, W., Olivier, N., & Pienaar, J. (1991). Nuwe grondmaatreëls. *SA Public Law*, pp. 255–269.
Eisenberg, A. (1995). Public purpose and expropriation: Some comparative insights and South African Bill of Rights. *South African Journal Human Rights, 11*(2), 207–221.
Flemmer, M. (1976). *Sir William H Beaumont and the Native land commission 1913–1916*. A Master's Degree of Arts in History, University of Natal, Durban.
Hornby, D., & Royston, L. (2017). *Untitled: Securing land Tenure in urban and rural South Africa*. Durban: UKZN Press.
Jacobs, M. (1982). *Law of expropriation in South Africa*. Cape Town: Juta & Co.
Klopper, H., & Pienaar, G. J. (2014). A historical context of land reform in South Africa and early policies. *Potchefstroomse Elektroniese Regsblad, 17*, 685–688.
Lahiff, E. (2007). Willing buyer, willing seller: South Africa's failed experiment in market-led agrarian reform. *Third World Quarterly, 28*(8), 1577–1597.
Lewin, J. (1944). The native in South Africa, Witwatersrand university press, Johannesburg. In M. De Klerk (Ed.), *A harvest of discontent: The land question in South Africa* (pp. 99–111).
Loveland, I. (1999). By due process of law: Racial discrimination & the Right to Vote in South Africa 1855–1960. Oxford: Hart, pp. 242–243.
Marais, E. J., & Maree, P. J. H. (2016). At the intersection between expropriation law and administrative law: Two critical views on the Constitutional Court's Arun judgement. *Potchefstroomse Elektroniese Regsblad, 19*(1), 1–54.
Murray, C., & Williams, G. (1994). Land and freedom in South Africa. *Review of African Political Economy, 61*, 315–324.
Parliament of South Africa. (1936). *Native Trust and Land (Act 18 of 1936)*. Pretoria: Government Printer.
Pienaar, J. M. (2015). Land reform embedded in the constitution: Legal contextualization. *Scriptura, 114, 1*–20.

PMG. (2019). *Committee Report on Amending Section 25 of the Constitution*. Available https://pmg.org.za/committee-meeting/28123/. Accessed May 2019.
Republic of South Africa. (1950). *Group Areas (Act No. 41 of 1950)*. Pretoria: Government Printer.
Republic of South Africa. (1965). *The Expropriation (Act No. 55 of 1965)*. Pretoria: Government Printer.
Republic of South Africa. (1966). *Group Areas (Act No. 36 of 1966)*. Pretoria: Government Printer.
Republic of South Africa. (1975). *The Expropriation (Act No. 63 of 1975)*. Pretoria: Government Printer.
Republic of South Africa. (1991). *Abolition of Racially Based Land Measures (Act No. 108 of 1991)*. Pretoria: Government Printer.
Republic of South Africa. (1993). *The Provision of Certain Land for Settlement (Act No. 126 of 1993)*. Pretoria: Government Printer.
Republic of South Africa. (1994). *Restitution of Land Rights (Act No. 22 of 1994)*. Pretoria: Government Printer.
Republic of South Africa. (1994). White Paper on Reconstruction and Development, Notice No. 1954 of 1994. Available https://www.gov.za/sites/default/files/governmentgazetteid16085.pdf. Accessed December 2018.
Republic of South Africa. (1996a). *Land Reform (Labour Tenants) (Act No. 486 of 1996)*. Pretoria: Government Printer.
Republic of South Africa. (1996b). *The Constitution of the Republic of South Africa of 1996*. Pretoria: Government Printer.
Republic of South Africa. (1997). *The Extension of Security of Tenure Act (Act No. 62 of 1997)*. Pretoria: Government Printer.
Republic of South Africa. (2000). *The Promotion of Administrative Justice (Act No. 3 of 2000)*. Pretoria: Government Printer.
Republic of South Africa. (2004). *Communal Land Rights (Act No. 11 of 2004)*. Pretoria: Government Printer.
Republic of South Africa. (2008, May). *Land Reform in South Africa, Getting Back on Track—CDE Research No. 16*.
Republic of South Africa. (2012, June). *Land Reform Policy Discussion Document*. Pretoria: Government Printer.
Republic of South Africa. (2012). *Land Reform Policy Document*. Available https://www.sahistory.org.za/sites/default/files/landpolicyproposals_june2012v_1.pdf. Accessed December 2018.
Republic of South Africa. (2016). *Diagnostic report on land reform in South Africa*. Available http://www.parliament.gov.za/storage/app/media/Pages/2017/october/High_Level_Panel/Commissioned_Report_land/Diagnostic_Report_on_Land_Reform_in_South_Africa.pdf. Accessed December 2018.

Republic of South Africa. (2018a). *Cabinet approves expropriation bill*. Available https://www.gov.za/sites/default/files/b4-2015_150213_edited.pdf. Accessed November 2018.

Republic of South Africa. (2018b). *Green Paper on land reform*. Available http://www.gov.za/sites/www.gov.za/files/land_reform_green_paper.pdf. Accessed November 2018.

Republic of South Africa. (2018c). *State of the nations address*. Available https://www.gov.za/speeches/state-nation-address-2018. Accessed November 2018.

Republic of South Africa. (2018d). *President Cyril Ramaphosa: State of the Nation Address: South African Government*. Available https://www.gov.za/speeches/president-cyril-ramaphosa-2018-state-nation-address-16-feb-201 8pdf. Accessed December 2018.

Robinson, L. G. (1997). Rationales for rural land redistribution in South Africa Brooklyn. *Journal of International Law, 23*, 465–484.

Rugege, S. (2004). Land reform in South Africa: An overview. *International Journal of Legal Information, 32*(2), 283–312.

SA History. (2018). *Natives Land Act (Act 27 of 1913)*. Available https://www.sahistory.org.za/archive/natives-land-act-act-no-27-1913. Accessed November 2018.

Slade, B. V. (2014). Public purpose or public interest and third party transfers. *Potchefstroomse Elektroniese Regsblad, 17*(1), 167–206.

Union Parliament. (1913). *Natives Land (Act 27 of 1913)*. Pretoria: Government Printer.

Van Dalsen, A. (2017). *Land reform—Presidential policy statements on expropriation without compensation*. Available https://hsf.org.za/resource-centre/hsf-briefs/landreformpresidential-policy-statements. Accessed on 17 May 2017.

Van der Walt, A. J. (2005). *Constitutional property law*. Landsdowne: Juta & Co.

Van der Walt, A. J., & Pienaar, J. M. (2009). *Introduction to the law of property*. Landsdowne: Juta & Co.

Wentzel, W. (2005). *The draft Expropriation Bill, 2013 and the Constitutional Court's decision in White Paper on Reconstruction and Development. 1994*. Gen N 1954 in GG 16085 of 23 November 1994.

Wickins, P. (1981). The Natives Land Act of 1913: A cautionary essay on simple explanations of complex change. *South African Journal of Economics, 49*, 105–129.

CHAPTER 3

Globalization of South African Land Reform Scheme: An Interrogation

Adeoye O. Akinola and Irrshad Kaseeram

Introduction

In colonial, apartheid and post-apartheid South Africa, land and land-related issues have dominated public discourse and policymaking. The apartheid government monopolized land, a very basic asset, resources and capital, and continued to reproduce inequality in the country. Land was used as an instrument of disempowerment during apartheid; thus, the successive post-apartheid governments have seen land reform as a means to redressing historical injustice, bridging the inequality gap between the white minority and black majority, and empowering the black poor (Akinola, 2018a). Since apartheid, and up till the present, South Africa has remained one of the most unequal society in the world (Greenwood, 2018). Thus, land reform aims at underscoring the fact that agrarian

A. O. Akinola (✉) · I. Kaseeram
University of Zululand, KwaDlangezwa, South Africa
e-mail: AkinolaA@unizulu.ac.za; aoakinola@uj.ac.za

I. Kaseeram
e-mail: KaseeramI@unizulu.ac.za

A. O. Akinola et al. (eds.), *The New Political Economy of Land Reform in South Africa*,
https://doi.org/10.1007/978-3-030-51129-6_3

transformation is required to reallocate capital assets that had been disarticulated by the 1913 Natives' Land Act, which had generated a landless majority in the country (Department of Land Affairs, 1997).

The importance of land in the new global economic order has put pressures on governments to rethink land arrangements in many African countries. Their colonial legacies distorted the pre-colonial land administration in the continent. Land is an important source of capital, and a productive asset for the poor (Lipton, 2009). Thus, restricted access to land is the cause of protracted food insecurity, dwindling agro-allied industrial power, the developmental crises and the conflicts recorded in South Africa, as well as many other African countries (Moyo, 2007). In other words, "access to land, is fundamental to most households and remains the means of livelihood, 'centre of gravity' to communities, as well as sources of natural capital, social sustainability and spiritual fulfilment" (Akinola & Wissink, 2019: v).

Generally, there are three major approaches to land reform: a radicalization approach (Zimbabwe); a nationalization or state-ownership model (Nigeria) and a liberal-oriented or market-led approach (South Africa). Post-apartheid South Africa combines two of these models: a state-led model, which entails the nationalization of land and a liberal-oriented or market-led reform, which involves the willing buyer, willing seller land reform model. The entire reform project of the government was categorized into three elements: land redistribution, land restitution and tenure security (Department of Land Affairs, 1997). Despite the efforts of the state to correct the skewed-land arrangement in the country, there are both endogenous and exogenous restrictions. The most damaging is the influence of globalization on the sociopolitical and economic environment whereby the policy on land is determined.

Since the start of majority rule in 1994, emphasis has been placed on market approaches to land reform in Africa. The Brettonwood institutions, a powerful farmers' union (predominantly white) in South Africa, in particular, and traditional authorities have pressurized the government from adopting a radical approach to land reform (Cousins, 2015). The result was the insertion of Section 25 of the South African Constitution, which provides for the processes for "democratic" land reform programmes, in conformity with a global economic template. The liberalization of African economies, and influence of global capital on land reform, is one of the contradictions of globalization in Africa. Globalization has affected the course of national policies in developing countries, including South Africa.

The global economic order has constrained the sovereignty of state to control their national economies and embark on a bottom-up land policy approach. While the acclaimed African "economic miracle" is a product of globalization, globalization has catered for the needs of the affluent few, while ordinary Africans, particularly black South Africans, are still trapped in shacks, shanty towns, poverty and uncertainty, struggling with black African immigrants for survival. Cousins (2015) acknowledges the disappointing outcome of the post-apartheid land reform programmes and strongly believes in the continued relevance of land reform in the country's quest for redressing historical injustice, attainment of democratization and sustainable development.

Globalization of land, land dispossession during colonialism and apartheid, and failed land reform projects of the post-apartheid South Africa have generated growing conflicts over land use across sociocultural cleavages, class, gender and nationality. Therefore, this chapter interrogates the government's adoption of the neoliberal approach to land reform, which has engendered poverty and widened inequality in the country. Aside the use of literature, the chapter relies on primary data, through unstructured interviews of stakeholders in the South African land reform scheme in KwaZulu-Natal and Northern Cape provinces between September 2017 and August 2019. This was guided by the principle of anonymity.

A Glimpse into History

The anti-colonial struggle against apartheid domination was partly based on the objective of regaining the land which was violently taken from the black majority. The white minority government promulgated the Native Land Act of 1913, which allocated 13% of the land area of the country to the black population, which constituted about 80% of the national population, while the whites controlled more than 80% of the land (Rugege, 2004: 283). More than two centuries of subjugation of local communities by the European powers deprived black South Africans of most of their land resources, through coercion, and economic and legal instruments (Bosch, n.d.). Kariuki adopts a historical analysis to locate the central sources of discord in the land reform discourse thus:

> The process of settler occupation entailed the alienation of fertile agricultural lands and the creation of exclusive reserves for African occupation that were least arable and environmentally degraded. Thus, the struggle over land was fundamentally a struggle of rights over ownership, control, access and use of land. (Kariuki, 2009: 1)

In South Africa, land dispossession during apartheid, and the consistent denials of the rights of the majority to land, constituted one of the major motivations for the masses' support for liberation movements, led mainly by the African National Congress (ANC). Thus, at the advent of majority rule in 1994, the political leadership realized the imperative of implementing a land policy that would cater for the needs of black people and redress the injustices of the apartheid regime.

Land reform has now become a veritable instrument for the mass mobilization of the black majority during elections. Thus, the timing of the land expropriation without compensation (LEWC) "coincides" with the replacement of President Jacob Zuma, with the Vice President, Cyril Ramaphosa, and the 2019 general election in the country. The failed reform agenda and intensified agitations for policy shifts in the land and agricultural sector led to President Zuma's push for the attainment of LEWC by the state. This would involve the seizure of land from the white people and reallocation to the landless black majority for the purpose of redressing historical land inequality. While the Ramaphosa-led administration changed the narratives of LEWC, his administration continues to ride on its popularity among the predominantly black population. In general, populist utterances in respect to land redistribution have become elements of party manifestoes during election due to the preserved land inequality in the country.

Land inequality is a decisive indicator of the wide economic gap between the elite (mostly white) and the masses (constituting the black majority). Therefore, land reform became the major policy drive of the Cyril Ramaphosa's administration. It is important to note that South Africa operates a dual economy with two distinct sectors: a white urban and capitalist agrarian system and a rural poor African sector (Alexander, 2015: 19). However, the underdevelopment of the poor rural African population cannot only be attributed to the legacy of land dispossession but located within the dictates of the new international economic order.

Despite the efforts of the post-apartheid administrations to redistribute the land resources, the adoption of liberal policy template founded on the willing buyer, willing seller approach and monetization of land, there are compelling evidences of policy failure, land hunger and invasions, denials of land rights and land inequality in the democratic South Africa (Akinola, 2018a). It was soon clear that the liberalization of the land reform was a policy error and, thus, the admission by the government of its failure, as far back as 2016, and the urgency to radicalize land policy in the country.

Based on the White Paper on Land Reform (1997), the overreaching "objectives of land reform are to redress the injustices of apartheid, foster national reconciliation and stability, underpin economic growth; and improve household welfare and alleviate poverty" (Department of Land Affairs, 1997). Indeed, "the post-1994 government land reform project conceived land reform as a liberationist agenda designed at addressing inequities of the hitherto political dispensations" (Akinola, 2018a: 3).

The ANC-led state has failed to implement effective land reform in the post-apartheid South Africa. A disjointed land reform programme would struggle to attain the lofty objectives highlighted in the 1997 White Paper on Land Reform, which becomes the foundations upon which the reform agenda stands. For instance, the implementation of LEWC may reinforce both racial divisions and social fragmentation in the country, while many black South Africans still live in shacks and many others are subjected to undignified lifestyles in many illegal and legal settlements across the country. Failed land reform has jeopardized food security due to land and farm unproductivity. Although there are debates whether LEWC would increase the employment in the agricultural sector, it is not also clear how LEWC would address the lack of support for emerging farmers and land beneficiaries, which largely results in land and farm unproductivity. While the government has identified LEWC as the best, and fastest, route to effective reform, it is pertinent to revisit the pre-colonial land tenure system and see how to modernize the indigenous land arrangement.

The issue of land reform is located in the broad discourse of colonialism in South Africa. At the advent of majority rule in 1994, there was a serious disagreement between the Africanists and ANC with respect to presenting the best approach to the land question. The ANC founded land reform on a colonial paradigm, while the Africanist favoured a more inclusive and locally driven land arrangement that would effectively benefit the disadvantaged in the country.

In reality, and in terms of driving agrarian reform, alleviating poverty and igniting rural development and combating rural–urban migration, the prevalent land policy has no foundation to achieve these objectives.

As noted by Moyo (2007: 2), "increased struggles for land reflect the absence of a development capable of absorbing the employment and consumption needs of growing populations into industrializing and diversified economies. The agrarian transition has so far failed to materialize, while the home market remains disarticulated" (Moyo, 2007: 2). This aligns with the reality of land relations in other post-colonial African countries, like Zimbabwe.

It is germane to understand that land relations in the pre-colonial Africa were based on communalism, in opposition to the individualist nature of modernity. Lands were entrusted to the communities through traditional and family leaders. Land ownership and the importance of title deeds or other formal documents in support of land ownership was alien to pre-Africa. In that period, land use was synonymous with ownership.

Globalization of Land and Land Reform

Globalization increases the worldwide interconnectedness of people and their engagements through markets, information and capital flows, human migrations, and sociopolitical institutions (Lambina & Meyfroidt, 2011). The interconnectivity makes it easy to transfer western sociopolitical and economic systems (liberal ideology) to other societies. Globalization aims to universalize the human environment and subject every system to the dictate of capitalist countries under the leadership of the United States and other advanced capitalist countries (Akinola, 2018b). Globalization "increases the influence of large agri-business enterprises and international financial flows on local land use decisions, in some cases weakening national policies intended to promote a public good" (Lambina & Meyfroidt, 2011: 3465). Globalization is understood to represent the height of liberal ideology, reflected in the universalism of Western political (democracy) and economic (capitalism) systems.

While liberalists relate democratization to sustainable peace and security, based on the proposition of the democratic peace theory (Akinola, 2018b), the liberalization of the South African land reform and the democratic regime's stability, since 1994, has not resulted into corresponding peace and security in the country. Land conflict has escalated, while land-related public dissent and mass disillusionment have continued to be heightened. The persistent land conflict has reinforced racial hostility, which resulted in about 160 racism-related violent incidents on farms in January 2016, which was the highest occurrences of farm conflict since 1994 (Sieff, 2016). By 2019, farm attacks and murders have been racialized.

In practical terms, particularly in post-apartheid South Africa, liberal approaches to land reform have failed bridge the gap between the rich white farmers or land owners and the poor or landless blacks. It was not designed to redistribute land wealth on the principle of equity and justice. It is a system promoted by individual accumulation in place of communalism, which characterized pre-colonial Africa. The evolution of globalization predated colonialism in Africa. It started with imperialism around the fifteenth century, which later led to the political subjugation of African societies and governance structures. The contradictions of the integration of the African economy to the advanced capitalist world, which started with imperialism and was consolidated by colonialism, became evident in Africa. African resources were explored and exploited, leading to land dispossession in countries like South Africa and Zimbabwe.

Colonialism directly integrated the economies of African into that of the advanced European powers. This created two opposing classes: the core and the periphery, the developed and the underdeveloped, the industrial and the consumer economies. The same stratification is replicated in national economies, which institutionalize the capitalist class and the masses. Capitalism has replaced feudalism and overthrown communism. It has also replaced African modes of economic interaction, communalism and trade-by-barter. Capitalism and market economy, therefore, have become the economic system most compatible to the development of globalization.

There is a big difference between land use, possession and land ownership; successive South African governments have failed to reconcile these differences. In pre-colonial Africa, land ownership by individuals was limited and relegated as secondary. Land was a communal property, rather than individual, under the control of traditional authorities, clan leaders and family heads. The nature of African societies made land ownership remote; lands were allocated to users periodically. For instance, no land was allocated or reserved for those who had no immediate use of land. Land occupation, land use and utility were synonyms for "land ownership" in pre-colonial African communal societies. This is starkly different from the modern-day commercialization of land that places critical importance on land ownership and the possession of title deeds.

Contrary to the commercialization, monetization and commodification of land by liberal ideology, land is not just a commodity: it encompasses everything that defines black South Africans. Establishing the importance of land to black people, Rugege (2004) presents the viewpoint of an old man, which emphasizes the perspectives of the majority of black South Africans,

> The land, our purpose is the land, that is what we must achieve. The land is our whole lives, we plough it for food, we build our houses from the soil, we live on it and we are buried in it. When the whites took our land away from us, we lost the dignity of our lives, we could no longer feed our children. We were forced to become servants; we were treated like animals. Our people have many problems, we are beaten and killed by the farmers, the wages we earn are too little to buy even a bag of mielie-meal. (Rugege, 2004: 284)

As consistently argued by radical political economists, capitalists are not in the business of creating desired jobs in societies but are driven by profit maximization and capital accumulation. While the National Development Plan (NDP), which aimed at poverty elimination and reduction of inequality, highlighted how improved land use in communal areas has the propensity to improve the livelihoods of about 300,000 South Africans, the means to achieve this is lacking (National Planning Commission, 2012). Thus, the targets remain unachievable.

The NDP, a policy template for a better South Africa by 2030, enumerated other government targets. Other aims of the policy documents were to increase employment from 13 million in 2010 to 24 million in 2030; realize a developmental, capable and ethical state that treats citizens with dignity; broaden social cohesion and unity, while redressing the inequities of the past; and realize a food trade surplus, with one-third produced by small-scale farmers or households (National Planning Commission, 2012). Furthermore,

> Rural economies will be activated through improved infrastructure and service delivery, a review of land tenure, service to small and micro farmers, a review of mining industry commitments to social investment, and tourism investments" while the government was to create "an additional 643 000 direct jobs and 326 000 indirect jobs in the agriculture, agro-processing and related sectors by 2030. (National Planning Commission, 2012: 57–58)

The realization of these aims, within the liberal framework of land policy in South Africa, is questionable.

The nature of globalization ensures a shift from an agricultural market directed at ensuring food security, to the integration of South African agricultural market with that of global agricultural economy. In relation to land use, the global shortage of productive land motivated agricultural and financial actors at the global level to delve into the internal land policies of states towards the realization of the optimal use of arable land.

The World Bank, which advocated market-led land reform, suggested the delivery of 30% of land back to black South Africans within five years (Cousins, 2015; Hall, 2004; Walker, 2017). The ANC-led government adopted this and ran into problems. As posited by Moyo (2003), the liberal approach to land arrangement favoured the predominantly white farming elites, who could easily access the required capital (both local and foreign) to engage in successful large-scale farming. Thus, the lack of support to emerging black farmers engendered land unproductivity and deepened the socio-economic gap between white and black people, and thereby, ironically, reinforcing the asset and land inequality that land reform aimed at addressing. While the government later realized the lack of support system for land beneficiaries and established the Recapitalisation and Development Policy Programme, which replaced all previous forms of funding for land reform (Cousins, 2015), institutional assistance to the emerging black farmers remains grossly inadequate.

A vital component of liberalization policy, the Structural Adjustment Programme (SAP), with its insistence on subsidy removal, aggravated the struggles in the land and agricultural sectors, which led to what Moyo (2007: 2) calls "the collapse of Africa's nascent agro-industrial base". Farm produce was directed at the international market, rather than national markets. This is possibly because of the higher income accruable from operating globally rather than in the unstable national economic space. This could be advantageous to large-scale commercial farmers, but the local farmers do not have the capacity to operate and compete at this level. As noted by Moyo (2007: 5), "for the middle-sized farm to realise its potential of redirecting production to the national market and hence to synergise dynamically with domestic wages, a reversal of neo-liberal policies would be required". The present South African government has realized the imperative of abandoning liberal ideology and have seen LEWC as a policy choice, but there has not been any clarity on the policy direction in this regard.

As experienced across Africa, SAP has remained one of the basic instruments of liberalization, which engenders free trade (Akinola, 2018b). The South African border is opened, not only to exportation of agricultural produce, but for the importation of farm products, skills and labour, which disadvantages local farmers. As revealed by the participant, in the South African sugarcane industry, local farmers have struggled to negotiate better with sugarcane entrepreneurs who dictate the prices due to their exposure to quality and cheaper sugarcane from the neighbouring Southern African countries. Indeed, local farmers are more likely to concentrate on national food consumption, while large-scale farmers are predisposed to targeting both the national and the international markets. As revealed by a participant, this is because of the higher income accruable from operating on the global stage than on the unstable national economic space. Many of the participants, mostly local farmers, hold that large-scale farming could be advantageous to the large-scale commercial farmers, but local farmers did not have the capacity to operate and compete at this level.

Land reform tailored towards large-scale farming is not entirely bad for local economies, but the peculiarity of the respective national economies should be taken into consideration before adopting such agricultural policy. Globally, "at least 1.5b people today have some farmland as a result of land reform, and are less poor, as a result. But huge, inefficient land and land inequality remains, or have re-emerged in low income countries" (Lipton, 2009: 8). This may be related to the market-led land reform, based on the willing buyer, willing seller approach. This was well captured by Hall, who maintains that,

> Reliance on the market and on willing sellers to make land available for redistribution, and a relatively 'hands-off' state, means that land reform falls short of confronting and transforming entrenched forms of exclusion and marginality. While providing crucial resources to some, land reform is proceeding alongside the deepening of capitalist relations of production in the countryside. In this context, a focus on transferring assets to the poor is anomalous, since they lack the means to engage in capital accumulation in commercial agriculture. (Hall, 2004: 225)

Globalization has reduced the capacity of the Southern African states to act independently. Global capital consistently hits at the sovereign power of the state to implement locally devised and national-driven economic policy. Factually, "the African state, situated within the context of neo-colonial class formation processes and extroverted economic structures, is itself shaped by differentiated internal social forces that define political power and accumulation, but these remain subordinated to external capital and markets" (Moyo, 2007: 7).

While South Africa has projected itself as a regional power, the state is subjected and subordinated to global capital (Ogunnubi & Akinola, 2017). A participant in Kimberley, Northern Cape, engages the weakness of the state thus:

> The government think they are in control, far from it. They are not. Government officials have continued to shy away from sharing uncomfortable truths among themselves. Government have lacked the capacity to control and outwit powerful interests in the land sector. In many instances, non-governmental elites have been able to assemble experts in all fields (economics, surveying, real estate, agro-economist), who have succeeded to manipulate the government to accede to their demands. For instance, when the former President spoke about embarking on 'radical economic transformation', he was staunchly challenged by powerful forces that were under him and many of them have controlled governments for more than a century. Eventually, the President tactically dropped the idea and the use of the term 'radical'.

Liberalism creates a strong interlink between the state and the capital, and it follows that whoever controls the state, controls the capital, and vice versa. Therefore, the white owners of capital have a strong hold on the post-apartheid state to the detriment of the majority black population. As argued by political economists, and reinforced by Cousins (2015), while the capitalist elites created a little space for entry, it is very difficult for emerging black land or farm owners to break into this "status" in the present South Africa. This is in tandem with the elite[1] theory, popularized by Mosca and Pareto (Delican, n.d.). It is ironic to think that an elitist political institution—the state—in a developing society could effectively champion the cause of the masses.

Globalization results in the urbanization of some parts of the country, through industrialization and exploration of natural resources. The emergence of the cities (core) and rural areas (periphery) became a reality

[1] The elites, referred to as "higher stratum" by Pareto, comprise of people who are on top of other classes (Delican, n.d.).

in the country. Through the sophistication of the cities and attractive employment opportunities for migrant labour, there was rural–urban bulge during apartheid. A participant notes that post-apartheid South Africa continued to reinforce the rural–urban movement due to the failure of land reform to resolve agrarian transformation and the development of the rural areas towards achieving reversed migration. This brings to the fore the link between land reform and rural–urban migration. South Africa's industrial economy absorbs labour from the hinterland, thereby promoting rural–urban movement. Khan (2015: 9) describes the reason for the urban migration bulge as the "tendency to extract raw materials from the rural hinterland and transfer it to urban processing zones wherein the manufacturing sector is primarily located". Land reform could be used to drive the development of the rural areas and ensure migration reversals.

Globalization and the Reality of Land Reform

The post-apartheid land reform, based on liberal ideology, was subjected to the dictates of the global market. According to Moyo and Yeros (cited in Moyo 2007), market-driven land policy framework has had two implications for national development in Africa. Firstly, it abandons the integration of agriculture and industry at the national level, enhancing instead their integration into the global markets. Secondly, it aggravates economic and social insecurities, strengthens migration to urban centres and produces a deepening mode of maldevelopment.

Moyo (2007) further explains that capitalist relations of production have displaced feudal-type relations in Europe and elsewhere, but the level of industrial growth in the developing countries has been very minimal. These trends have increased popular dependence on land for social reproduction, while agrarian productivity potentials remain unrealized. He declares that with the failure to resolve the agrarian question, the national question remains unresolved. Land reform is an instrument of political struggles and land control has become a "key source of mobilizing power through electoral politics in which capital and class power direct struggles for democratisation and development" (Moyo, 2007: 8). The apartheid government used land ownership and access to enrich the whites, while the black majority experienced denials of land rights and access to productive resources.

There was high optimism among black people that land reform would be the mechanism to redress historical inequality, eradicate poverty and improve agricultural productivity. Over two decades after the minority rule of apartheid, questions continue to be raised about the effectiveness of land reforms as a poverty elimination instrument, especially in the remote arid areas like the Southern Kalahari (Bradstock, 2007: 23). In their study, Dikgang and Muchapondwa (2015) establish the link between land access and household economic well-being. In the Southern Kalahari, Khomani San beneficiaries have gained more access to land but the use of restituted land has neither increased per capita income nor reduced the high rate of poverty in Southern Kalahari (Dikgang & Muchapondwa, 2015). Instead, the use of restituted land has heightened poverty. The Khomani San community is characterized by land underutilization due to the complexity generated by the administration of the restituted land and the lack of support systems for the farming communities. For instance, electricity supply to the region was disconnected for more than a decade, while access to basic infrastructures (schools, market, and hospitals) was greatly restricted.

The World Bank has been very critical about the South Africa's level of poverty and inequality (Calland, n.d.). More than half of South Africans (55.5%) lived in poverty in 2018 (Wilkinson 2018). The report further revealed that 9 out of every 10 poor South Africans (93%) were black, while that of the white population was estimated at 1%. One of the big challenges of the reform agenda at the formative stage was what Hall (2004) refers to as "big policy and the shrinking state". The state adopted its land reform model without careful consideration of the economic and sociopolitical environment through which the policy was to be actualized. Dikgang and Muchapondwa (2015: 13) claim that "a general weakness of many land reform projects is the lack of attention to continuities between pre- and post-transfer livelihoods strategies". Under the land restitution legal framework, the government had an option to award the successful claimants either alternative land or cash compensation if it was not possible to award them their ancestral land. Most urban claims were settled financially through the willing buyer, willing seller approach (Dikgang & Muchapondwa, 2015).

Out of the 77, 149 land claims resolved by the state, more than 92% of the claimants (71, 292) preferred monetary compensation over land ownership (DA, 2013). By 2015, only about 8% of land claimed through redistribution or restitution have been settled. Of the 69, 119 urban restitution claims that have been settled, the majority of these were through the payment of cash compensation (Cousins, 2015: 6). Based on the National Development Plan 2011, the scope of land reform has been expanded to include the creation of jobs, improved livelihood of rural population and agricultural productivity (Cousins, 2015). Policy failure directly explains the slow pace of reform, land unproductivity and food insecurity in the country. Based on the estimation, about 90% of agricultural land transferred to black emerging farmers has not been utilized productively (Khan, 2015). Ashton (2012) argues that

> it is fruitless to hand over huge parcels of land to new, emerging farmers with inadequate capital resources and no means to leverage land for capital collateral. Most of the land presently being transferred to new owners is not even transferred, but leased, almost setting the system up for failure. (Ashton, 2012)

The willing buyer, willing seller approach is an expensive route to land reform. Different land entrepreneurs, lawyers, estate valuers and financial bodies were paid for each transaction through the willing buyer, willing seller approach. The Treasury stated that,

> The department plans to settle 2 851 claims over the MTEF period. R10.8 billion is allocated over the period in the Restitution programme for settling claims, constituting 32.3% of the department's total budget, while R331.6 million is allocated in the same programme for spending on consultants. (National Treasury, 2018: 4)

Despite the high costs of implementing land reform, inadequate budgetary allocation for land reform was evident in the first decade, whereby the budget for land reform was below 0.5% of the national budget (Hall, 2004: 221). More than two decades after, Hall has observed that the situation remains the same. Thus, the propensity for people to opt for financial settlement in place of land access complicated the entire process and made the implementation of the policy too expensive for the government, which could explain policy failure. As revealed by Walker (2017: 19), "consistently small budgets certainly positioned land reform as a minor program of government, and one that constitutes the most contentious public debate. While fluctuating over the years is evident, funds allocated for reform never exceeded 1 percent of budgetary allocations".

Furthermore, the government policy of acquiring or buying and redistributing land to those in need has raised other issues in terms of identifying the "genuine" beneficiaries in need of land. Ineffective redistribution may engender neo-land capture, whereby the ruling elites and the civil servants and land entrepreneurs are in a collusion to accumulate the gains of the land reform. There have been cases of land reform corruption across the country. This has created contradictions, as government has allegedly acquired land, which has not been redistributed. The state lacks the required financial power to buy, and, in some cases, there are difficulties in determining market value of land. Government also faces persistent opposition from the black minority, led by the leader of the Economic Freedom Fighters (EFF) leader, Julius Malema, to implement land expropriation without compensation (LEWC). LEWC is expected to make land available for the emerging black farmers and others interested in small farming.

Recently, there have been calls for increased small-scale farming by black people, but the drivers of land reform had prioritized large-scale farming. Under President Thabo Mbeki, "the land reform program actively favored more commercially oriented aspirant farmers; productivity, measured in terms of market participation, became the new catchphrase" (Walker, 2017: 19). This highly disfavoured black small-scale farmers and relegated them to the background in terms of accessing government largesse for the agricultural sector. President Thabo Mbeki's approach favoured the new international economic order, which celebrates large-scale commercial farming and downgrades the contribution of small-scale farming. Although many black small-scale farmers have benefited from land reform,

> Overall, the major beneficiaries of processes of agrarian change have been the owners of large-scale commercial farming and agribusiness enterprises. This reflects in part the poor performance of land reform, but it is also consonant with broader trends in society towards the concentration of economic power in a few large corporations. (Cousins, 2015: 7)

The capitalization of farms or large-scale agriculture, a fallout of globalization and integration of South African agricultural economy into the global markets has led to the evictions of farm workers and a drastic decline in farm labour. Indeed, machines have replaced humans on large-scale commercial farms. This has further put pressures on the country's rising unemployment and the urgency for rethinking the prevalent land reform programmes.

There is a direct relationship between the rising unemployment and land conflict. South Africa has witnessed rising farm conflicts, resulting in the loss of lives and property. Global finance capital, which has penetrated Africa, has become one of the drivers of land-related conflicts, as the exploitation of natural resources, such as oil and minerals, has expanded into new African enclaves, which have highlighted the foreign dimension of underdevelopment of the continent. Most conflicts in Africa revolve around issues of land and/or resources over land. As noted by Akinola and Uzodike (2017: 2),

> Certain groups' desire to control power and resources at the expense of others explains the racism, ethnic conflict, genocide, xenophobia, civil wars, and armed insurrections experienced by many African states, particularly those like South Africa that experienced prolonged foreign domination.

These realities have reinforced the significance of land in the political economy of South Africa. As noted by Moyo (2003), "variegated struggles at varying scales and localities over escalating unequal access to and control of land represent Africa's real land question", which translates to sociopolitical and economic challenges. Civil wars, inter-country conflicts in the region, migration and involuntary displacements are symptoms of rising land conflicts, which manifest in violent conflicts over access to key natural resources, by both domestic and external forces.

Conclusion

The chapter has engaged the influence of globalization on South African land reform programmes and revealed the challenges of adopting neoliberal ideology to redress historical injustice and land dispossession in post-apartheid South Africa. An adoption of liberalization policy, without effective implementation capacity, explains policy failure. The willing buyer, willing seller approach failed due to a lack of finance and the unwillingness of many to sell. When land was available for sale, the price was above market value. Thus, land market contradicts the logic of the law of supply and demand or "invisible hand", which ought to ensure the effective regulation of the market.

As capitalism is evolving so also is the development of strategies for manipulating market functioning by the capitalist class, to the detriment of the impoverished masses. The chapter reinforced the correlation between the lopsided land arrangements and poverty in South Africa. Land is an asset, a resource, a capital and a source of wealth and livelihood. Thus, the denial of land is a prerequisite for poverty. This is more peculiar to the rural population who made their living from land and land-related endeavours, either as farmers or farm workers. Land is not just a resource, like crude oil, timber and gold. It is not just an economic commodity, like automobiles or shoes. It constitutes a basic and social resource that binds societies to a universal heritage and also acts as an instrument of social stability and national security.

The chapter located the land reform discourse in historical exposition, and posited that the historical land dispossession by the apartheid regime and the unequal land relations between the white and black population, motivated for the implementation of land reform by successive post-apartheid governments. Despite the efforts of the state in the reform regime, it is unanimously accepted that the reform agenda has failed.

The willing buyer, willing seller approach (which is the pillar of land redistribution) has been jettisoned by the government, while evidence of land hunger and conflict has prevailed. Indeed, land inequality persists. This has called into question the wisdom of the choice of liberal approach to land reform, and, thus, the attempt of the ANC-led government to draw supports for the radicalization of land reform in South Africa, under the "land expropriation without compensation" slogan. Based on the character of the state and its approach to the policy shift, it is doubtful whether expropriation without compensation is the magic wand required to effectively redistribute land resources for the benefits of the majority, without threatening the social stability and economic growth of South Africa.

Land reform in South Africa is very complex, both in the draft of the policy and its implementation. There have also been concerns about its nature and reality. Indeed, the policy on land and the viewpoints of reform actors needs to be decolonized. The present arrangement reinforces the policy template adopted during colonialism and continues to enhance inequality of land relations in the country. Generally, colonialism in Africa and under the apartheid regime in South Africa has distorted the pre-colonial land arrangement and land tenure system, and imposed upon society a modern or state-inclined model of land administration.

South Africa experienced racial capitalism during apartheid and the weight of neoliberal capitalism in the post-apartheid dispensation. The political and socio-economic institutions that were established to promote racial discrimination were destroyed by post-apartheid successive governments; however, the existing land administration still reinforces racial divisions and elitism. This is compatible with liberalism, which always upholds the division of society into core (rich) and periphery (poor). We strongly argue for the reform of the prevalent land reform and the localization or domestication of any ideology adopted in the state's quest for a policy shift on land reform.

References

Akinola, A. O., & Uzodike U. O. (2017). Ubuntu and the quest for conflict resolution in Africa. *Journal of Black Studies*, 1–23. https://doi.org/10.1177/0021934717736186.

Akinola, A. O., & Wissink, H. (2019). Introduction. In A. O. Akinola & H. Wissink (Eds.), *Trajectory of land reform in post-colonial African states: Quest for sustainable development and utilization* (pp. v–ix). Cham: Springer.

Akinola, A. O. (2018a). South African land reform: An appraisal. *Africa Review, 10*(1), 1–16.

Akinola, A. O. (2018b). *Globalization, democracy and oil sector reform.* New York: Palgrave Macmillan.

Alexander, A. (2015). *Democracy dispossessed: Land, law & the politics of redistribution in South Africa.* PhD thesis, Graduate School of Arts and Sciences, Columbia University.

Ashton, G. (2012). *Land Reform in South Africa: An Unfulfilled Obligation.* Available at https://sacsis.org.za/site/article/1475.

Bosch, D. (n.d). *Land conflict management in South Africa: Lessons learned from a land rights approach.* FAO Corporate Document Repository. Food and Agriculture Organization of the United Nations. Available http://www.fao.org/3/j0415t/j0415t0a.htm.

Bradstock, A. (2007). *Land restitution and livelihood: The Khomani San.* Farm-Africa Working Paper Number 6. Available http://www.farmafrica.org/downloads/resources/WP%206%20Land%20Restitution%20and%20Livelihoods%20The%20Khomani%20San.pdf. Accessed on 29 August 2016.

Cousins, B. (2015). 'Through a glass, darkly': Towards Agrarian reform in South Africa. In B. Cousins & C. Walker (Eds.), *Land divided, land restored: Land reform in South Africa for the 21st century.* Auckland Park: Jacana.

Delican, M. (n.d.). *Elite theories of Pareto, Mosca and Michels*. Available http://dergipark.gov.tr/download/article-file/9789.

Democratic Alliance. (2013). *DA policy on land reform*. Available http://www.da.org.za/wp-content/uploads/2014/01/Land-Reform1.pdf.

Department of Land Affairs. (1997). *Department of land affairs White Paper on land policy, 1997*. Pretoria: Department of Land Affairs.

Dikgang, J., & Muchapondwa, E. (2015). The effect of land restitution on poverty reduction among the Khomani San "Bushmen" in South Africa. *South African Journal of Economics*, 1–18. https://doi.org/10.1111/saje.12088.

Greenwood, X. (2018, 4 April). South Africa is the most unequal country in the world and its poverty is the "enduring legacy of apartheid", says World Bank. *Independent*. Available https://www.independent.co.uk/news/world/africa/south-africa-unequal-country-poverty-legacy-apartheid-world-bank-a8288986.html.

Hall, R. (2004). A political economy of land reform in South Africa. *Review of African Political Economy, 31*(100), 213–227.

Kariuki, S. (2009). Agrarian reform, rural development and governance in Africa: A case of Eastern and Southern Africa. *Policy Brief 59*. Rosebank: Centre for Policy Studies.

Khan, S. (2015). Sustainable local economic development (LED) and rural land reform challenges and prospects in post-apartheid South Africa—A policy perspective. *Journal of Economics, 6*(1), 8–17.

Lambina, E. F., & Meyfroidt, P. (2011). Global land use change, economic globalization, and the looming land scarcity. *PNAS, 108*(9), 3465–3472.

Lipton, M. (2009). *Land reform in developing countries: Property rights and property wrongs*. New York: Routledge.

Moyo, S. (2003). The land question in Africa: Research perspectives and questions. Draft paper presented at *CODESRIA Conferences on Land Reform, the Agrarian Question and Nationalism* in Gaborone, Botswana (18–19 October 2003) and Dakar, Senegal (8–11 December).

Moyo, S. (2007). Land in the political economy of African development: Alternative strategies for Reform. *Africa Development, 32*(4), 1–34.

National Planning Commission. (2012). *Our future—Make it work: National Planning Commission National Development Plan 2030: Executive summary*. Available https://www.gov.za/sites/www.gov.za/files/Executive%20Summary-NDP%202030%20-%20Our%20future%20-%20make%20it%20work.pdf.

National Treasury. (2018). *2018 budget estimates of national expenditure: Vote 39 rural development and land reform*. Available http://www.treasury.gov.za/documents/National%20Budget/2018/enebooklets/Vote%2039%20Rural%20Development%20and%20Land%20Reform.pdf.

Olusola, O., & Akinola, A. (2017). South Africa and the question of hegemony in Africa. *Journal of Developing Societies, 3*(4), 1–20.

Rugege, S. (2004). Land reform in South Africa: An overview. *International Journal of Legal Information, 32*, 283–312.

Sieff, K. (2016). *South Africa: Trial of four white farmers and a policeman for the murder of two black men highlights the racial divisions still haunting the rainbow nation.* Available http://www.independent.co.uk/news/world/africa/south-africa-trial-of-fourwhite-farmers-and-a-policeman-for-the-murder-of-two-black-men-highlights-a6879751.html.

Walker, C. (2017). The land question in South Africa: 1913 and beyond. *Oxford Research Encyclopedia of African History*. https://doi.org/10.1093/acrefore/9780190277734.013.79.

Wilkinson, K. (2018, 20 February). Ramaphosa right about 'big difference' between Black & White unemployment in South Africa. *Africa Check*. Available https://africacheck.org/spot-check/ramaphosa-right-about-big-difference-between-black-white-unemployment-in-sa/.

CHAPTER 4

The Expropriation of Land Without Compensation in South Africa: A Strategy for Alleviating or Worsening Poverty?

Mandla Mubecua and Victor H. Mlambo

Introduction

Since the twentieth century, there have been increasing calls for the acceleration of land reform in South Africa. While, the emergence of multiparty politics in South Africa in the year 1994 promised to usher in a new era for governance and democracy, sadly, little has been achieved with reagrds to the equal ownership of land, especially agricultural land, which is seen as one of the pro-poor initiatives (Kalabamu, 2019). The unequal ownership of land in South Africa has been associated with poverty, unemployment, and the inability of black South Africans to emancipate themselves from the above mentioned issues. There is a correlation between land inequality and increasing poverty in South Africa (Akinola, 2018). Land inequality in South Africa can be traced back to the

M. Mubecua · V. H. Mlambo (✉)
University of Zululand, KwaDlangezwa, KwaZulu-Natal, South Africa

A. O. Akinola et al. (eds.), *The New Political Economy of Land Reform in South Africa*,
https://doi.org/10.1007/978-3-030-51129-6_4

apartheid period, where the aparthied government designed and implemented laws that were aimed at dispossesing the land from the black majority, in favour of the white minority (Berry, 2018).

Despite the optimism associated with land reform, the willing buyer, willing seller approach has failed to redress the historical land-related injustice; it is this failure that has given rise to the rhetoric of expropriating land without compensation. Lumumba-Kasongo (2015) notes that land redistribution has been slow in the country and the willing buyer, willing seller approach has failed to fast-track the land redistribution process. It is for that reason that there are increasing calls for the amendment of Section 25 of the South African Constitution, which permits land expropriation without compensation (Thwala, 2018).

The ruling party, the African National Congress (ANC), during its December Conference in 2017, took a decision to amend Section 25 of the South African Constitution for the purpose of LEWC. The ANC revealed that the constitutional amendment is important to guarantee policy sustainability and economic stability. By 15 November 2018, the Constitutional Review Committee, inaugurated by the government, took a decision to amend Section 25 of the Constitution (Merten, 2018).

There is growing concern that government's rush to implement land expropriation has become highly politicized. This further creates a feeling of uncertainty in the country and puts pressure on financial institutions who have granted loans to farmers and for the purchase of land. The growth and consolidation of the Economic Freedom Fighters (EFF) has further increased the rhetoric of expropriating land without compensation (Thwala, 2018). Therefore, it is important to explore the cost-benefits LEWC in the country, particularly its place in poverty alleviation and the socio-economic development of the country.

Conceptualizing Land Expropriation Without Compensation

There is no universal conceptualization of land expropriation without compensation. The concept 'land expropriation without compensation' comprises of the two terms: 'land expropriation' and 'without compensation'. Firstly, land expropriation relates to the act whereby the government or an appointed authority dispossesses privately owned property, specifically land for the benefit of the public (Guo, 2001). Secondly, the concept 'without compensation' means the denial of incentives or compensation in exchange for that asset of land. Thus, LEWC is defined as the process of taking privately owned land for the benefits of the public or collective without providing any incentive or compensation whatsoever. The privately owned land or farmland is forcefully taken without the expected inducements for the current owners.

To further understand the concept, it is necessary to examine different aspects of the political, economic and social situations in South Africa. Private properties in South Africa are mostly owned by white people, which includes industries, game parks/reserves, hotels resort centres and farms (Williams, Williams, Fitzgerald, Sheppard, & Hill, 2018). Therefore, in respect of the political aspect, should LEWC eventually come to light most white people in South Africa will lose their lands and property without incentives. Based on the colonial and apartheid reality of land dispossession of black South Africans by white people, the former lost possession of their arable lands to the whites without any form of compensation (Andrews, 2018).

The economic aspect relates to the land ownership system, which, under the auspices of neoliberalism, will be to undergo transformation into the radicalization of land reform scheme. Neoliberalism, otherwise known as limited government, is a system that promotes economic liberalization through privatization, deregulation and commercialization (Bond, 2019). The existing willing buyer, willing seller approach reinforces the liberalization of South Africa's land reform approach. Although the EFF is trying to push for state's ownership of land (which will translate to socialism), the ANC leadership has completely rejected this. Under the social impact, South African citizens will be afforded the opportunity of equality of land and property ownership. This will translate to wealth redistribution and the improvement of the livelihood of underprivileged black South Africans.

History of Land in South Africa

Having understood the concept of land expropriation without compensation in general and what it means and its socio-economic and political dimensions, it is of utmost importance to understand South Africa's land conflict and its drivers in a historical context. In South Africa, colonialization can be traced back to the seventeenth century with the arrival of Europeans (Roberts, 2001). Initially, they resided in the Cape area of South Africa (Assari, 2018). The arrival and the domination of Europeans in the north and east, as well as the arrival of the British in Xhosa-land and Natal, brought pressures and intimidations on the Bantu-speaking native South African groups (Roberts, 2001).

The conflict between the Europeans and the Bantu-speaking groups was centred on land dispossession. Africans were forced to abandon their land and farms, while others were forcefully converted to labourer's on their own lands (Roberts, 2001). Moreover, the discovery of gold in the nineteenth century increased the demand for black people to work as cheap labour (Wolpe, 2018). Black South Africans were driven from resourceful, arable land onto barren land.

The apartheid government passed laws and policies that oppressed black people. For instance, the Natives Land Act (No. 27 of 1913) enforced that only 7% of arable land was to be allowed for black South Africans and the more arable land was reserved for white people (Bradstock, 2006; Roberts, 2001). The law prohibited black people to own any given land and property. Approximately 80% of the arable land was removed from the hands of black people and given to white people, who were less than 20% of the country's population (Roberts, 2001).

The Natives Land Act also relocated the black population to live in areas which were classified as reserves, provided they were going to be employed by white farmers. The discovery and exploration of natural resources like gold in South Africa by the apartheid government made people from South Africa, Lesotho, Swaziland and Mozambique, rely on the whites for survival as they were the ones who owned and operated the mines (Adepoju, 2003). Black South Africans who had their arable land taken away from them, working in the mines became the only option in the quest to provide for thier families. The Natives Urban Areas Act of 1923 promoted that local authorities should demarcate urban dwellers according to their race (Woolard & Klasen, 2005). Furthermore, there was poor and inadequate service delivery in black communities. For instance, blacks were restricted to settlements without healthcare services. Even the education system favoured whites more than blacks. In schools, all subjects were studied in the Afrikaans language, all this was done to consolidate white dominance at the expense of the black majority (Alberts, 2018).

The unavailability of arable land for the black majority led to the increase of racial poverty in South Africa (Roberts, 2001). Currently, there is no act or law separating blacks and whites, but there is still a wide and growing economic gap between whites and blacks (Maylam,

2017). Public services were mostly provided to white people compared to black people, and hence, the mortality rate declined among whites and increased significantly for blacks (Tate & Fink, 2019). In 1993, the primary representative household and living survey showed that blacks were highly affected by poverty compared to whites. Similarly, the current rate of poverty and unemployment rate favours white people compared to black South Africans. In terms of wages, the majority of blacks earn less than their white counterparts (Assari, 2018).

The year 1994 signified the abolition of apartheid and the emergence of majority rule through multiparty politics. The end of the apartheid left in its trail a high rate of inequality, poverty and the inability of black South Africans to socio-econimically develop themselves (Özler, 2007). Black South Africans were denied assets, like land. The denial of land rights engender poverty because of people's inability to generate a livelihood, and also results in feelings of dependency because it made the black majority depend on whites for their survival and welfare (Carter & May, 2001).

From 1996 to 2006, the government executed a land redistribution programme for South African residents through a grant-based system, wherein residents applied for a grant from the state to assist in the purchase of the land (De-Satgé & Cousins, 2019). This government initiative (grant-based system) was very successful and sustainable because it also encouraged economic growth at the same time. However, the pace and process of land transfer fell below the public and government expectations (Spierenburg, 2019).

In 2006, the South African government introduced a proactive strategy of buying land and took custody of it, for the land to be given to beneficiaries for agricultural production (Vorster, 2019). However, such an approach was not successful and, as a result, the High-level Panel on the Assessment of Key Legislation and Acceleration of Fundamental Change noticed that the process of acquiring land by the government gradually decreased from 2009 (De-Satgé & Cousins, 2019). It is believed that one of the reasons was the changing of the Department of Land Affairs to the Department of Rural Development and Land Reform, which resulted in many changes in the way government went about purchasing the land (Hall & Kepe, 2017).

The changing of the Department of Land Affairs to the Department of Rural Development and Land Reform led to the diversion of the funds that were allocated for land reform to other activities (Musakwa, 2018).

Moreover, the slow pace of land reform was due to the incapacity of the ruling party (ANC) to enforce the proposed strategy for expropriating the land with equitable compensation. The failure of the South African government to give back the land to its rightful owners led to the persistence of inequality and the increased poverty rate among the blacks (Mango, Makate, Tamene, Mponela, & Ndengu, 2017).

Historically, the concept of land expropriation without compensation started to gain prominence under the leadership of former South African president, Jacob Zuma. The ANC's national conferences held in 2012 and 2017 saw the possibility of implementing LEWC because of the ineffectiveness of the willing buyer, willing seller approach (Boshoff, Sihlobo, & Ntombela, 2018). The subsequent president of the country, Cyril Ramaphosa, in his first State of the Nation Address (SONA), which had been approved by parliament, strongly advocated for LEWC. The intention was to resolve the historical injustices in land ownership, while ensuring sustainable reconciliation (Thwala, 2018).

According to the ANC, there are justifiable and compelling reasons to push for the amendment of the Constitution which has been seen as a barrier to the implementation of LEWC. However, there are current debates regarding the amendment of Section 25 of the South African Constitution, which hitherto makes provisions for the administration of land reform (Hlomendlini & Makgolane, 2017). Indeed, the government has announced the amendment of Section 25 of the Constitution; thus, it is important to discuss the motivations for government's advocacy of LEWC and reveal the intended beneficiaries of the policy shift.

Land Expropriation Without Compensation: Motivations and Beneficiaries

Ntsebeza and Hall (2007) argue that since the advent of a democratic South Africa, in 1994, it became clear to the incoming government that the land ownership, reform and land-related issues had to be given priority in a bid to curtail land inequality and make land available to previously disadvantaged groups which saw their lands taken away from them forcefully. Cousins and Walker (2015) state that immediately after 1994, the ANC-led government agreed on ensuring that land was redistributed, but this was never really carried out, mainly because of investor concerns and fear of potential economic sanctions. Derman, Hellum and Sandvik (2013) argue that from 1994 to 2018, little has changed in terms of land ownership patterns in South Africa, with minority whites still owning over 65% of commercial land.

The major motivating factor behind the increasing rhetoric of land expropriation is the assumption that the majority of black South Africans are living below the poverty line, mainly because they do not own or have access to land. Ownership of commercial land would have created opportunities to undertake farming activities, engage in productive use of land and use the land as an instrument to eradicate poverty.

Cirolia, Görgens, van Donk Smit and Drimie (2017) hold that the issue of landownership in South Africa is quite complex as there are many stakeholders who are directly and indirectly involved. For example, commercial farmers in South Africa are heavily indebted to commercial banks, which explains the opposition of the banking sector to the proposed policy. Implementation of LEWC will make it impossible to retrieve these loans (Ngubane, 2018). Lahiff (2007) argues that the willing buyer, willing seller approach has failed to meet the desired results anticipated by the government, as the government had hoped that farmers (predominately white) would be willing to sell their farms to emerging black farmers and government was willing to provide the funds. However, the process has not contributed significantly to land redistribution in the country. Furthermore, those who managed to sell their farms often charged above market-values, which costs government billions.

Kloppers and Pienaar (2014), however, maintain that the issues of land expropriation in South Africa have been largely underpinned by political ideologies, rather than the consideration for socio-economic development. Eche (2013) also posits that the theory that land expropriation will reduce poverty and inequality is highly questionable, and the people making such claims are doing so for political gains at the expense of the poor. Drawing lessons from Venezuela, Howard-Hassmann (2015) reveals that, in the early 2000s, President Hugo Chavez made land expropriation his top priority, in order to address the growing inequality that was engulfing the country. However, Spanakos (2014) alludes that modern Venezuela depends mostly on imported foods stuffs, mainly because productive agricultural land was given to people who were unskilled, which led to food insecurity. Furthermore, corruption within the political elite of the country further impacted the effective distribution of the land.

While this initially was a good idea, it was flawed by procedural loopholes and 'cronyism' within the country prevailed at the expense of ensuring stable food security and effective distribution of the land (Spanakos, 2014). Venezuela has experienced political and economic issues linked to land policy. Alexander (2009) states that the economic sanctions, levelled against the country, are another contributing factor to the land unproductivity in the country. Santarcángelo, Justo and Cooney (2016) attribute the decline of Venezuela's agricultural output to the failure of the state to effectively ensure the proper allocation of land. Land beneficiaries were not equipped with the necessary skills needed to enhance land and farm productivity. It remains unclear if South Africa will follow in the footsteps of Venezuela.

According to Groenewald (2018), the government has continuously stated that land expropriation in South Africa will be different to that of Zimbabwe, due to constitutional backing. However, de Wet (2018) states opposition to this perspective. He maintains that the process will be marred by widespread corruption, and land expropriation and redistribution will be marred by cronyism and corruption, thereby further jeopardizing the socio-economic development of the country. Chidede (2016) states that the political rhetoric engulfing South Africa regarding land issues is putting South Africa not only against the international community but also creating the feeling of uncertainty within the polity. For instance, investors are anxious to understand how this process will unfold and the real motivation for the policy.

Shaw (2003) states that in developing countries, particularly in Africa, Zimbabwe has been the most widely cited case of failed land reform programmes. In the 2000s, President Robert Mugabe was vocal on the slow rates at which ordinary black Zimbabweans were not benefiting from the vast availability of land in the country (Shaw, 2003). He also decried the dominance of land by white farmers. The Zimbabwean government thereafter adopted a policy which entailed expropriating land without compensation. White farmers were forcefully evicted from their farms, costing billions of dollars to the Zimbabwean economy and resulting in economic sanctions and crisis. The major highlights of the reform were the fact that most of these farms were given to political allies and family members who had no idea on how to utilize them; unemployment soared, inflation increased drastically and the ramifications were immense (Rutherford, 2016). Presently, Zimbabwe is still plagued by those events, as white farmers have not returned to the country, and the country is experiencing chronic food security issues (Hughes, 2010).

In South Africa, the concept of land expropriation is clouded by issues of uncertainty and secrecy. The government continues to display its resolve to implement the policy, and it does not seem as if the opposition has significantly impeded the actualization of LEWC. Page and Tarp (2017) raise critical questions, based on South Africa's low levels of economic growth, how will land expropriation without compensation accelerate its economic growth? Furthermore, based on the activism of government officials in support of LEWC, they seem more positioned to be the main beneficiaries of LEWC. The poor, who ought to be the target of the policy, may continue to experience land hunger. This then begs the question as to whether this will be for the benefit of black South Africans or the few who are politically connected, as was observable in the cases of Venezuela and Zimbabwe, where it caused a significant decline in terms of economic competitiveness and led to high poverty and rising unemployment rates.

These case studies have created pessimism among many on the probable success of implementing a similar programme in South Africa (although the South African government states that this will be done in accordance with the law). Although the strategy can be successfully implemented at the initial stage, it may face the problem of sustainability in the future.

The South African case is also unique to other case studies. In view of South Africa's history, the land was forcefully taken from the blacks (Moyo, Jha, & Yeros, 2019). For that reason, the question that arises is that should land remain under the control of the minority, or should it be divided to benefit the majority? Regardless of the response, the central question is what implications will this have on socio-economic development. Moreover, why should the landowners (mainly whites) be compensated for forcefully removing the black from their arable land? Considering those points, Kilian (2018) argues that even though the implementation of LEWC can be problematic in the future, it will help resolve the land inequality and historical injustices of land dispossession. Furthermore, Kilian (2018) also believes that LEWC would create employment opportunities and redress poverty. Kilian maintains it will increase agricultural production and ensure food security in the country.

The Land Audit Report released in 2018 shows that, presently, whites own 72% of the land, coloureds (mixed race) have 15%, Indians own 5%, but blacks only own 4% of the land (Kilian, 2018). Focusing on the inequality in the landownership as the Land Audit Report shows, Kilian

(2018) asserts that the idea that LEWC may, after all, lead to an economic disaster may not be valid. Assuredly, the policy would play an important role in improving the economy of the country (Phakathi, 2018). To further understand land expropriation, the subsequent section explores the place of political rhetoric in the LEWC scheme.

The Political Rhetoric Driving Land Expropriation Without Compensation

Moyo and Yeros (2005) attest to the fact that the issue of land expropriation has become highly politicized, which impedes a constructive engagement with relevant stakeholders. Neethling (2015) supports this assertion by stating that the growing rhetoric of LEWC has been motivated by the emergence and growth of the EFF political party. The left-wing party has made LEWC their primary mandate in their efforts to replace the ANC as the ruling party. The party has won the hearts of many people in South Africa, especially in rural areas where people feel marginalized by the current government (Phakathi, 2018). The EFF has also appealed to those who feel the government has failed to accelerate the redistribution of land to the previously disadvantaged (Moyo & Yeros, 2005).

Due to the vociferous stance of the EFF on LEWC, the ANC has had no choice but to adopt the radicalization of land reform as the most appropriate model of land reform that would benefit the poor and landless (Mkokeli, 2018). Ntsholo (2018) alludes that the EFF's militant posture and their disregard for the socio-economic implications of land grabs has enabled it to infiltrate the strongholds of the ANC, which has further pressured the ANC to share similar views of land expropriation. The ANC, unlike the EFF, has made it clear that the proposed policy would not jeopardize socio-economic and political stability of the country.

Li, Gubo and Lixia (2012) state that agricultural economy plays an important role in South Africa. According to the authors, the agricultural forest and fishery sector contributes significantly to South Africa's GDP. Oosthuizen (2003) reveals that the agricultural sector creates a staggering 39,000 jobs and with adequate support, the National Development Plan estimates that by 2030, the sector can employ up to a million people.

The Department of Agriculture, Forestry and Fisheries (2016) states that the sector contributed significantly as it was the leading sector in terms of performance in the country in 2016. Therefore, it is undeniably clear that the agricultural sector plays a vital role in South Africa, and therefore, the issue of LEWC should be carefully weighed against the contributions that the sector makes to the country's development (Maumbe, 2009). From the EFF's point of view, land expropriation will benefit the poor (Mkokeli, 2018).

However, Ngubane (2018) recalls instances where farms have been bought by the government and redistributed to black farmers without providing the required support and skills acquisition programmes. This has hampered the productivity and sustainability of these farms of which many ended up becoming idle and unproductive, resulting in billions of losses to the farmers and government. Xaba (2015) supports this position and reiterates that running a farm requires a complex set of skills that are acquired over a period of time. For instance, in Zimbabwe, farms were given to farm beneficiaries who lacked the skills needed to ensure the full operational capacity of these farms. This explains the failure of the Zimbabwean land reform scheme and the ensuing, and continuing agricultural and economic crisis experienced in the country. In South Africa, this means that emerging black farmers should be provided with these skills beforehand, before pushing the agenda of land expropriation, which will surely impact the country's economy (Mabaya, Tihanyi, & Karaan, 2011).

Merten (2018) also states that the 2019 general elections would further exert pressures on the ANC to implement a populist land reform agenda, which has become top agenda of the ANC's opposition party, the EFF. With the rise and consolidation of the EFF, it has become inevitable for the ANC to also support LEWC. Rather than trying to find a balance between the needs of the people and economic development of the country, the land issue is usually used as a political tool by political parties to mobilize supporters and gain votes during elections (Merten, 2018).

Similarly, the 2019 elections set a precedent for the land issue to be used as a political campaigning tool. For the ANC to ensure victory in the 2019 electoral process, it had to outwit the EFF by supporting the acceleration of land redistribution, even if this means implementing LEWC. Hans and Zungu (2018) therefore conclude that the battle of control and power in the country has seen the debate around land becoming an instrument of mobilization and electioneering.

Ntsebeza and Hall (2007) agree that land reform has been slow in South Africa but it is also very important to ensure South Africa undertakes this in line with the provisions of the Constitution and international law. While the rhetoric has been that LEWC would contribute towards poverty alleviation, Phakathi (2018) argues to the contrary. He maintains that expropriating agricultural land could negatively impact the competitiveness of the South African agricultural sector, increase food insecurity, leading a constraint in economic growth. It is also undeniable that the increasing political rhetoric around land has caused a lot of feeling of uncertainty among investors in South Africa (Ntsebeza & Hall, 2007). According to the Department of Agriculture, Forestry and Fisheries (2016), from 1993 to 2007, farming units in the country decreased from 57,980 to 39,982, but this may support the argument that LEWC will reverse this trend (Fig. 4.1).

The department also argues that, on a positive note, there has been increasing investments in the agricultural sector from 2016, when the value of investments in the sector stood at a record 427. The implementation of LEWC is likely to jeopardize this growth (Fig. 4.2).

However, Phakathi (2018) states that one of the most important elements to consider regarding LEWC is the debt owed by farmers to

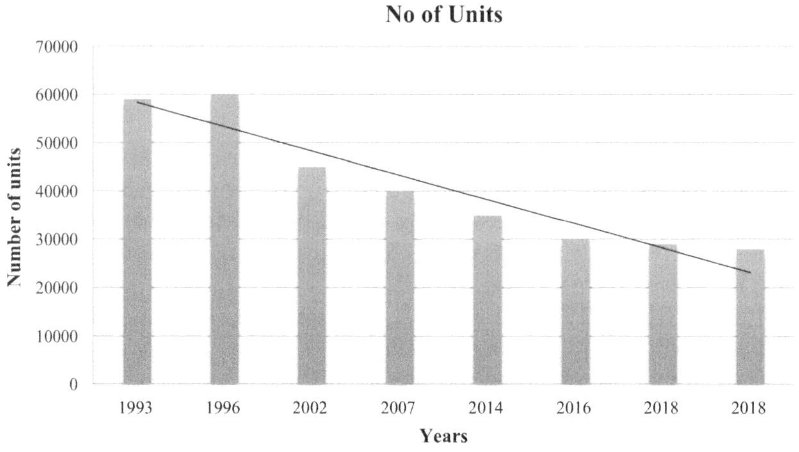

Fig. 4.1 Number of farming units in South Africa (*Source* Hlomendlini and Makgolane [2017: 4])

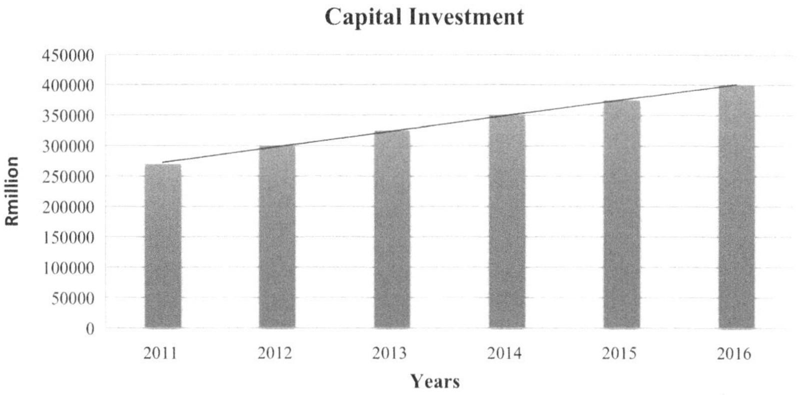

Fig. 4.2 Capital investments inflow into the agricultural sector (*Source* Hlomendlini and Makgolane [2017: 5])

lenders. The Department of Agriculture, Forestry and Fisheries (2016) states that, in 2016, a staggering R145 billion was owned by farmers, of which an astounding R89.38 billion was owed to banks (Fig. 4.3).

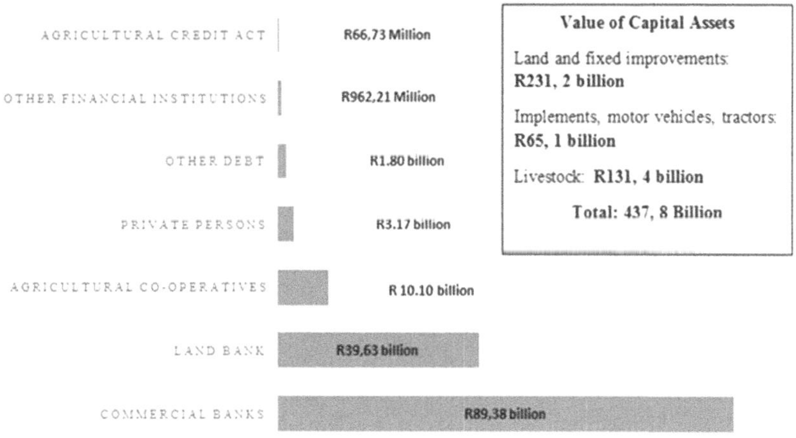

Fig. 4.3 *Farming debt in 2016—R145 billion* (*Source* Hlomendlini and Makgolane [2017: 6])

The NDP sees agriculture as a very sensitive sector which must be prioritized by the government, in terms of support and development. However, with the increasing rhetoric of LEWC, it is difficult to foresee this sector creating a million jobs as envisioned by the National Development Plan (NDP). Kirton and Larionova (2018) argue that while there are concerns in relation to the existing land reform, it is undeniably crucial to understand the importance of the sector. Reversal of development of the sector would have colossal implications for the country's socio-economic development, poverty levels and unemployment. Kirton and Larionova (2018) reveal that it is imperative that the agenda concerning land expropriation should ensure that all stakeholders should be integrated into the planning and implementation processes, to ensure fairness and give people the opportunity to significantly contribute to the feasibility and cost-benefits of the programmes. Merten (2018), however, concludes that people are desperate for a change in the country and many are desperate for the review of land reform. Therefore, this frustration has set a dangerous precedent under which important decisions regarding the land issue may not be taken into consideration. One of which is how to ensure that LEWC does not constitute a breach of international law.

Lumumba-Kasongo (2015) argues that the growing uncertainties around LEWC have brought with it confusion and left many questions unanswered. This confusion has aggravated opposition to land expropriation to such an extent that they have waged a campaign to discredit the proposed policy of land expropriation. For example, lobby groups such as Afri-forum, Freedom Plus and even the Zulu king have become strong oppositions to the actualization of LEWC. These actors have also taken their campaign internationally to create awareness and have generated hostility regarding its implementation. While the issues have gained traction in South Africa, internationally, the land issue has not received the required global attention favourable for the opposition (Makinana, 2018).

The LEWC discourse has created feelings of uncertainty not only with farmers but also within other political interests in the country, especially in terms of its implementation and legitimacy. Byrnes and Munro (2018) also argue that South Africa has laws and is also part of many international agreements (treaties, conventions and intergovernmental agreements), which guarantee property rights and thus, these conventions do not support LEWC. For instance, the Protection of Investment Act,

Vienna Convention on the Law of Treaties and The International Centre for Settlement of Investment Disputes (ICSID).

Modise and Mtshiselwa (2013) posit that while pre-apartheid legislation, such as the Native Land Act benefited the white people without hindrances, post-apartheid South Africa has become a signatory to numerous treaties which hinders the country from radicalizing land reform. Leon (2018), therefore, warns that the implementation of LEWC could expose the country to lawsuits, due to a breach of international law. Leon (2018) further states that in Zimbabwe, for example, land grabs have resulted in lawsuits against the government. In Zimbabwe, a particular group of Dutch nationals, whose farms were seized, sued the government through the ICSID. Also, German and Swiss landowners were awarded $195 million because of land grabs in Zimbabwe. The lesson here is that South Africa has a responsibility to respect international laws, and the regulations of treaties to which the country is a signatory (Leon, 2018).

LEWC: A Recipe for Disaster or a Remedy for Sustainable Development?

It has been discussed that the fundamental aim of LEWC is to redistribute land (which was apparently stolen or taken forcefully) to the majority of black South Africans who are still perceived as landless despite being the majority in South Africa (Ntsebeza & Hall, 2007). However, one cannot simply ignore the political rhetoric that has clouded the issue of LEWC. Mojo and Yeros (2005) comment that when such a delicate and highly important issue becomes politicized, it then raises serious questions as to the implications (socio-economically and, by extension, politically) this could have for the country.

House (2012), for example, argues that when Venezuela announced its policy of LEWC in the early 2000s, it was largely because many people in the country were angry at the fact that most of the land was owned by a few multinational corporations and they were sidelined when it came to the ownership of large swathes of land. In 1999, President Hugo Chavez amended the Constitution to declared that "the predominance of large idle estates (*latifundios*) was contrary to the interests of society". In 2001, Chavez introduced a land law which permitted the expropriation of such *latifundios* (Cameron, 2018).

Brewer-Carías (2010) comments that initially this was a great plan to ensure equality in landownership, but when the issue became politicized, corruption, nepotism and elitism took over; land was given to connected businesses and individuals. The land was also allocated according to political criteria, with those who supported the government (*chavistas*) far more likely to receive it than those who were apolitical or supported the opposition. What ordinary Venezuelans had hoped would be an opportunity for them to own land, quickly turned into an era of sadness and misery and, until today, Venezuela depends highly on imports of agricultural products (Brewer-Carías, 2010).

The flawed execution of the LEWC policy increased food insecurity, poverty, unemployment and contributed to the stagnation in the agricultural sector (Hausmann & Rodríguez, 2014). Furthermore, Hausmann and Rodríguez (2014) state that while indeed the flawed policy of LEWC impacted Venezuela negatively, the impact was cushioned by an open-border policy and the vast oil reserves in the country. Nonetheless, the impact on the livelihoods of the people was significant.

Moreover, when one talks about LEWC that had an observable political connotation to it, undoubtedly Zimbabwe comes to mind. Havnevik, Matondi and Beyene (2011) argue that from its initial planning, assuming it would have followed the strict codes of the Constitution and rule of law, the policy was meant to ensure that everyone would had a say in the economy through the ownership of land. However, Mugabe's hatred for the West gave way to the politicization of the process, which led to unlawful evictions, seizures, the handing over of farms to allies and a total disregard for human rights, which then gave way to the economic issues Zimbabwe is experiencing today.

Moore, Kriger and Raftopoulos (2013) affirm that what followed after was a true reflection of what happens when issues regarding land redistribution are controlled by few who have ulterior motives. Economic sanctions by Western countries further impacted negatively on the Zimbabwean economy, with limited investments in the sector, increased inflation, unemployment, poverty and political isolation internationally (Moore et al., 2013). Naki (2018) states that while the ANC has for long underscored the need for land redistribution, the development and growth of the EFF, which has seen that party gaining popularity in the country by mainly pushing the issue of land expropriation, has indirectly exerted tremendous pressure on the ruling party to follow suit (Naki, 2018).

Ensor (2018) notes that poverty and unemployment will increase significantly if the process of LEWC is politically compromised, to benefit politically connected individuals, as evident in Zimbabwe. Farming, for example, requires a combination of skills and knowledge, and the lack of such skills from the recipients of expropriated farms may result in retrenchments and the eventual closure of such farms. Ensor (2018) also comments that besides poverty and unemployment, a politically compromised LEWC policy will surely result in economic stagnation, the loss of farmers' skills, experience and knowledge ('brain drain'), inflation concerns and the fear of downgrading by rating agencies. The combination of these issues will cripple the output from the agricultural sector in southern Africa (Ensor, 2018).

One may, therefore, conclude that while there is indeed a need to redistribute land in South Africa, it must be undertaken within the confines of the law and the recipients ought to know what they are going to do with the land. The process must be politically independent and must not be used to benefit individuals as this will lead to an agricultural decline in the country, which will then threaten food security, and thus further contribute to hunger, poverty and capital flight.

Conclusion

The problem of land in South Africa may be traced back to the arrival of the colonial powers, even before the emergence of apartheid. The racist, nationalist government introduced acts like the Natives Land Act (1913) that was oppressive to the blacks and favourable to the whites. The impact of this in post-apartheid South Africa is evident in the data that reveals that more than half of black South Africans are living below the poverty line.

The chapter has revealed that, since from 1994 to 2018, very little has been achieved in terms of addressing the land-related historical injustice in the country. Some of the government strategies to return the land back to black people through restitution or redistribution were not effective. For instance, the willing buyer, willing seller approach has failed. Despite the decades of land reform in the post-apartheid era, poverty, land inequality and land unproductivity continue to increase. This has led to the call for LEWC and the approval of the amendment of Section 25 of the South African Constitution.

The ineffectiveness of the same strategy (LEWC) in Venezuela and Zimbabwe casts doubts about the sustainability of the strategy in South Africa. However, land was forcefully taken from the black people and it is imperative to implement policy to locate the vulnerable and dispossessed in the land reform programmes. That is the reason Killian (2018) asserts that LEWC could help in alleviating poverty and inequalities because blacks have been the most vulnerable group. Moreover, the chapter has discussed that the issue of land in South Africa has been used as a strategy to mobilize the masses for electoral purposes.

The government's rhetoric of LEWC has neglected an important question: How will the government pay back the loans many of the farm and land owners have obtained from banks? The Department of Agriculture, Forestry and Fisheries (2016) reveal, that in 2016, a R145 billion was owned by farmers, of which a staggering R89 million is to banking institutions. There is no clear strategy on how the South African government aims to pay the money owed. Moreover, LEWC will scare off investors from the country because of the jettisoning of property rights and policy uncertainty.

That approval for the amendment of Section 25 of the Constitution increases the likelihood that LEWC would be implemented very soon. With that reason, the chapter suggests that proper skills acquisition programmes should be provided to the new beneficiaries. Moreover, an effective monitoring and evaluation of the processes and implementation of LEWC should be put in place for effectiveness, accountability and transparency. Furthermore, since the land may be expropriated without compensation, future research may focus on the implementation of the policy without threatening the socio-political and economic stability of South Africa.

References

Adepoju, A. (2003). Continuity and changing configurations of migration to and from the Republic of South Africa. *International Migration, 41*(1), 3–28.

Akinola, A. O. (2018). Land reform in South Africa: An appraisal. *Africa Review, 10*(1), 1–16.

Alberts, C. (2018). Afrikaner and coloured school-going adolescents negotiating ethnic identities in a post-colonial South African educational context: A dialogical self interpretation. In *The Dialogical Self Theory in Education* (pp. 129–142). Cham: Springer.

Alexander, K. (2009). *Economic sanctions: Law and public policy* (1st ed.). United Kingdom: Palgrave Macmillan.

Andrews, D. (2018). *Capitalism and nature in South Africa: Racial dispossession, liberation ideology and ecological crisis*, PhD thesis, University of Cape Town.

Assari, S. (2018). Health disparities due to diminished return among black Americans: Public policy solutions. *Social Issues and Policy Review, 12*(1), 112–145.

Berry, S. (2018). Who owns the land? Social relations and conflict over resources in Africa. *GLOCON Working Paper Series*, 7.

Bond, P. (2019). Neoliberalism, state repression and the rise of social protest in Africa. *The Palgrave handbook of social movements, revolution, and social transformation* (pp. 213–231). London: Palgrave Macmillan.

Boshoff, T., Sihlobo, W., & Ntombela S. (2018). *Redistribution of agricultural land: Expropriation without compensation debate*. Available: https://agbiz.co.za/uploads/AgbizNews18/Expropriation_Without_Compensation_debate.pdf.

Bradstock, A. (2006). Land reform and livelihoods in South Africa's Northern Cape province. *Land Use Policy, 23*(3), 247–259.

Brewer-Carías, A. R. (2010). *Dismantling democracy in Venezuela: The Chávez authoritarian experiment*. Cambridge: Cambridge University Press.

Byrnes, W. H., & Munro, R. J. (2018). *Money laundering, asset forfeiture and recovery and compliance—A Global guide*. New York: LexisNexis.

Cameron, J. (2018). *MUST READ! Scary lessons for ANC about Venezuela-style land grab plans—Anthea Jeffery*. Available: https://www.biznews.com/thought-leaders/2018/07/18/lessons-anc-venezuela-land-grabs-plans. Accessed 12 January 2019.

Carter, M. R., & May, J. (2001). One kind of freedom: Poverty dynamics in post-apartheid South Africa. *World Development, 29*(12), 1987–2006.

Chidede, T. (2016). *Legal protection of foreign direct investment: A critical assessment with focus on South Africa and Zimbabwe*. Branding: Anchor Academic Publishing.

Cirolia, L. R., Görgens, T., van Donk, M., Smit, W., & Drimie, S. (2017). *Upgrading informal settlements in South Africa: Pursuing a partnership-based approach*. Cape town: Juta and Company (Pty) Ltd.

Cousins, B., & Walker, C. (2015). *Land divided, land restored: Land reform in South Africa for the 21st century*. Johannesburg: Jacana.

De Satgé, R., & Cousins, B. (2019). *Rural land redistribution in South Africa: Contrasting visions and models*. Available: https://www.africaportal.org/publications/rural-land-redistribution-south-africa-contrasting-visions-and-models/.

de Wet, P. (2018). *Could banks be the biggest losers in expropriation without compensation?* [ONLINE]. Available at: https://www.businessinsider.co.za. Accessed 4 November 2018.

Department of Agriculture, Forestry and Fisheries. (2016). *Trends in the agricultural sector* [ONLINE] Available at: https://www.daff.gov.za/Daffweb3/Portals. Accessed 13 November 2018.

Derman, B., Hellum, A., & Sandvik, K. (2013). *Worlds of human rights: The ambiguities of rights claiming in Africa*. Netherlands: Brill.

Eche, D. M. (2013). *Land degradation, small-scale farms' development, and migratory flows in chiapas: Case study: Tapachula* (Vol. 4). Kassel: Kassel University Press.

Ensor, L. (2018). Land expropriation without compensation spells 'economic disaster'. *Business Day Live*. Available: https://www.businesslive.co.za. Accessed 13 February 2019.

Groenewald, Y. (2018). *Could banks be the biggest losers in expropriation without compensation?* Available: https://www.fin24.com/Economy/. Accessed 12 November 2018.

Guo, X. (2001). Land expropriation and rural conflicts in China. *The China Quarterly, 166*, 422–439.

Hall, R., & Kepe, T. (2017). Elite capture and state neglect: New evidence on South Africa's land reform. *Review of African Political Economy, 44*(151), 122–130.

Hausmann, R., & Rodríguez, F. R. (2014). *Venezuela before Chávez: Anatomy of an economic collapse*. Pennsylvania: Pennsylvania State Press.

Hlomendlini, H., & Makgolane P. (2017). *Land expropriation without compensation: Possible impact on the South African agricultural economy*. Available: https://agrigauteng.com/index_htm_files/2017%20July%20Possible%20impact%20of%20land%20expropriation%20on%20the%20agric%20sector%2027%20July.pdf. Accessed 25 September 2018.

Havnevik, K., Matondi, P. B., & Beyene, A. (2011). *Biofuels, land grabbing and food security in Africa*. New York City: Zed Books/Nordiska Afrikainstitutet.

House, F. (2012). *Countries at the crossroads 2011: An analysis of democratic governance*. Lanham: Rowman & Littlefield Publishers.

Howard-Hassmann, R. (2015). The right to food under Hugo Chávez. *Human Rights Quarterly, 37*, 1024.

Hughes, D. (2010). *Whiteness in Zimbabwe: Race, landscape, and the problem of belonging*. London: Springer.

Kalabamu, F. T. (2019). Land tenure reforms and persistence of land conflicts in Sub-Saharan Africa-The case of Botswana. *Land Use Policy, 81*, 337–345.

Kilian, A. (2018). Land expropriation without compensation key for economic growth. *Masondo, Polity news*. Available: http://www.polity.org.za/art

icle/land-expropriation-without-compensation-key-for-economic-growth-masonda-2018-03-06. Accessed 25 September 2018.

Kirton, J., & Larionova, M. (2018). *BRICS and global governance*. Abingdon: Routledge.

Kloppers, H. J., & Pienaar, G. J. (2014). The historical context of land reform in South Africa and early policies. *Potchefstroom Electronic Law Journal/Potchefstroomse Elektroniese Regsblad, 17*(2), 676–706.

Lahiff, E. (2007). 'Willing buyer, willing seller': South Africa's failed experiment in market-led agrarian reform. *Third World Quarterly, 28*(8), 1577–1597.

Leon, P. (2018). *Land expropriation without compensation: SA risks breaching international law, being massively sued*. Available: https://www.biznews.com/. Accessed 7 November 2018.

Li, X., Gubo, Q., & Lixia, T. (2012). *Agricultural development in China and Africa: A comparative analysis*. Abingdon: Routledge.

Lumumba-Kasongo, T. (2015). *Land reforms and natural resource conflicts in Africa: New development paradigms in the era of global liberalization*. Abingdon: Routledge.

Mabaya, E., Tihanyi, K., & Karaan, M. (2011). *Case studies of emerging farmers and agribusinesses in South Africa*. Stellenbosch: African Sun Media.

Makinana, A. (2018). *FF Plus goes international with campaign to stop land expropriation*. Available: https://www.timeslive.co.za/politics. Accessed 4 November 2018.

Mango, N., Makate, C., Tamene, L., Mponela, P., & Ndengu, G. (2017). Awareness and adoption of land, soil and water conservation practices in the Chinyanja Triangle, Southern Africa. *International Soil and Water Conservation Research, 5*(2), 122–129.

Maumbe, B. (2009). *E-Agriculture and e-government for global policy development: Implications and future directions: Implications and future directions*. India: IGI Global.

Maylam, P. (2017). *South Africa's racial past: The history and historiography of racism, segregation, and apartheid*. London: Routledge.

Merten, M. (2018). *The politics of land expropriation without compensation in the ANC constitutional review proposals*. Available: https://www.dailymaverick.co.za/article/2018-11-0. Accessed 4 November 2018.

Mkokeli, S. (2018). The EFF is in charge—The ANC follows us: Malema has Ramaphosa 'where he wants him'. *Timeslive*. Available: https://www.timeslive.co.za. Accessed 7 November 2018.

Modise, L., & Mtshiselwa, N. (2013). The natives land act of 1913 engineered the poverty of black South Africans: A historic-ecclesiastical perspective. *Studia Historiae Ecclesiasticae, 39*(2), 359–378.

Moore, D., Kriger, N., & Raftopoulos, B. (2013). *Progress' in Zimbabwe? The past and present of a concept and a country*. London: Routledge.

Moyo, S., Jha, P., & Yeros, P. (2019). The scramble for land and natural resources in Africa. *Reclaiming Africa* (pp. 3–30). Singapore: Springer.

Moyo, S., & Yeros, P. (2005). *Reclaiming the land: The resurgence of rural movements in Africa, Asia and Latin America*. New York City: Zed Books.

Musakwa, W. (2018). Identifying land suitable for agricultural land reform using GIS-MCDA in South Africa. *Environment, Development and Sustainability, 20*(5), 2281–2299.

Naki, E. (2018). ANC cosying up to EFF 'to redress imbalances'. *The Citizen*. Available from: https://citizen.co.za/news/1842753/anc-cosying-up-to-eff-to-redress-imbalances/. Accessed 04 January 2019.

Neethling, T. (2015). The coming revolution: Julius Malema and the fight for economic freedom, Floyd Shivambu (Ed.): Book review. *Journal for Contemporary History, 40*(1), pp. 208–211.

Ngubane, M. (2018). Why so many new black farmers in SA are bound to fail. *The Citizen*. Available: https://citizen.co.za/talking-point/. Accessed 7 November 2018.

Ntsebeza, L., & Hall, R. (Eds.). (2007). *The land question in South Africa: The challenge of transformation and redistribution*. Pretoria: HSRC Press.

Ntsholo, L. (2018). *Mainstream media's shockingly antagonistic attitude to the EFF*. Available: https://www.dailymaverick.co.za. Accessed 13 November 2018.

Oosthuizen, M. (2003). *Expected labour demands in South Africa 1998-2003*. Cape Town: Development Policy Research Unit.

Özler, B. (2007). Not separate, not equal: Poverty and inequality in post-apartheid South Africa. *Economic Development and Cultural Change, 55*(3), 487–529.

Page, J., & Tarp, F. (2017). *The practice of industrial policy: Government—Business coordination in Africa and East Asia*. Oxford: Oxford University Press.

Phakathi, M. (2018). *Land expropriation plan will be very bad for agricultural finance, Agbiz tells MPs*. Available at: https://www.businesslive.co.za/bd/national. Accessed 6 November 2018.

Roberts, B. J. (2001). Chronic and transitory poverty in post-apartheid South Africa: Evidence from KwaZulu-Natal. *Journal of Poverty, 5*(4), 1–28.

Rutherford, B. (2016). *Farm labor struggles in Zimbabwe: The ground of politics*. Indiana: Indiana University Press.

Santarcángelo, J. E., Justo, O., & Cooney, P. (2016). *Latin America after the financial crisis: Economic ramifications from heterodox perspectives*. Berlin: Springer.

Shaw, W. H. (2003). 'They stole our land': Debating the expropriation of white farms in Zimbabwe. *The Journal of Modern African Studies, 41*(1), 75–89.

Spanakos, A. (2014). Venezuela before Chávez: Anatomy of an economic collapse. *Americas Quarterly, 8*(3), 129.

Spierenburg, M. (2019). Living on other people's land; Impacts of farm conversions to game farming on farm dwellers' abilities to access land in the Eastern Cape, South Africa. *Society & Natural Resources*, pp. 1–20.

Tate, S. A., & Fink, K. (2019). Skin colour politics and the white beauty standard. *Beauty and the Norm* (pp. 283–297). Cham: Palgrave Macmillan.

Thwala, W. D. (2018). *Land expropriation without compensation is long overdue freedom park.* https://www.freedompark.co.za/stay-informed/opinion-pieces/3380-land-expropriation-without-compensation-is-long-overdue.html. 02 October 2018.

Vorster, N. (2019). Land and identity in South Africa: An immanent moral critique of dominant discourses in the debate on expropriation without compensation. *HTS Teologiese Studies/Theological Studies, 75*(4), 9.

Williams, K. S., Williams, S. T., Fitzgerald, L. E., Sheppard, E. C., & Hill, R. A. (2018). Brown hyaena and leopard diets on private land in the Soutpansberg Mountains, South Africa. *African Journal of Ecology, 56*(4), 1021–1027.

Wolpe, H. (2018). Industrialism and race in South Africa. In S. Zubaida (Ed.), *Race and Racialism* (pp. 151–180). Routledge: British Sociological Association.

Woolard, I., & Klasen, S. (2005). Determinants of income mobility and household poverty dynamics in South Africa. *Journal of Development Studies, 41*(5), 865–897.

Xaba, G. (2015). *Identifying entrepreneurial skills required by South African black farmers-an entrepreneurial model.* PhD thesis, University of the Witwatersrand, Johannesburg.

CHAPTER 5

South African Land Question and the Dilemma of Land Expropriation Without Compensation: A Critical Examination

Mzingaye Brilliant Xaba

Introduction

South Africa's land reform programme, one of the country's most ambitious social engineering programmes, continues to limp on more than two decades after it was initially introduced. Largely due to poor outcomes, land reform has become a controversial, sensitive, politicised and to some extent, a racially polarising issue in post-apartheid South Africa (Cousins, 2015; Hendricks, 2013). This is because South Africa's history is laced with racism, wherein black communities were systematically forcibly removed from their lands, the basis of their livelihoods, with the arrival of white settlers, leading to the impoverishment of black communities

M. B. Xaba (✉)
Postdoctoral Research Fellow - SARChI Research Chair in the Sociology of Land, Environment and Sustainable Development, Department of Sociology and Social Anthropology, Stellenbosch University, Cape Town, South Africa

A. O. Akinola et al. (eds.), *The New Political Economy of Land Reform in South Africa*,
https://doi.org/10.1007/978-3-030-51129-6_5

(Cousins, 2016b; Xaba & Roodt, 2016). This explains why there is such a demand for land acquisition, and the return of land to the 'rightful owners' (black people), especially by radical left-leaning groups and landless black communities. The post-apartheid government soon realised the necessity of implementing land reform to address the historical injustice and land inequality in the county.

However, since 1994, the three pillars of land reform (redistribution, restitution and tenure reform) have barely achieved their goals. In the midst of the slow pace of land reform, there have been claims by some scholars, politicians, civil society groups and landless communities that the 'willing buyer, willing seller' approach for land acquisition has been ineffective. These claims especially started at the 2005 Land Summit where delegates overwhelmingly rejected that the state solely uses this approach when purchasing land (Aliber, 2015: 145–148; Hall & Ntsebeza, 2007; Ntsebeza, 2007). Thus, there has long been a call for the removal of the willing buyer, willing seller approach to speed up land reform. It is important to note that the ruling African National Congress (ANC) has been using this market-based approach to appease investors, but pressures within and outside the ANC by other stakeholders, especially by the left-leaning militant Economic Freedom Fighters (EFF) and some land-based groupings, popularised the 'land expropriation without compensation' (LEWC) approach.

In the context of losing votes, legitimacy and credibility, the ANC has no doubt been using the land question not only to correct land injustice, but for political survival by trying to appease black communities, albeit clumsily and without clarity, because of the pressures from the EFF (Ntsebeza, 2018). The EFF has seemingly been successful in positioning themselves as champions of the poor black communities. Ever since the EFF started calling for LEWC and the scrapping of the willing buyer, willing seller approach after their formation in 2013, the ANC has been in a panic mode, eventually leading them to introduce this radical stance on land reform. Indeed, in 2017, the ANC endorsed the LEWC policy under its 'radical economic transformation' (RET) motto to speed up land reform, although the then newly elected ANC President, Cyril Ramaphosa, argued that the policy should not upset the markets (Mahlakoana, 2017).

However, in the midst of all the hype around land acquisition and the politicised nature of the land question, the state, populist politicians and many other commentators have created an impression that LEWC will make land reform cheaper and more effective. This is partly due to the fact that over 20 years of existing land reform programmes have hardly shaken the core of racially skewed land arrangements. Because of the emotive nature of the historic land dispossession, which resulted in the impoverishment of black communities, the political class has related to the land debates with passion, bias, anger and distortion of facts (Coleman, 2018). Whether LEWC is feasible, effective and an improvement on existing land policy is still unclear and debatable, especially at a time when the processes of the Constitutional Review Committee to provide constitutional clarity on expropriation, are still ongoing. Evidently, social media, public talks and debates have been awash with land jokes, the need for the return of 'stolen land', with white farmers being labelled as rich, selfish and not wanting to share wealth with black communities.

I argue that while there is some fact regarding the recalcitrant attitude of some white farmers on land acquisition, and that there is a need to provide legal clarity on expropriation, the political rhetoric on land acquisition problems dissuades the public from understanding the real issues on land reform processes. LEWC has been partly used by the ANC to outdo the left-leaning militant (EFF) in order to woo voters. However, my argument is not an attempt to imply that land acquisition is not important; it is. The point is that there needs to be more focus in land reform conversations on what happens when land has been identified, gazetted and transferred, as well as aligning all land stakeholders to improve provision of post-settlement support (PSS). An effective land reform requires strong institutions and cooperative stakeholders.

I start by briefly explaining land reform programmes in the post-apartheid dispensation. The next section on the emergence of expropriation then helps to explore the reasons behind the adoption of LEWC as the most appropriate solution for sustainable land reform. From there, I explain the legal and political connotations of LEWC to show that it is an instrument for electoral mobilisation for both the ANC and EFF in their attempt to outdo each other in the 2019 general elections. The subsequent section is less optimistic about the success of LEWC. The next section then situates the LEWC in the broader context of international law and reveals possible problems that the implementation of LEWC might face. In the last section, I emphasise that the state needs to focus on struggling land beneficiaries and unproductive farms, and most importantly, provide a better alignment amongst land reform stakeholders for an effective land reform programme.

Land Reform Since 1994: A Struggling Land Reform

In 1994, the ANC inherited a racially-based system of landownership, access and use, owing to the history of land dispossession, domination and colonisation that started in 1652 (Ntsebeza, 2018; Xaba & Roodt, 2016). To reverse the racially-based landownership patterns, the ANC government introduced the three-pronged land reform components (redistribution, restitution and tenure reform) based on the willing buyer, willing seller approach. Land was to be purchased from willing white farmers for redistribution to black communities. This approach was based on the advice of the neoliberal World Bank (WB), together with other economists (Hall, 2004, cited in Hall, 2010a). Land restitution was meant to return the land to those who lost land after 1913, whereas land redistribution focuses on redressing landownership imbalances by giving land to black South Africans for residential and production purposes. Tenure reform was meant to protect tenure for those people who live in areas where their tenure is insecure, such as farmworkers and dwellers, labour tenants and those who live in former 'reserves' (Alexander, 2015, cited in Akinola, 2018: 2; Ntsebeza, 2007: 118; Ntsebeza, 2018).

In 1994, the government set out to redistribute 30% of farmland (through restitution and redistribution) by 1999; the target date was later shifted to 2014. But by 2018, only about 8–9% of farmland had been given to black beneficiaries, although other academic estimates project a higher figure (Cousins, 2015: 254–255; Cousins, 2016b; Lodge, 2018; Sihlobo & Kapuya, 2018). The literature on land reform shows that most land reform projects have failed, and that about 50% of rural land reform projects have brought some benefits to beneficiaries, although these are often quite small (Cousins, 2016b). Thousands of land claims that were lodged have not been finalised and tenure reform has failed to stop evictions, retrenchment of farmworkers and insecurity of tenure as landowners have mastered how to evade the tenure laws. In rural areas, some people remain prone to evictions because of reported corruption of traditional leaders (Cousins, 2016a, 2016b; High Level Panel, 2017: 204; PLAAS, 2016).

After over 20 years of democracy, South Africa is characterised by disillusioned citizens, rising unemployment, poverty and inequality. The increasing populism, which is evidenced by the recent #FeesMustFall and the #RhodesMustFall protests from 2015 onwards, as well as the continuing violent service delivery protests, is evidence of a massive anger from the black communities who long for a break from the racial past. For the radical/left-leaning groups and some radical elements within the ruling ANC who are against what they call 'white monopoly capital', the return of land to the 'rightful owners' (black people) has been the rallying call for decolonisation and breaking from the racist past. The EFF and other left-leaning groups such as Black First Land First (BLF) have successfully presented themselves as champions of the black poor, and they see white landownership as illegitimate because it derives from the proceeds of colonisation, apartheid and white domination of the black race (Kepe & Hall, 2018). LEWC and the increasing popularity of the calls for radicalism and decolonisation can be traced to the formation of the EFF in 2013.

In 2012, the ANC expelled its Youth League leadership; these expelled Youth League members formed the EFF party in 2013 (Ntsebeza, 2018), and land LEWC was to become their rallying call for decolonisation. Indeed, the EFF has popularised radicalism in South Africa (Kepe & Hall, 2018: 128–129) and their influence is growing, especially amongst the youth. Seeing that the EFF was growing and popularising the radical conversation, particularly its calls for LEWC, the ANC responded by adopting the same radical stance on land policy (Bendile, 2017). This is because the ANC government is between a rock and a hard place, and they are pushed to populist policy spaces because land has been so politicised and debated in during electioneering. The call for LEWC is largely an act of survival on the part of the ANC to appease the populist politicians and poor black voters, and less to do with real issues on land reform. According to Ntsebeza (2018), the EFF has been so powerful, so much so that they have pressured the ANC to adopt a radical approach to land reform to appease black voters, many of who are poised to vote for the EFF or other opposition parties. Lodge (2018) shares the same sentiment by arguing that LEWC is somehow an attempt by the ANC to deflect political pressure from the left-leaning/radical politicians.

By 2017, the ANC had started initiating a radical stance on land reform. In doing so, the ANC also initiated a change of the 1913 start-off date, so that restitution claims can include the pre-apartheid land dispossession that happened before the 1913 Lands Act was promulgated (Bendile, 2017). The Minister of Rural Development and Land Reform at the time, Gugile Nkwinti was quoted saying,

> the bottom line is that we are in trouble. We need to fast-track the decisions we took. We just need to bite the bullet, in my view. Just remember, the ANC has always been careful. Now people say, 'you are too slow'. (Bendile, 2017)

The Minister indirectly referred to the ANC's subjection of land reform to the markets, which was purportedly to protect the economy and the young South African democracy.

The ANC's radical stance on land reform happened at a time when it was losing supporters because of many issues, including perceptions of corruption, inefficiency, arrogance and poor service delivery. The ANC performed badly in the 2016 local government elections, largely because the then leader of ANC, President Jacob Zuma, was allegedly involved in many corruption scandals, and the service delivery protests showed that the masses were disillusioned and angry with the government for poor governance. Thus, as a strategy for political survival, regime consolidation and democratic survival, the ANC realised the need to adopt radical steps to undo the racially-based inequalities on land reform (Ntsebeza, 2018). Therefore, the ANC's radical stance is largely about deflecting rising popularity of the EFF and preventing the opposition party from becoming the voice of the majority poor South Africans.

Emergence of LEWC Conversation

There have always been scholarly arguments that Section 25 (s25) of the Constitution slowed land reform, implying that it needed to be amended, and that the willing buyer, willing seller approach had to be scrapped because it was slowing land reform. Ntsebeza (2007, 2018) and other scholars such as Ntsholo (2015) have long argued that the property clause in s25 of the Constitution is contradictory and conflictual. It protects white properties, but at the same time, seeks to redistribute land, thereby impeding accelerated land reform projects. The willing buyer willing seller approach remains the ugly representation of the property clause (Aliber, 2015: 145). Under Section 25, of the 1996 Constitution, proponents of LEWC argue that the market-based approach protects white farmers and that white farmers have some kind of veto powers on land reform. While recognising that the Constitution is problematic, the High Level Panel, a Parliamentary initiative, through its report that was published in 2017, revealed that the Constitution was not a hindrance to land reform.

According to the report, what has been lacking is the political will or courage of conviction to implement land reform and combat land-related corruption by state officials (High Level Panel, 2017). This demonstrates the importance of strong and cooperative institutions (stakeholders) for the realisation of an effective land reform.

The property clause in s25 was inserted into the Constitution as a result of compromises during the early negotiations for a democratic South Africa. During the Convention for a Democratic South Africa (CODESA) in the early 1990s when the National Party (NP) was preparing to cede political power, the inclusion of a property rights clause in the Constitution was the main issue which was meant to protect the properties of the minority white class from future majority rule (Hall, 2010a: 20; Ntsebeza, 2007). Hall (2010b: 199) succinctly observes that during the controversial clause negotiations, the quandary,

> was whether or not property, already regulated through statute and common law, should be given constitutional protection in a Bill of Rights and, if so, how the powers of the state to enact land reform and the rights of citizens to claim land rights would be balanced against the rights of existing property rights.

After its formation in 2013, the EFF repeatedly claimed that s25 of the Constitution has slowed land reform and argued for its amendment. In early 2017, the EFF moved a motion to amend s25, but the ANC used its majority to thwart the EFF's motion to remove the provision that the state must pay 'just and equitable compensation' after expropriation (Kepe & Hall, 2018: 129; Leon, Ripley-Evans, Burnell & Kota, 2018). The chairperson of the Rural Development and Land Reform Committee in Parliament, Phumuzile Ngwenya-Mabila, an ANC member, said,

> We are not going to be told what to do. We are not in alliance with anyone...expropriation of land should be done for public purpose and public interests, not for the EFF purpose and EFF interests. Secondly, expropriation without compensation is unconstitutional. (Merten, 2018a)

Ngwenya-Mabila's statement came at a time when the ANC was sharply divided between a faction led by Zuma, which was pushing for what they called 'radical economic transformation' (RET) which included LEWC, and Cyril Ramaphosa's faction which seemingly did not support LEWC.

Eventually, LEWC was adopted in the ANC's December 2017 Conference, but the newly elected President Cyril Ramaphosa was reluctant to accept the proposed policy due to the notion that LEWC might ruin the economy. In 2018, the EFF capitalised on the ANC's adoption of the LEWC, and brought a motion in Parliament to amend s25 and introduced the language of LEWC, including removing the requirement that the state must pay 'just and equitable' compensation after expropriation. Eventually, LEWC was adopted by Parliament, leading to the formation of the Constitutional Review Committee (CRC) (Merten, 2018a).

Although the EFF and ANC seem to have agreed on expropriation, the EFF wants nationalisation wherein the state becomes the custodian of land, whereas the ANC (although unclear) seems to be leaning towards using acquisition for redistribution to people, and a system of mixed ownership patterns (Hall, 2018; Manona, 2018; Merten, 2018a; Merten, 2018b). Essentially, the ANC wants LEWC to be included amongst the options that they currently have, which includes purchasing land on the market, negotiating, expropriating and paying compensation (Hall, 2018). The next section builds on this by discussing the nature of the political and legal meanings of LEWC and how it is presented as a solution.

The Political and Legal Interpretations of LEWC

The evident challenge with expropriation is that it is being debated at a time when many black communities are tired of waiting for their land and bitter about their living conditions in the context of increasing unemployment, poverty and inequalities, over 20 years after independence. The reality is that the state has failed to use their expropriation powers enshrined in the Constitution under s25. The ANC cannot afford to create an impression that the Constitution has been the barrier to meaningful land reform when they have largely not tested it. But the ANC is cornered by increasing populism politics. Legal experts and scholars have correctly argued that the state has ignored its powers to expropriate under s25 of the South African Constitution. What has been lacking on the part of the state is political will, strong institutions and courage of conviction to implement meaningful land reform (High Level Panel, 2017). One of the senior ANC leaders, and ANC Parliamentary Chief Whip, Jackson Mthembu, correctly argued that the ANC cannot blame the Constitution for the failures of land reform, and tweeted, 'blaming the Constitution for the slow pace of land reform is both disingenuous and scapegoating. We failed, finish en klaar' (du Toit, 2017).

Importantly, the former deputy Chief Justice of the Constitutional Court, Dikgang Moseneke, maintained that it was legal to expropriate land, and that the willing buyer, willing seller does not appear in the Constitution (Pithouse, 2015). According to Ngcukaitobi (2018), a respected lawyer, expropriation entails the obligatory (compelled by law) acquisition of land from an individual by the government to meet constitutionally circumscribed purposes, subject to 'just and equitable' compensation. The scope of compensation must be agreed on by the state and the landowner, failure of which a court of law can determine the amount of compensation. As provided under the s25, expropriation should be undertaken only for 'public purpose' or 'public interest'. In determining the value of compensation, the following criteria are taken into consideration by the courts: the market value of the property, what would be 'just and equitable' compensation, the history of acquisition of such land and the current use of that land (Ngcukaitobi, 2018). The available piece of legislation on expropriation is the Expropriation Act 63 of 1975 and it is still law for as long as it does not violate other provisions of the Constitution (Manona, 2018). In fact, legal experts have long argued that under the current legal framework, LEWC is legally possible, because the amount of compensation could possibly be zero. Section 25 (8) of the Constitution makes it possible for the state to avoid paying compensation (Ngcukaitobi, 2018).

In understanding the calls for LEWC, it is important to illustrate how the ANC government has neglected its expropriation powers by using the Mala Mala restitution case (Hall, 2018). The Mala Mala restitution case has demonstrated the ANC government's lack of political will and courage of conviction to implement s25 and their general political cowardice, or maybe their fear of market reaction. In 2013, the Mala Mala restitution case was dragged to the Constitutional Court in 2013 for the Court to determine what is 'just and fair' compensation. However, the then Minister of Land Reform, Mr. Gugile Nkwinti, withdrew the case, opting to pay compensation of about R1 billion to one white family. This demonstrates the fear of using expropriation powers on the part of the state, and it reveals that the payment of such a huge amount of compensation was not a problem generated by the Constitution. In general terms, the state has failed to fully explore s25, and thus, the calls for LEWC are premature (Hall, 2018; Hull, 2018). The Mala-Mala case was a demonstration of the ANC's double standards, wherein by amending the Constitution they would create an impression that the Constitution has been a stumbling block, yet they have ignored the use of state's powers as enshrined in the Constitution.

Even the Parliamentary debates on LEWC are characterised by 'lack of debate in a debate', wherein politicians merely espouse rhetoric without substance. Although land acquisition is important for land reform, the public is being misled by the EFF and the ruling ANC who have turned LEWC to an instrument of public manipulation. The lack of substance on the debates on LEWC is often shaped in a way that those pushing for LEWC want to be seen as champions of the poor, whereas those who feel that expropriation is possible with the current Constitution are labelled as 'sellouts' by populist politicians. For instance, Inkatha Freedom Party's (IFP) vocal Member of Parliament (MP), Mkhuleko Hlengwa, strongly argued that the ANC was dissuading the public from real issues and argued that compensation less expropriation was an attack on the democratic gains of South Africa and that LEWC was possible within the current provisions of the Constitution (Merten, 2018c). Later in the same sitting, an EFF MP used the debate to invoke racial politics and said, 'Your time is up, white people!' (Merten, 2018c). This was pure grandstanding by the EFF, to create an impression that as the pushers of LEWC they are pro-poor and champions of black people, while those who are against LEWC are regarded as liberation 'sellouts'.

This is because the support for LEWC is an emotive, moral and political demand that is rooted in bitterness against the racial past and precipitated by the current increasing levels of unemployment, poverty and social inequality that has characterised the new South Africa. There is a sense that white people must pay for exploiting black communities (through land dispossession) and that the return of land to black communities will lessen black poverty. Thus, Lodge (2018) concludes that LEWC is much more about punishment and retribution because many black people hold that the white community is responsible for their protracted poverty. In the next section, I seek to engage the reality of the implementation of LEWC and the misconception that LEWC will possibly result in effective land reform.

LEWC: A Solution to Successful Land Reform?

There is no doubt that expropriation is important, and that the easy availability of land for land reform will be an added advantage for land reform processes, but all that is dependent on strong state institutions for an effective land reform. Besides the populist rhetoric in public and Parliamentary debates, proponents of LEWC have not presented clear, meticulous and coherent evidence to demonstrate that such a policy will be less costly to the government and resolve other land-related issues. Aliber (2015: 145–146) admits that the willing buyer, willing seller approach is clearly problematic, but decries that the calls for its scrapping have created an impression that there are other superior alternatives which must replace the market-based willing buyer, willing seller and that proponents of LEWC present little evidence of the unfeasibility and impracticality of the market-based approach. Additionally, Sihlobo and Kapuya (2018) have meticulously explained why LEWC does not mean land acquisition will be cheaper or effective. Firstly, it is not clear how the LEWC will cater for assets on the farm and improvements on the land (Sihlobo & Kapuya, 2018: 3).

And then there is the question of the debt incurred by white farmers. It is widely known that many white farmers are in debt, with poor farming returns estimated to be about 6% in a good season. In fact, national farm debt was estimated to have increased to R160 billion by 2018. A big portion of this debt, about 62%, is owed to commercial banks, while about 27% is owed to the Land Bank, while agricultural cooperatives are owed 7% by farmers and the rest are private individuals and other institutions (Sihlobo & Kapuya, 2018: 2). Thus:

> The question then becomes, should a property owner continue servicing their loan when they no longer have ownership rights to that property or a component therefore, and the bank has no security to fall back on? Furthermore, should financial institutions-and the real-estate corporations-simply write off their assets on their balance sheets? (Sihlobo & Kirsten, 2018)

Proponents of LEWC have failed to directly engage on the question of debt and how it would be resolved. Again, given the anxiety and uncertainty amongst white farmers, it is likely that white farmers will withdraw their investments on land, which will result in high food prices.

Moreover, LEWC may lead to extremely complex technical and administrative challenges for the state, which will stall land reform (Lodge, 2018; Sihlobo & Kapuya, 2018: 4). Research shows that land reform-related departments are characterised by red tape, incompetence, ineptitude and poor policy alignments, which has slowed land reform, especially the delivery of PSS. The Department of Rural Development and Land Reform (DRDLR) is one of the weakest government departments in the country (Cousins (2016b). In this way, with the impending LEWC, it is likely that the value of land and investments (both internally and externally) on land will be reduced, which means that the land beneficiaries will inherit low-priced land, low farm asset prices and high costs of borrowing (Lodge, 2018; Sihlobo & Kapuya, 2018). Therefore,

> There is no such thing as expropriation without compensation in a quasi-capitalist economy, because what the government refuses to pay in compensation will effectively be paid for through the negative effects that the beneficiaries experience, as well as the ripple effects in the wider economy. (Sihlobo & Kapuya, 2018: 4)

Moreover, as shown in the next section, the debates on expropriation seem to have drawn little from international jurisprudence, and when one considers international laws and treaties, it seems the implementation of the LEWC may be problematic.

LEWC, International Laws and Treaties: Lessons from Zimbabwe

By international standards, and indeed in South Africa, the area of compulsory acquisition of property by governments against private parties has been one of the most highly litigated of case laws (Manona, 2018). It is important to draw from international law in implementing the LEWC because South Africa is a signatory to those treaties and part of the broader world. It becomes important for one to examine what LEWC would mean from the perspectives of international law. For instance, Leon (2018) states that,

> Under customary international law, each sovereign state expects other states to treat its nationals and their property in accordance with certain

> basic standards, collectively known as the 'international minimum standard of treatment'. This standard entails that expropriation may only be undertaken for a legitimate public purpose, in accordance with non-discriminatory due process, and accompanied by compensation.

Thus, Leon (2018) fears that LEWC may contradict customary international law and other treaties to which South Africa is party to, which may create global hostility against the country and undermine investors' confidence. It is important to add that according to current geopolitics anchored on neoliberalism, private property rights and the respect for markets is very important. The Bilateral Investment Treaties (BITs) that South Africa signs with other countries will likely have an effect on LEWC (Leon, 2018). For instance, in the matter between *Bernhard von Pezold and others v. Republic of Zimbabwe* in 2015 in which the Zimbabwean government had grabbed land from white farmers, a Tribunal awarded market value compensation to the white family farmers (who are dual Swiss and German citizens), which was to be paid by Zimbabwean government, based on the BITs with Switzerland and Germany. The Tribunal found that the Zimbabwean government, through its fast-track land reform programme, breached expropriation, fair and equitable treatment (FET) and other provisions of the Zimbabwean BITs with Switzerland and Germany. This is because upon the signing of international treaties, there is usually a clause that implies that legal issues can be settled in an international commercial tribunal, which, in this case, meant that they are not subjected to any domestic legislation, such as the Constitution of Zimbabwe for instance.

There is the possibility of a similar outcome if LEWC is eventually implemented in South Africa. Such legal cases have serious implications for the effectiveness of LEWC in South Africa due to the reality that international law can still supersede the workings of LEWC. Surely, a country cannot use its domestic legislation to contradict its commitments to international law (Leon, 2018). Initially, the Zimbabwean government tried to ignore the *Bernhard von Pezold and others v. Republic of Zimbabwe* ruling in 2015; a later court order ruled that since Zimbabwe was bound by the BIT, property owned by the government could be sold in execution of the order to pay von Pezolds. After the collapse of the Mugabe-led government, the new Zimbabwean government has called on white commercial farmers, whose farms were expropriated, to return (Mavhunga, 2018; Sihlobo & Kapuya, 2018: 3). Most importantly, the present Zimbabwean government has shown commitment in compensating the white commercial farmers by establishing a Compensation Committee under the Land Acquisition Act (Mavhunga, 2018; Sihlobo & Kapuya, 2018: 3).

In a related judgement in 2018, the Constitutional Court of South ruled that the former President Jacob Zuma's action to sign the Southern African Development Community (SADC) Protocol in 2014 to 'remove the rights of individuals, both in South Africa and the entire region to access the tribunal for legal redress' (which sank the SADC Tribunal) was unconstitutional, unlawful and irrational (*Law Society of South Africa and Others v President of the Republic of South Africa and Others*, 2018). From a legal point of view, these cases will also have a serious impact on the LEWC in South Africa. Whether the South African land LEWC will be aligned to international laws and treaties still remains speculative and a matter that requires further discussion. This case emanated from the LEWC or the fast-track land reform programme in Zimbabwe, and the SADC Tribunal was the last court of appeal for the Zimbabwean white farmers whose farms were expropriated after the Zimbabwean government removed the powers of domestic courts to handle the matter. The SADC Tribunal then ruled against the Zimbabwean government regarding land reform and found that the Zimbabwean government violated certain sections of the SADC treaty. Rather than forcing the Zimbabwe government to comply with the Tribunal's ruling, SADC leaders decided to strip the Tribunal of its powers, thereby replacing it with a new protocol; the Zimbabwean government ignored the Tribunal ruling (*Law Society of South Africa and Others v President of the Republic of South Africa and Others*, 2018).

Sihlobo and Kapuya (2018: 3) conclude that 'the Zimbabwean experience tells us that expropriation without compensation is a catastrophically a bad idea', and that 'there is no such thing as expropriation without compensation'. This is due to the fact that, directly or indirectly, the state will pay for LEWC through job losses, market instability, de-industrialisation and loss of agricultural export revenues. Thus, 'if the government declines to compensate its commercial sector for land improvements-at the very least-then someone else will have to pay for it indirectly' (Sihlobo & Kapuya, 2018: 3). Therefore, there is the need to consult widely and engage all parties towards presenting a balance between the adoption of LEWC and international law.

Zimbabwe's socio-economic crisis after radicalising its land reform scheme presents the disastrous consequences of manipulating the markets in the context of a geopolitical and economic order that is dominated by neoliberalism. This was the argument advanced by South African white farmers and commercial farmers' unions during the 2005 Land Summit in South Africa (Hall & Ntsebeza, 2007). By 2018, roughly 18 years after implementing LEWC in Zimbabwe, a lot of Zimbabweans were dependant on food imports, foreign aid and financial assistance from donor organisations (Nyarota, 2018), whereas in the same year the Zimbabwean government lifted a ban (temporarily) on imports and published a list of basic commodities that companies and individuals could import, of which the majority were agricultural products, indicating the collapse of the economy due to the adoption of LEWC (Thompson, 2018). This is a lesson for South Africa. A consultative, pragmatic, legal and systematically implemented 'expropriation', without any political jargon is likely to yield positive results.

Policy Direction for Land Reform

Although land acquisition is important, the biggest problem with the prevalent land reform is not solely the lack of access to land per se, but concerns the complex interactions that unfold when land is claimed or identified, gazetted, and when such land is eventually awarded to beneficiaries (Xaba & Roodt, 2018). The possibility of massive legal land acquisition by the state will still not resolve the challenges of post-settlement and poor alignment of land stakeholders. Land transfer without proper PSS is setting up beneficiaries for failure. Indeed, there are cases where land has been given to beneficiaries but the government was unable to provide PSS services, thereby restricting land and farm productivity (Xaba & Roodt, 2016). Furthermore, there is evidence that the state is sitting on 4000 farms which have not been awarded to beneficiaries because of administrative issues and social conflict amongst beneficiaries (George & Eybers, 2017). Hence, there is more to land reform than land acquisition.

The calls for LEWC create an impression that there is a shortage of available land and that prices for land are excessively high. Although this could be partly true, the picture is multifaceted and not simplistic. The high land prices argument was popularised, especially leading up to the promulgation of the Land Reform Property Valuations Act 17 of 2014 (LRPVA) (Aliber, 2015: 150). The promulgation of the LRPVA was based on the view that land prices in the open markets are high, leading to the setting up of the Office of the Valuer General to intervene in the skyrocketing prices. While the rising prices of land argument are accepted, Cousins (2016b: 13) argues that if the state could increase their budgets for land reform from 0.4 to 2%, they will be able to purchase farms at slightly below market value.

Furthermore, the High Level Panel that was published in 2017 found that state departments have derailed land reform through collusion, ineptitude and corruption. Land sales are characterised by the collusion between state officials, estate agents and landowners, which inflated prices (High Level Panel, 2017). Again, in a judgement between *Msiza v Director-General for the DRDLR and Others* in 2016, Judge T Ngcukaitobi questioned the reasons behind government's payment of market value as compensation, when the Constitution requires a 'just and equitable' compensation. In other words, the 'compensation' requirement is not an impediment to land reform and does not justify the cancellation of the 'compensation' clause attached to land expropriation. The state has largely failed to use its appropriating powers appropriately.

Moreover, evidence on land reform projects indicates that many beneficiaries lack the required infrastructure, inputs, agricultural extension services and other post-settlement services that are needed to ensure proper agricultural production. A lot of effort needs to be invested in empowering state departments that are related to land reform such as municipalities, agricultural provincial offices and other land reform departments to eradicate slow delivery of PSS and improve policy coherence and information flow amongst all land reform stakeholders. Thus, Cousins (2016b: 17) and Lodge (2018) recommend that in order for land reform to be manageable and successful, there is more need for a major expansion of extension services. Secondly, there is a need to break up large farms into small holder units that are manageable, in order to avoid group dynamics problems.

It is also important to revitalise the bureaucracy and improve institutional structures, procedures and systems of data collection and analysis towards the development of land reform programmes. All these efforts will generate positive outcomes if the government can increase its budget for land reform. Xaba and Roodt (2018) question the push for LEWC when the government has not directed much effort towards financing land reform projects. Even when the government passed the Restitution of Land Rights Amendment Act of 2014, which was eventually struck off by the Constitutional Court in 2016, the government had not shown strong enthusiasm to increase the state's budget for land redistribution and restitution.

Conclusion

There is no doubt that the land debates have been captured by the political elites, albeit without substance and debated in an electioneering mode. The land reform narrative has been largely characterised by populism by public officials as they jostle to appease black communities that have been at the receiving end of ineffective land reform. However, there exists the wider perspective of the failure, of market-based willing buyer, willing seller approach to land reform over 20 years of implementation. While I do not disagree with the need to provide legal clarity on expropriation and the importance of land acquisition, the land chorus has hidden the most important and meticulous aspects of land reform. Scholars and stakeholders are not clear about which alternative model should replace the willing buyer, willing seller approach; however, the LEWC has been presented by the government as a solution to the land reform. In contrast to the Zimbabwean government that is still reeling from the LEWC or fast-track land reform that was implemented in the early 2000s, the South African government has chosen to go ahead with the implementation of LEWC and to provide constitutional clarity on the matter.

There is clearly a disjuncture between the political discourse and rhetoric on expropriation, what expropriation represents in legal terms, and the possible practicalities of implementing LEWC. Proponents of LEWC often create an impression that market model of land reform is entirely erroneous and that radicalisation of land policy will make land reform effective and meaningful. I have demonstrated that the debate on LEWC misses the meticulous aspects of land reform because it has been explored as an instrument of political mobilisation for electoral gain. In conclusion, I believe that land acquisition is important for land reform, but even if the LEWC was to be implemented, it may not resolve the diverse problems generated by the state's intervention in the land sector, and in particular, it may not redress post-settlement crisis.

Acknowledgements M. B. Xaba is currently a Postdoctoral Fellow at Stellenbosch University in the Sociology Department. He received funding from

DST-NRF Centre of Excellence in Human Development that is based at Wits University for his PhD thesis at Rhodes University in Sociology Department.

The PhD funders are acknowledged as follows:

"*The support of DST-NRF Centre of Excellence in Human Development at the University of Witwatersrand, Johannesburg in the Republic of South Africa towards this research is hereby acknowledged. Opinions expressed and conclusions arrived at, are those of the author and are not to be attributed to the CoE in Human Development.*"

References

Akinola, A. O. (2018). Land reform in South Africa: An appraisal. *Africa Review, 10*(1), 1–16.

Aliber, M. (2015). Unravelling the 'willing buyer, willing seller' question. In B. Cousins & C. Walker (Eds.), *Land divided, land restored: Land reform in South Africa for the 21st century*. Jacana Media: Auckland Park.

Bendile, D. (2017). ANC plans 'constitutional revolution' on land. *Mail and Guardian*, 3 February. Online: https://mg.co.za/article/2017-02-03-00-anc-hits-warp-speed-on-land. Accessed on 12 December 2018.

Bernhard von Pezold and others v. Republic of Zimbabwe. (2015). (ICSID Case No. ARB/10/15). Available: https://icsid.worldbank.org/en/Pages/cases/casedetail.aspx?CaseNo=ARB/10/15.

Coleman, M. (2018). *Credible land reform outcome requires reliable, accurate information-Weekend Argus*. South African Institute of Race Relations, 30 June 2018. Online: https://irr.org.za/media/credibleland-reform-outcome-requires-reliable-accurate-information-weekend-argus. Accessed on 30 April.

Cousins, B. (2015). 'Through a glass, darkly': Towards agrarian reform in South Africa. In B. Cousins & C. Walker (Eds.), *Land divided, land restored: Land reform in South Africa for the 21st Century*. Jacana: Auckland Park.

Cousins, B. (2016a). Why South Africa needs fresh ideas to make land reform a reality. *The Conversation*, 1 June. Online: http://theconversation.com/why-south-africa-needs-fresh-ideas-to-make-land-reform-a-reality-60076/. Accessed on 6 June 2016.

Cousins, B. (2016b). *Land reform in South Africa is sinking. Can it be saved?* Council for the advancement of the South African Constitution. Nelson Mandela Foundation. Hanns Seidel Foundation. Available: https://www.nelsonmandela.org/uploads/files//Land__law_and_leadership_-_paper_2.pdf. Accessed on 22 November 2016.

du Toit, P. (2017). Jackson Mthembu on the ANC's land reform: We failed, finish en klaar. *Huffpost*, 3 March. Online: https://www.huffingtonpost.co.

za/2017/03/03/weve-failed-finish-and-klaar-says-ancs-jackson-mthembu_a_21872433/. Accessed on 15 December 2018.

George, L., & Eybers, J. (2017). Govt sits on 4000 farms, yet hints at expropriation. *Fin24*, 22 March. Available: https://www.fin24.com/Companies/Agribusiness/govt-sits-on-4-000-farms-yet-hints-at-expropriation-20170522. Accessed on 22 February 2018.

Hall, R., & Ntsebeza, L. (2007). Introduction. In L. Ntsebeza & R. Hall (Eds.), *The land question in South Africa: The challenge of transformation and redistribution*. Pretoria: HSRC Press.

Hall, R. (2010a). Reconciling the past, present and the future: The parameters and practices of land restitution in South Africa. In C. Walker, A. Bohlin, R. Hall, & T. Kepe (Eds.), *Land, memory, reconstruction, and justice: Perspectives on land claims in South Africa*. Athens: Ohio University Press.

Hall, R. (2010b). *The politics of land reform in post-apartheid South Africa, 1990 to 2004: A shifting terrain of power, actors and discourses*, PhD thesis, University of Oxford.

Hall, R. (2018). Land expropriation without compensation: What does it mean? *City Press*, 4 March. Available: https://m.news24.com/Columnists/GuestColumn/land-expropriation-without-compensation-what-does-it-mean-20180304-5. Accessed 11 December 2018.

Hendricks, F. (2013). Rhetoric and reality in restitution and redistribution: Ongoing land and agrarian questions in South Africa. In F. Hendricks, L. Ntsebeza, & K. Helliker (Eds.), *The promise of land: Undoing a century of dispossession in South Africa*. Jacana Media: Auckland Park.

High Level Panel (High Level Panel on the Assessment of Key Legislation and the Acceleration of Fundamental Change). (2017). *Report of the high level panel on the assessment of key legislation and the acceleration of fundamental change*. Parliament of South Africa. Available: https://www.parliament.gov.za/storage/app/media/Pages/2017/october/High_Level_Panel/HLP_Report/HLP_report.pdf. Accessed on 07 May 2018.

Hull, S. (2018). Of the necessity of, and mechanisms for, expropriating land without compensation. *Daily Maverick*, 11 June. Available: https://www.dailymaverick.co.za/article/2018-06-11-on-the-necessity-of-and-mechanisms-for-expropriating-land-without-compensation/. Accessed on 12 December 2018.

Kepe, T., & Hall, R. (2018). Land redistribution in South Africa: Towards decolonisation or recolonisation? *Politikon*, *45*(1), 128–137.

Law Society of South Africa and Others v President of the Republic of South Africa and Others. (2018). Constitutional court of South Africa. Available: https://collections.concourt.org.za/bitstream/handle/20.500.12144/34610/Full%

20judgment%20Official%20version%2011%20December%202018.pdf?sequence=57&isAllowed=y. Accessed on 12 December 2018.

Leon, P. (2018). Land EWC may breach international law. *PoliticsWeb*, 25 July. Available: http://www.politicsweb.co.za/comment/expropriation-of-land-without-compensation-may-bre. Accessed on 11 December 2018.

Leon, P., Ripley-Evans, J., Burnell, M., & Kota, M. (2018). Expropriation of land without compensation. *Herbert Smith Freehills*, 25 July. Available: https://www.herbertsmithfreehills.com/latest-thinking/expropriation-of-land-without-compensation. Accessed on 12 December 2018.

Lodge, T. (2018). Thinking about land South African land reform. *Focus*, 83 December. Available: https://hsf.org.za/publications/focus/focus-83-on-land/focus-83-04-13.pdf. Accessed on 11 December 2018.

Mahlakoana, T. (2017). *ANC goes radical on land question*. Business Day, 21 December. Available: https://www.businesslive.co.za/bd/politics/2017-12-21-anc-goes-radical-on-land-question/. Accessed on 07 January 2018.

Manona, S. (2018). Is it discord or is it a matter of different hymn books? Post facto paper presented at: *The Land Reform debate—Realising expropriation of land without compensation through constitutional amendments* held at Rhodes University, Makhanda, 17 July.

Mavhunga, C. (2018). Zimbabwe sets aside $53 million to compensate displaced white farmers. *VOA News*, 6 December. Available: https://www.voanews.com/a/zimbabwe-sets-aside-53-million-to-compensate-displaced-white-farmers/4689069.html. Accessed on 11 December 2018.

Merten, M. (2018a). Explainer: Everything you want to know (or would rather not have known) about expropriation without compensation. *Daily Maverick*, 10 September. Available: https://www.dailymaverick.co.za/article/2018-09-10-explainer-everything-you-wanted-to-know-or-would-rather-not-have-known-about-expropriation-without-compensation/. Accessed on 11 December 2018.

Merten, M. (2018b). The politics of Land Expropriation Without Compensation in the ANC constitutional review proposals. *Daily Maverick*, 8 November. Available: https://www.dailymaverick.co.za/article/2018-11-08-the-politics-of-land-expropriation-without-compensation-in-the-anc-constitutional-review-proposals/. Accessed on 6 December 2018.

Merten, M. (2018c). Land expropriation, the final push: Constitutional amendment drafting committee set up, Cabinet approves draft Expropriation Bill. *Daily Maverick*, 7 December. Online: https://www.dailymaverick.co.za/article/2018-12-07-land-expropriation-the-final-push-constitutional-amendment-drafting-committee-set-up-cabinet-approves-draft-expropriation-bill/. Accessed 11 December 2018.

Msiza v Director-General for the Department of Rural Development and Land Reform and Others (LCC133/2012) [2016] ZALCC 12 (5 July 2016).

Ngcukaitobi, T. (2018). How land expropriation would work. *Mail and Guardian*, 08 June. Available: https://mg.co.za/article/2018-06-08-00-how-land-expropriation-would-work/. Accessed on 08 June 2018.

Ntsebeza, L. (2007). Land redistribution in South Africa: The property clause revisited. In L. Ntsebeza & R. Hall (Eds.), *The land question in South Africa: The challenge of transformation and redistribution*. Pretoria: HSRC Press.

Ntsebeza, L. (2018). This land is our land. *FP*, 3 May. Available: https://foreignpolicy.com/2018/05/03/this-land-is-our-land/. Accessed on 6 December 2018.

Ntsholo, L. (2015). The land and agrarian question: a call to think. *Daily Maverick*, 08 September. Available: http://www.dailymaverick.co.za/opinionista/2015-09-08-the-land-and-agrarian-question-a-call-to-rethink/#.VjUgGyuTQXh. Accessed on 31 October 2015.

Nyarota, G. (2018). *The graceless fall of Robert Mugabe: The end of a dictator's reign*. Cape Town: Penguin Books.

Pithouse, R. (2015). *Land, dignity and democracy: South Africa's constitution does allow for expropriation*. Available: http://sacsis.org.za/site/article/2298. Accessed 12 December 2018.

PLAAS (Institute for Poverty, Land and Agrarian Studies). (2016). *Diagnostic report on land reform in South Africa*. Commissioned report for High Level Panel on The Assessment of Key Legislation and The Acceleration of Fundamental Change, an initiative of Parliament of South Africa. Institute for Poverty, Land and Agrarian Studies (PLAAS), University of Western Cape.

Sihlobo, W., & Kapuya, T. (2018). Why land 'expropriation without compensation' is a bad idea. *View Points*, Centre for Development and Enterprise, 2 July.

Sihlobo, W., & Kirsten, J. (2018). EFF's strategy will destroy the asset value of a large portion of SA's land. *Business Day*, 30 July. Available: https://www.businesslive.co.za/bd/opinion/2018-07-30-effs-strategy-will-destroy-the-asset-value-of-a-large-portion-of-sas-land/. Accessed on 25 December 2018.

Thompson, J (2018). Zimbabwe lifts ban on imports of basic commodities. *TimesLive*, 23 October. Available: https://www.timeslive.co.za/news/africa/2018-10-23-zimbabwe-lifts-ban-on-imports-of-basic-commodities/. Accessed on 11 October 2018.

Xaba, M. B., & Roodt, M. J. (2016). South Africa's land reform efforts lack a focus on struggling farmers. *The Conversation*, 5 December. Available: https://theconversation.com/south-africas-land-reform-efforts-lack-a-focus-on-struggling-farmers-69249. Accessed on 6 December 2018.

Xaba, M. B., & Roodt, M. J. (2018). The populist rhetoric around land acquisition in South Africa obscures a number of significant factors on land reform. *The Thinker Journal, 78*.

CHAPTER 6

Land Expropriation, Food Security and Local Economic Development (LED) in South Africa

Nokukhanya N. Jili and Mfundo M. Masuku

Introduction

Since the end of minority rule in 1994, the land question has remained an unresolved issue in South Africa. The apartheid regime was characterised by land inequalities and denials of land rights, especially for the African group. In 1997, the White Paper on South African Land Policy was adopted as a policy which aimed to address the land question in the country. The White Paper introduced land redistribution, land restitution and tenure reform as the three key elements of land reform programme. Initially, the South African government set a target of 30% of land redistribution by 1999, which was later deferred to 2014. Government's failure to meet the 2014 target resulted in resetting the date to 2025 (Kepe &

N. N. Jili (✉)
University of Zululand, KwaDlangezwa, South Africa
e-mail: JiliN@unizulu.ac.za

M. M. Masuku
University of Mpumalanga, Mbombela, South Africa

A. O. Akinola et al. (eds.), *The New Political Economy of Land Reform in South Africa*,
https://doi.org/10.1007/978-3-030-51129-6_6

Hall, 2016). This is evidence that there are major challenges with the execution of the land reform programme, identifiable by the strategies and approaches used (Gopal, 2013).

The South African government adopted and promoted the willing buyer, willing seller approach, which was based on the interpretation of its successes and failures elsewhere, notably in Kenya in the 1960s and Zimbabwe in the 1980s. This approach was also not successful due to white farmers' unwillingness to sell their farms. In 2011, Proactive Land Acquisition Strategy (PLAS) was introduced and was based on the state's buying up land and retaining ownership of it, with the intention of leasing rather than transferring it to beneficiaries (Antwi & Nxumalo, 2014; Ranwedzi, 2013). This created fears in the South African food industry, as the South African government proposed to buy the farms below the market price which most farmers referred to as 'expropriation without compensation', which violated the expropriation act of 1975 (Holmes, 2014).

Sachikonye (2003) maintains that land redistribution is a tool for addressing poverty in the rural areas, noted for subsistence and small-scale farming. Rigg (2006) stated that agriculture is essential for rural and urban communities for ensuring food security and economic development. Due to the economic crisis experienced by many households, there has been a resurgence of agriculture for sustenance and improved livelihoods. Indeed, food security cannot be separated from sociopolitical issues like access to land as well as other natural resources (Gopal, 2013; Reddy & Moletsane, 2011). As emphasised by many, the land reform programme has failed to meet its aims and objectives because of the strategies and approaches that were poorly executed (Aliber & Cousins, 2012; Qalam & Lumet 2012). Moreover, Qalam and Lumet (2012) state that the failure of the land reform programme as a whole is purely because of the undesirable government approach, the choice of policies and the rigid South African Constitution. Therefore, land reform has not resolved the high rate of poverty in the country.

Aliber (2003) states that poverty, especially in rural areas, results from lack of access to productive land. Those that have access to land as a productive resource do not derive economic benefits from it, which denies them the financial independence that follows land access. Holden (2014) holds that access to land is not enough if support is not provided for the people, which includes financial support, training, access to markets and ensuring adequate amenities. The highest prevalence of household food insecurity is in sub-Saharan Africa at 23.2%, followed by South Asia (15.7%) with 40% of the rural population in South Africa being dependent on the land for their livelihoods (Burchi, Scarlato, & d'Agostino, 2018). Coetzee (2018) reveals that it is estimated that 14 million people in South Africa are food insecure because they are net consumers of purchased food and not producers of food.

Food security is a basic human right that is entrenched in the Constitution of 1996 and the Constitution, Section 25, commits to bring about equitable access to land for all South Africans (Mubangizi & Mubangizi, 2005). Republic of South Africa (2002) points out that food security is an economic and social right enshrined in the Constitution, and a vital aspect of well-being and socio-economic development in poor rural and urban communities. Breslin, Delius, and Madrid (1997) state that the majority of people who are affected by high unemployment and vulnerable to inadequate basic services are black people in rural areas. By 1997, the South African government had formulated development strategies to strengthen or support vulnerable households through a programme of food support to assist marginalised communities. However, domestic food products are being supplemented by food import options such as fuels and fertilisers; this also affects access to food due to high costs. In the light of this background, this chapter argues for a robust policy of land expropriation, which is an essential mechanism for wealth redistribution, local economic development and food security in South Africa. The chapter is divided into seven sections. The first is the introduction, followed by government strategies to address food insecurity, the importance of land for food security, land distribution and redistribution within small-scale farming, land reform, economic growth and development, politics of land expropriation without compensation and land expropriation and food security.

Government Strategies for Addressing Food Insecurity

Ncube and Kang'ethe (2015) insist that governments have an obligation to address food crises to bolster and secure the lives of their people through formulation and implementation of policies. Kepe and Tessaro (2012) assert that an understanding of South African food security policies clearly shows that the government has adopted the issue as a matter of urgency, particularly in rural areas where the majority are vulnerable to food insecurity. However, Aliber and Hart (2009) indicate that these food security policies do not have clear guidelines on how food security projects, based on smallholder agriculture, should align with land and agrarian reform projects in rural areas. The argument is that food security policies intend to improve nutritional safety nets by introducing food programmes which have balanced diets and provide food aid in collaboration with the private sector and social organisations. Local communities are also encouraged to invest in agriculture as a vehicle towards local economic development (LED), by providing support services that will increase their production, especially in outlying areas. Qureshi, Dixon, and Wood (2015) argue that policies should influence how people, various sectors and institutions communicate with each other and provide incentives to improve food security.

The main aim of food security policies is to ensure sufficient food production at all levels, increase food availability, access and food utilisation, and increase the efficiency and sustainability of food production, with the extension of improved processes through investment in agricultural infrastructure. Food security policies also focus on enhancing access to productive inputs including seeds, fertiliser supply and access to credit (Fukuda-Parr & Taylor, 2015). Altman, Hart, and Jacobs (2009) reveal that South African food policies focus on rural food insecurity, with an emphasis on food production, not food access. South Africa has progressively engaged in the fight against hunger and poverty through its policies and programme interventions. However, they further point out that in South Africa social and economic policies become conceptually delinked and, as a consequence, practical programme interventions to address food insecurity are reduced to a residual relief role. Furthermore, Alemu (2015) noted that national policy planning is limited and government is silent on the spatial dimensions of food insecurity in the country. It is important to facilitate spatial studies of food insecurity, which would facilitate evidence-based policy planning that depends on reliable data to determine which areas, populations and households are food insecure. The sub-topics below engage specific policy drives regarding food security in the country.

White Paper on Agriculture (1995)

The Agriculture White Paper (1995) commits the South African government to address both national food security and household food security. The government decided to formulate a national food security strategy that would streamline, harmonise and integrate the diverse food security programmes into the Integrated Food Security Strategy (IFSS) that was established in 2002. The South African food security policies and strategies exist to ensure that relevant and important stakeholders reach a consensus on food security diagnosis. Food security policies are meant to improve South Africa's adequacy and stability of access to safe and nutritious food at both national and household levels (Department of Agriculture, Forestry and Fisheries, 2012; Department of Social Development and Department of Agriculture, Forestry and Fisheries, 2013). According to the White Paper on Agriculture (RSA, 1995) 'agricultural policy exists to ensure equitable access to agriculture and promote the contribution of agriculture to the development of all communities, society at large and the national economy, in order to enhance income, food security, employment and quality of life in a sustainable manner'. The White Paper was developed to create an enabling environment which is more accessible to all role-players in this sector, such as different state departments, farmers, agro-industrialists and farmers' organisations, in order to participate in policy formulation.

Hendriks and Olivier (2015) maintain that the main purpose of the White Paper is to ensure unbiased access to agriculture and promote the influence of agriculture in the development of all communities and society at large to build the national economy, in order to improve income, food security, employment and quality of life. Altman et al. (2009) reveal that agricultural programmes concentrate on other sectors, including commercial and small-scale emerging commercial farmers and increasing production, competitiveness and land reform. This has not been achieved because little effort is made to improve agricultural support services, and the consequence has been that they remain very weak. Qureshi et al. (2015) emphasise that policies should ensure the provision of public goods, including technology, to facilitate changes in farming practices and ensure a sustainable farming sector that meets societal demands with the intention to reduce the level of food insecurity.

Furthermore, the White Paper (1995) states that the role of agriculture in the rural community must be coordinated with the roles of the other relevant government departments, NGOs and private enterprises involved in strengthening and developing rural communities by alleviating food insecurity. However, Rodriguez-Pose and Hardly (2015) note that rural and small farmers are still unable to afford or access new technologies, while it is well proven that farming production is increasingly technology intensive, requiring both education and upfront investment. The White Paper (1995) also outlines to the importance of developing rural infrastructure for agricultural development and services such as access to proper roads, telephone services, electricity and others that are invisible or inadequate in most rural areas, and make difficult for rural dwellers to compete in the market. In terms of production, the White Paper clearly states that the government is responsible to put in place agricultural production systems, and implementation should also be organised in such a way that it brings improvement to national as well as household food security. It further illustrates that in the case of natural disasters such as floods, runaway veld fires and severe drought, the government should assist farmers with farming and agricultural financing systems.

Food Security Policy for South Africa, 1997 and 2012

This policy was enacted in order to align agriculture and land reform towards economic development, particularly of the poor and marginalised. The main objective of this policy is to further improve market participation of the emerging agricultural sector and improve food distribution to ensure access to food. During apartheid, the black majority were intentionally denied access to assets such as land, livestock and markets (Koch, 2011). As a result of this, the democratic government has reprioritised its public spending to focus on improving the food security situation for previously disadvantaged populations. Therefore, the food security policy of the Department of Rural Development and Land Reform (DRDLR) in 1997 focused on providing strategies on how to achieve food security at national and household levels by interrogating the concept of food availability, accessibility and utilisation as basic way of obtaining food security. It clearly indicated that most South African households still experience poverty, which is manifested in food insecurity.

The food security policy of 2012 (DSD & DAFF) asserts that the role of the government is to ensure that citizens are food secure through creating an enabling environment where all communities would be able to produce food and have control over its production. Drawing on the work of Poulton and Chinsinga (2018), this could be achieved through increased production of affordable food, and enhancing opportunities for entry into commercialised agriculture by subsistence and smallholder farmers. This policy highlights the importance of grain marketing infrastructure relating to questions of access, pricing and the issue of public investment as being priorities, including productive infrastructure, health services and education, particularly in rural areas.

Integrated Food Security Strategy (IFSS – 2002)

Most previous food security policies in South Africa had failed because, at household levels, people were still food insecure. Therefore, the government decided to formulate the IFSS, with a focus on land reform, production of food, marketing of food products and access to food legislation (DoA, 2002). This strategy was based on the approach of integrating public-private-civil society partnerships and focuses on household food security without overlooking national food security. It further alluded that the expected outcomes of this strategy are greater ownership of productive assets and participation in the economy by the food insecure, and increased competitiveness and profitability of farming operations and rural enterprises that are owned and managed by, or on behalf of, the food insecure. Other important outcomes are improved levels of governance, coordination, financial administration and management of food security improvement interventions in all spheres of government, and between government and the private sector and civil society (DoA, 2002). However, Drimie and Rugsemok (2010) identify five institutional constraints that limited the success of the IFSS:

a. The Department of Agriculture, tasked to coordinate and facilitate the integrated strategy within government, was unable to do so in an effective manner. It basically focused on developing the agricultural sector to reinforce food availability rather than on land accessibility and utilisation.
b. The government had limited administrative capacity to coordinate food security programmes; as such, the management had no instrument to drive the process or resources to ensure that other departments contributed towards alleviating food insecurity according to their expertise. The emphasis remained on agriculture and relationships or collaboration with other sectors remained unclear due to poor coordination of directorates.
c. There were no budgets for government spending on food security at any of the administrative levels. All funds were allocated by sector and financed by one entity, preventing the emergence of joint projects and programmes.

d. The major challenge that was identified was the minimal communication between various stakeholders, including government and civil society.
e. The lack of food security policy or legislative frameworks prohibited the government from providing a clear line of authority, as well as a means of preventing non-collaboration and implementation of relevant programmes in a disjointed manner. An emerging policy established later by the national DoA does not appear to adequately address these institutional constraints.

Based on the limitation of IFSS, the Zero Hunger programme was then initiated in 2009 to strengthen and assist in the actualisation of the IFSS, which was to increase food production and trade. Furthermore, the emphasis is on the utilisation of land and agrarian reform that ensures land tenure for food security and improvement of food production. This programme is aimed at reducing incidences of food insecurity through improving the capabilities of all South Africans to access nutritious food and to guarantee the basic human right of access to adequate food; through this programme, South Africa should contribute towards the Millennium Development Goals (DAFF, 2012).

Furthermore, Zero Hunger was established to address food insecurity by improving collaboration among national and provincial organisations and NGOs, as well as coordination of inputs and resources to increase household food security and rural development (Fukuda-Parr & Taylor, 2015). They further indicate that the focus was to improve access to food, advance the food production capacity of households and resource-poor farmers and foster partnerships with relevant stakeholders within the food supply chain. As indicated on the programme, the needs of people living in rural areas are different from those of people living in urban areas—that means a specific set of interventions is required for each case. However, Hendricks (2013) states that a major challenge to achieving food security is failure to implement policies and absence of broad partnerships. However, De Cock et al. (2013) uncover the truth that through the Zero Hunger strategy, households were able to provide themselves with adequate food for 10.28 months on average.

The Importance of Land for Food Security

Denial of access to land for the black majority of South Africans during apartheid led to one of the greatest challenges the country faces today. This necessitated the inclusion of the property rights, which was contained in Section 25 of the South African Constitution to redress the imbalances of the past. Moyo (2007) asserts that land is the most important asset and forms the foundation for all human survival in terms of social and economic development. He further states that food security is achieved through direct production from the land and that access to land is important for the livelihoods of people. As stipulated in Section 26 of the South African Constitution of 1996, 'the state must take reasonable legislative and other measures, within its available resources, to foster conditions which enable citizens to gain access to land on an equitable basis'. Toulmin and Quan (2000) correctly posit that land is a primary means of subsistence and income generation in rural economies; access to land and security of land rights are of primary concern in the eradication of food insecurity.

In rural areas, land is a basic livelihood asset, the principal form of natural capital from which people produce food and earn a living. Access to land enables family labour to be put to productive use in farming, generates a source of food and provides a supplementary source of livelihood for rural workers and the urban poor. Gathering fruits, leaves and wood from common land is an important regular source of income for women and poorer households. Moyo (2007) has suggested some critical strategies to improve food security by improving access to land by the majority of the black population, supported by appropriate tenure policies. Another strategy suggested is further improving agricultural production through expansion of cropping areas by opening up virgin land and irrigation, increasing the cropping intensity or the proportion of cropping area in relation to other agricultural uses, and intensifying agricultural productivity through improved farming systems and inputs.

Land Distribution and Redistribution Within Small-Scale Farming

It is well recognised that severe land inequalities persist in South Africa between smallholders, large-scale and state farms. Hence, it is crucial for the South African government to encourage optimum use of land within commercial farming areas, especially via conservation agriculture/climate-smart agriculture and land redistribution. The smallholder farm sector is typically characterised as small but relatively 'un-modal' and equitably distributed land holdings are situated within a 'bi-modal' distribution of land between the large-scale farming sector (Jayne et al., 2003). Jayne, Mather, and Mghenyi (2010) assert that redressing these inequalities is an important element of an effective rural poverty reduction strategy, yet despite widespread acceptance that 'pro-poor' agricultural growth is strongly associated with equitable asset distribution, surprisingly little attention has been devoted to quantifying land distribution patterns within South Africa's small-scale farming sector. He further states that the productivity increases in smallholders, and that successful reduction of poverty in China, India and Taiwan is largely due to the equal distribution of land.

Mbedu (2014) holds that the South African government committed itself to taking a lead in the programme for the redistribution of land, trying to reach a target of redistributing 30% of white-owned agricultural land by 2014. This author further confirms that this process should be well planned, efficiently managed and fully financed in order to enable fundamental social transformation to take place without disrupting food security initiatives and activities. On the other side, in order to create jobs, attention has to be given to the protection of high potential agricultural land for productive agricultural purposes. The importance of fertile land was also reinforced by Karriem and Hoskins (2016), who point out that in rural areas people are denied access to overall basic needs and fertile land for agriculture. On the other hand, Francis (2002) argues that those who are involved in agriculture and livestock projects are faced with challenges such as monitoring labour, flooded commodity markets and vulnerability to theft. Poverty is the biggest threat to South Africa's economic freedom. It prevents people from achieving a satisfactory minimum standard of living. Poverty reduction relies on the equitable distribution of resources such as land and ensuring that people are able to access other income-generating resources such as training/education and access to markets so that they can be financially independent (Ite, 2005).

Land Reform, Economic Growth and Development

Land use has the potential to contribute to local economic development and could be a veritable instrument to combat poverty in South Africa. Access to land alone is not enough in ensuring local economic development in South Africa. Thus, the necessity for human development initiatives such as training and educating citizens on how to use land productively would contribute to economic growth and development holistically. It is also germane for the government to offer financial support and create access to markets, especially in rural areas. This can contribute to the increase of agricultural produce, better management of natural and farm resources, and local economic development through the establishment of Small Medium Micro Enterprise (SMMEs). SMMEs have an important contribution to economic development through the promotion of food security, generation of wealth and job creation. Antoni and Umejesi (2014) concur that SMMEs are viewed as skills developers, employment generators, promoters of economic growth and alleviators of food insecurity. Du Toit, Erasmus, and Strydom (2009) state that SMMEs integrate the resources of societies efficiently to produce goods and services for the society in which they operate.

The South African government has established some policies to promote SMMEs in rural areas as a strategy to address poverty issues with local economic development (LED) and food insecurity as the major challenge in these areas. Stevenson and Lundstrom (2001) maintain that agricultural policies do not stimulate economic development particularly in rural areas and thus fail to strengthen income generation and purchasing power to enhance food security. Mmbengwa et al. (2012) point out that in many developing countries (including South Africa) where socio-economic problems are dominant, the farming sector plays a crucial role in enhancing food security and job and capital creation. They suggest that the South African government has to create an enabling environment for farmers and SMMEs, to eliminate socio-economic problems. It is equally important for the government to recognise the economic and social benefits of investing in farming and SMMEs, especially in rural areas with the intention of building the rural economy. Mago and Toro (2013) concur that it is incumbent upon government to support the producers and public through its policies and institutions that will improve outputs, particularly in the agricultural sector. The state should ensure that conditions enable agriculture to expand their operations and markets.

Economic analysis supports the view that the contribution of land to rural economic growth depends upon the security, duration and enforceability of property rights, since these provide an incentive for agricultural investment and help develop markets to rent and sell land (Deininger

& Feder, 1999). Fukuda-Parr and Taylor (2015) indicate that the land reform programme and associated support to emerging farmers are the major elements of government policy related to production-based entitlement. However, this does not confirm that land reform would benefit food-insecure households, which are the poorest of the poor. According to Toulmin and Quan (2000), conventional wisdom about rural development in South Africa has continued to favour the replacement of customary systems of land management with what are considered to be more secure forms of individual tenure through the issue of land titles.

Persuasive talks regarding radical economic transformation, including calls for radical land reform, dominated the South African political sphere (Jankielsohn & Duvenhage, 2017). This call for radical transformation has been the main focus of political debates around the country since 2018. Resulting from the robust debates, Parliament resolved to give it effect and the expropriation bill has now been gazetted meaning that once the bill has seen signed into law, it will provide legal basis to give effect to the amendments as far as Section 25 of the Constitution (1996) is concerned. Land expropriation without compensation is deemed to provide meaningful effect on the issue of land reform in South Africa. Efforts to fast track the issue of land reform are nothing new in South Africa. Post the 1994 democratic elections, the South African government has implemented intervention programmes aimed at addressing the inequalities and imbalances of the past through a number of land reform policies and programmes. This included the willing buyer, willing seller which many scholars and political analysts have argued failed dismally in fast-tracking radical land reform in a country with a history of apartheid (Lahiff, 2007).

Land expropriation without compensation is said to address problems of historical dispossession and rural poverty. The land issue and food security are important components in the alleviation of poverty, especially in rural areas. What does land expropriation entail as far as food security is concerned in South Africa? Different scholars hold different views taking into consideration the impact of past land reform policies in South Africa. Cousins (2016) weighed in on the overall impact of land reform to date. The author argued that land reform since its inception has barely changed the socio-economic landscape of rural livelihoods and that it has presented minimum impact as far as poverty reduction is concerned. The author further argued that the lack of systematic data on the impact of the land reform policies via monitoring and evaluation and other sources has brought about challenges in measuring its impact on food security.

Land Expropriation and Food Security

Pringle (2011) asserts that South Africa is a modern industrialised country that requires effective commercial farming to feed its increasing population and improve exports of agricultural produce. Aliber, Maluleke, Manenzhe, Paradza, and Cousins (2013) express great concern that the agricultural sector in South Africa is slightly less export oriented due to small-scale farmers who have been not able to compete in a formal market. Land expropriation must engage itself in establishing a viable, non-racial and sustainable commercial and small-scale farming sector to enhance food security. Du Plessis (2018) argues that land expropriation does not guarantee job creation, poverty reduction or food security if the expropriated land is not utilised and managed to bring the desired production to the table.

He further criticised the process of expropriation of land without compensation as an unlawful act which contravenes property rights, endangers the economy and creates an unconducive environment for investment. Mkhabela, Ntombela, and Mazibuko (2018) have a different interpretation of LEWC; they indicate that it attempts to bring about fundamental transformation of property rights in order to readdress the history of land dispossession and lay the foundations of the social and economic rights for the poor. Bonti-Ankomah (2001) and May, Stevens, and Stols (2002) maintain that land expropriation has an ability to alleviate poverty and lower vulnerability to food insecurity through equal access to productive land. Coetzee (2018) maintains that South Africa is still the most food-secure country in the African continent, but land expropriation without compensation will lead the country into hunger as happened in Zimbabwe.

The critical point is that equal access to land and resources is identified as a contributory factor towards food security. This simply means that land expropriation and equitable redistribution are anticipated to contribute towards food security in South Africa with particular reference to rural livelihoods. Access to land will ensure that the previously disadvantaged rural population will be provided with the opportunity of income generation through agricultural activities. It will also ensure easy and sustainable access to food for households with limited or with no purchasing power. It should, however, be noted that land reform policies or programmes without adequate implementation strategies seldom achieve their intended objectives. Past land reform has been deemed to have had a little impact in South Africa due to the fact that the government failed to devise effective strategies addressing issues such as methods of beneficiary selection, farm planning and post-settlement support (Lahiff, 2007). These factors are crucial in ensuring maximum positive impact as far as addressing land dispossession and poverty reduction is concerned.

Agricultural activities, as a major contributor to the country's economy, rely on effective planning and management of land. Therefore, it is imperative that government prioritises enhancing capacity among landowners. Lack of capacity with regard to agriculture can have adverse consequences, therefore crippling the impact of land redistribution. People can only sustain or remain food secure if they are in possession of effective farming skills which will in turn contribute greatly to the issue of employment creation and rural development. Thus, land expropriation without compensation can have positive and negative effects on food security depending on its implementation, pre- and post-settlements support rendered to the beneficiary. Strategies aimed at providing such support are the determining factors as far as the impact of the land reform is concerned. Pre- and post-settlement support is of primary importance in facilitating land planning and management. Effective land planning and management skills will ensure that landowners or beneficiaries of land reform contribute positively towards food security and overall rural economic development.

Conclusion

The South African Constitution, 1996 specifies that food security is a fundamental or basic human right (economic and social rights) that must be enjoyed by all citizens, regardless of their socio-economic profile. In a bid to achieve this, programmes of food security are mostly targeted at rural areas due to the underdeveloped nature of such societies and economies. The Constitution further specifies that people have a right to equitable access to land. The government has tried to defend these provisions by making positive contributions towards alleviation of food insecurity in the country. However, the government has faced many challenges in the enforcement of these rights due to institutional challenges.

South Africa's recent attainment of majority rule, under the weight of the apartheid legacy, has imposed a limitation upon the vibrancy of the state to achieve its lofty goals.

It is worth noting that improving availability and accessibility of land by previously disadvantaged and poor populations will have a significant impact on reduction of food insecurity through the assistance of the government. It is crucial for the South African government to formulate and implement policies to improve previously disadvantaged people's participation in the formal economy and to address barriers of access to productive land and to food security. South Africa is one of the countries that have critical challenges regarding land reform, due to the fact that the majority of citizens have inadequate access to, and ownership of, land. Most of the rural areas have insufficient development and poor service provision, such as inadequate access to credit or financial assistance and lack of formal employment—which consequently leads to food insecurity. Formation of cooperatives has been treated as an amicable strategy for the rural populace to create job opportunities and a source of income; however, one of the challenges is that the majority of cooperatives based in rural areas are struggling due to lack of entrepreneurship skills; hence, they are not sustainable.

Moreover, it is notable that South Africa has formulated good food security policies towards ensuring sufficient food production at national, provincial and local levels so as to fulfil constitutional rights. However, these policies are not well implemented because rural people are still vulnerable to food insecurity. Issues of food insecurity are mostly aligned with the agricultural sector, and as a result, most of the food security projects and policies are based on agriculture and access to land. This indicates the lack of effective coordination between various governmental institutions to work together within their expertise to achieve food security with full participation of local community members. Governmental institutions could advocate strategies to collaborate with the private sector towards reviving rural entrepreneurship as the catalyst to attract investors and mobilise local resources, in the form of benefitting local people, towards creating local economic hubs. This would encourage rural populations to commercialise their local resources and become more productive by developing other avenues to generate income and reduce poverty.

References

Alemu, Z. G. (2015). *Developing a food (in) security map for South Africa*. Tunis: African Development Bank.

Aliber, M. (2003). Chronic poverty in South Africa: Incidence, causes and policies. *World Development, 31*(3), 473–490.

Aliber, M., & Cousins, B. (2012). Livelihoods after land reform in South Africa. *Journal of Agrarian Change, 13*(1), 140–165.

Aliber, M., & Hart, T. G. B. (2009). Should subsistence agriculture be supported as a strategy to address rural food insecurity? *Agrekon, 48*(4), 434–458.

Aliber, M., Maluleke, T., Manenzhe, T., Paradza, G., & Cousins, B. (2013). *Land reform and livelihoods: Trajectories of change in northern Limpopo province, South Africa*. Pretoria: HSRC Press.

Altman, M., Hart, T. G., & Jacobs, P. T. (2009). Household food security status in South Africa. *Agrekon, 48*(4), 345–361.

Antoni, A., & Umejesi, I. (2014). Small towns and enterprises: A study of workplace relations in a rural town in South Africa. *Journal of Sociology and Social Anthropology, 5*(2), 141–152.

Antwi, M., & Nxumalo, K. K. S. (2014). Impact of proactive land acquisition strategy (PLAS). Projects on human capital livelihood of beneficiaries in the Dr Kenneth Kaunda district in South Africa. *Journal of Human Ergology, 44*(2), 161–169.

Bonti-Ankomah, S. (2001). Addressing food insecurity in South Africa. In *SARPN conference on land reform and poverty reduction in Southern Africa* (pp. 4–5). Pretoria.

Breslin, E. D., Delius, P., & Madrid, C. (1997). Strengthening institutional safety nets in South Africa: Sharing operation hunger's insights and experiences. *Development Southern Africa, 14*(1), 21–41. https://doi.org/10.1080/03768359708439948.

Burchi, F., Scarlato, M., & d'Agostino, G. (2018). Addressing food insecurity in sub-Saharan Africa: The role of cash transfers. *Poverty & Public Policy, 10*(4), 564–589.

Coetzee, K. (2018). How food-secure are we really? *Farmer's Weekly, 2018*(18039), 28–28.

Cousins, B. (2016). *Land reform in South Africa is sinking. Can it be saved?* University of Western Cape, PLAAS.

De Cock, N., D'Haese, M., Vink, N., Van Rooyen, C. J., Staelens, L., Schönfeldt, H. C., et al. (2013). Food security in rural areas of Limpopo province, South Africa. *Food Security, 5*(2), 269–282.

Deininger, K., & Feder, G. (1999). *Land policy in development countries (Rural development Note No. 3)*. Washington, DC: World Bank.

Department of Agriculture. (2002). *International training straining strategy for the agricultural sector*. Pretoria: Department of Agriculture.

Department of Agriculture, Forestry and Fisheries. (2012). *The framework of the zero hunger programme*. Pretoria: Department of Agriculture, Forestry and Fisheries.

Department of Rural Development and Land Reform. (1997). *Land redistribution for agricultural development*. Pretoria: Government Printers.

Department of Social Development and Department of Agriculture, Forestry and Fisheries. (2013). *National policy on food and nutrition security*. Pretoria: Department of Social Development and Department of Agriculture, Forestry and Fisheries.

Drimie, S., & Rugsemok, S. (2010). The integrated food security strategy of South Africa: An institutional analysis. *Agrekon, 49*(3), 316–337.

du Plessis, D. (2018). Expropriation will ruin SA's food security and prosperity. *Farmer's Weekly, 2018*(18028), 6–7.

Du Toit, G. S., Erasmus, B. J., & Strydom, J. W. (2009). *Introduction to business management* (7th ed.). Cape town: Oxford.

Francis, E. (2002). Rural livelihoods, institutions and vulnerability in North West province, South Africa. *Journal of Southern African Studies, 28*(3), 531–550. https://doi.org/10.1080/0305707022000006503.

Fukuda-Parr, S., & Taylor, V. (2015). *Food security in South Africa human rights and entitlement perspectives*. Cape Town: University of Cape Town Press.

Gopal, N. (2013). *South Africa's land reform challenges*. Sandton: South African Property Owners Association.

Hendricks, S. (2013). South Africa's National Development Plan and New Growth Path: Reflections on policy contradictions and implications for food security. *Agrekon, 52*(3), 1–17.

Hendricks, S. L., & Olivier, N. J. (2015). Review of the South African agricultural legislative framework: Food security implications. *Development Southern Africa, 32*(5), 555–576.

Holden, S. T. (2014). Boserup and beyond: Mounting land pressures and development strategies in Africa. *Food Policy, 48*, 88–97.

Holmes, T. (2014, June 23). New land reform bill, dangerous or not? *Mail and Guardian Newspaper*.

Ite, U. E. (2005). Poverty reduction in resource-rich developing countries: What have multinational corporations got to do with it? *Journal of International Development, 17*(7), 913–929.

Jankielsohn, R., & Duvenhage, A. (2017). Radical land reform in South Africa–a comparative perspective? *Journal for Contemporary History, 42*(2), 1–23.

Jayne, T. S., Mather, D., & Mghenyi, E. (2010). Principal challenges confronting smallholder agriculture in sub-Saharan Africa. *World Development, 38*(10), 1384–1398.

Jayne, T. S., Yamano, T., Weber, M. T., Tschirley, D., Benfica, R., Chapoto, A., & Zulu. B. (2003). *Smallholder income and land distribution in Africa:*

Implication for poverty reduction strategies (Working paper). Zambia Food Security Research Project, Lusaka.
Karriem, A., & Hoskins, M. (2016). From the RDP to the NDP: A critical appraisal of the developmental state, land reform, and rural development in South Africa. *Politikon, 43*(3), 325–343.
Kepe, T., & Hall, R. (2016). *Land redistribution in South Africa*. Commissioned report for High Level Panel on the assessment of key legislation and the acceleration of fundamental change, an initiative of the Parliament of South Africa.
Kepe, T., & Tessaro, D. (2012). *Integrating food security with land reform: A more effective policy for South Africa*. Waterloo, ON, Canada: Centre for International Governance Innovation.
Koch, J. (2011). *The food security policy context in South Africa*. International Policy Centre for Inclusive Growth, United Nations Development Programme.
Lahiff, E. (2007). 'Willing buyer, willing seller': South Africa's failed experiment in market-led agrarian reform. *Third World Quarterly, 28*(8), 1577–1597.
Mago, S., & Toro, B. (2013). South African government's support to small, medium and micro-enterprises (SMMEs): The case of King William's Town area. *Journal of Economics, 4*(1), 19–28.
May, J., Stevens, T., & Stols, A. (2002). Monitoring the impact of land reform on quality of life: A South African case study. *Assessing quality of life and living conditions to guide national policy* (pp. 293–312). Dordrecht: Springer.
Mbedu, N. (2014). Social cohesion for the unfinished business of land reform in South Africa. *International Journal of African Renaissance Studies: Multi-, Inter- and Transdisciplinarity, 9*(1), 100–114. https://doi.org/10.1080/18186874.2014.916881.
Mkhabela, T., Ntombela, S., & Mazibuko, N. (2018, September 25–27). *Pro et Contra of Agriculture Land Reform in South Africa: A policy brief*. 56th Annual Conference Agricultural Economics Association of South Africa. Somerset West.
Mmbengwa, V. M., Ramukumba, T., Groenewald, J. A., van Schalkwyk, H. D., Gundidza, M. B., & Maiwashe, A. N. (2012). Analysis of the socio-economic factors that contribute to land and agrarian reform which initiated and supported small, micro and medium farming enterprises (SMMEs) in South Africa. *African Journal of Business Management, 6*(24), 7158–7169.
Moyo, S. (2007). Land policy, poverty reduction and public action in Zimbabwe. In A. Haroon Akram-Lodhi, S. M. Borras Jr., & C. Kay (Eds.), *Land, poverty and livelihoods in an era of globalization: Perspectives from developing and transition countries* (p. 344). London: Routledge.

Mubangizi, J. C., & Mubangizi, B. C. (2005). Poverty, human rights law and socio-economic realities in South Africa. *Development Southern Africa, 22*(2), 277–290.

Ncube, N., & Kang'ethe, S. M. (2015). Pitting the state of food security against some millennium development goals in a few countries of the developing world. *Journal of Human Ecology, 49*(3), 293–300.

Poulton, C., & Chinsinga, B. (2018). *The political economy of agricultural commercialisation in Africa* (APRA, Working Paper 16). Available: https://opendocs.ids.ac.uk/opendocs/handle/20.500.12413/14027.

Pringle, E. (2011, January 28). Fixing land reform. *Farmer's Weekly.*

Qalam, I., & Lumet, J. (2012). *Failure of land reform in South Africa*. World Socialist Web Site. Available https://www.wsws.org/en/articles/2012/12/06/land-d06.html.

Qureshi, M. E., Dixon, J., & Wood, M. (2015). Public policies for improving food and nutrition security at different scales. *Food Security, 7*(2), 393–403.

Ranwedzi, E. N. (2013). *The potential and limits of the proactive land acquisition strategy: Land reform implementation in Gauteng province of South Africa* (Doctoral dissertation). University of the Western Cape.

Reddy, V., & Moletsane, R. (2011). *The gendered dimensions of food security in South Africa: A review of the literature: Policy brief*. Pretoria: HSRC Press.

Republic of South Africa. (1995). *White Paper on agriculture*. Pretoria: Department of Agriculture.

Republic of South Africa. (2002). *The integrated food security strategy for South Africa*. Pretoria: Department of Agriculture.

Rigg, J. (2006). Land, farming, livelihoods, and poverty: Rethinking the links in the rural south. *World Development, 34*(1), 180–202.

Rodriguez-Pose, A., & Hardly, D. (2015). Addressing poverty and inequality in the rural economy from a global perspective. *Applied Geography, 61,* 11–23.

Sachikonye, L. M. (2003). The situation of commercial farm workers after land reform in Zimbabwe. *Harare: Farm community trust of Zimbabwe.*

Stevenson, L., & Lundstrom, A. (2001). *Patterns and trends in entrepreneurship/SME policy and practice in ten economies* (Vol. 3). Elanders Gotab. Available http://eng.entreprenorskapsforum.se/wp-content/uploads/2011/02/Patternsandtrends.pdf.

Toulmin, C., & Quan, J. (2000). Evolving land rights, policy and tenure in sub-Saharan Africa. In C. Toulmin & J. Quan (Eds.), *Evolving land rights, policy and tenure in Africa*. London: DFID/IIED/NRI.

CHAPTER 7

South Africa and the Quest for Land Reform: Implications for Integrative Food Security and Nation-Building

Stella Chewe Sabi

Introduction

The land question has become central to both the apartheid and post-apartheid South Africa. Apartheid describes a system of government with unjust laws and policies of radical racial segregation in South Africa that began in 1948 and ended in 1994. In the Afrikaans language, apartheid means 'apartness'. The term 'land question' borders on the system of land ownership in a given area such as a country, community, or society. It is well documented that following the conquest of Africa (in the nineteenth century) and its subsequent colonisation by Europeans (in the twentieth century), the colonial governments dictated land ownership and land use (Rugege, 2004). In southern Africa, much of the land grab and ownership was characterised by displacing the native Africans from their traditional lands and replacing them with white farmers as agrarian

S. C. Sabi (✉)
University of Zululand, KwaDlangezwa, South Africa
e-mail: SabiS@unizulu.ac.za

A. O. Akinola et al. (eds.), *The New Political Economy of Land Reform in South Africa*,
https://doi.org/10.1007/978-3-030-51129-6_7

property owners (Kariuki, 2009; Rugege, 2004). This unequal ownership of land was more pronounced in countries like Zimbabwe, Namibia, and South Africa, which suffered land dispossession and the radical racial domination that consigned the majority of black Africans to marginal 'homelands' or native 'reserves'. During the early years of colonisation, Africans made futile efforts to confront the Europeans occupiers and resist land dispossession; however, the use of sophisticated weapons and skills in warfare ensured the subjugation of Africans (Rugege, 2004).

Ultimately, the black majority became mere peasants, as the white minority owned large parcels of agrarian land. This was the case for countries like Zimbabwe, formerly known as Southern Rhodesia, where, in 1914, the few white farmers, numbering 23,730, occupied 19 million hectors of land (Mutasa, 2015; Shulika & Sabi, 2018). South Africa, being a country with the most Europeans, experienced not only racial domination but the worst form of state-managed land repression policies in Africa (Rugege, 2004).

While the degree of land inequality has reduced since after the end of apartheid, the reality in the country shows that land is still racially defined. A report by the Department of Rural Development and Land Reform revealed that, by the end of 2017, white minority owned land equals 26,663,144 ha or 72% of the total of 37,031,283 ha farms and agricultural holdings by individual landowners. This ownership is followed by coloured people (in South Africa, coloured is used to describe a person of mixed race), who owned 5,371,383 ha or 15%, while Indians owned 2,031,790 ha or 5% of the land in South Africa (Department of Rural Development and Land Reform, 2017). According to the report, at 4% or 1,314,873 ha, indigenous South Africans were the least in land ownership. Since 1994, the start of democracy, successive South African governments, led by the African National Congress (ANC), have prioritised land reform as an integral part of the nation's development agenda and as an instrument of socio-economic stability.

The chapter begins with an overview of the major concepts related to the topic in discussion, presents a historical context of land issues in contemporary South Africa, and evaluates the government's land reform policies since the colonial dispensation. The chapter proceeds to discuss the attempts made by the ANC led government, post-1994, regarding land reforms as one of the key policy instruments to address past injustices, ensure food security and promote the developmental agenda of South Africa.

An Overview of Major Terms

Land ownership: The term ownership simply refers to the state or the condition of having exclusive rights and control over property, which may be land, real estate or an equipment. Ownership involves having several rights, collectively known as titles (Appalachian Land Ownership Task Force, 2015). The titles may be separated by or held by different parties or individuals. The process and techniques of ownership are complex. Regarding land ownership, it can be gained, transferred and lost, for instance, in various ways. That is, to acquire it as property, one has to purchase it with money, or trade it with other properties, or inherit it, find it, or receive damages for it. Ownership can also be acquired through services' performance. Ownership can be transferred through legal means, such as eviction, exchanging it with other property, giving it as a gift, or having it taken from one ownership through legal means, such as eviction, foreclosure, seizure, taking or 'takeovers'. Ownership is self-propagating. This implies that the owner of any property will also own the economic benefits of the property (Chaddad & Cook, 2004).

Land reform: In an African context, land reform is predominantly linked to the colonial history of land dispossession, and the repressive and discriminatory laws which impoverished indigenous Africans. From this perspective, land reform can be defined as the restitution and redistribution of the rights to land to the people, mostly the poor, and those who had been disposed of their property owing to colonial and apartheid injustice laws (in the case of South Africa) of land appropriation and restructuring (Currie-Alder, Kanbur, Malone, & Medhora, 2014; Derman, 2006; De Villiers, 2003). More specifically, land reform is a variable resource and an important economic value for states, societies and development, whose process surpass statutory division of arable land and its allocation to the landless (Derman, 2006). The need for land reform is associated with reducing economic inequalities as a form of social justice and welfare (Kloppers & Pienaar, 2014).

Nation-building: In simple terms, nation-building means unifying the people within the state for its political stability and viability in a sustainable way (Kloppers & Pienaar, 2014). Additionally, nation-building is a process through which majority rule is constructed, whereby the state takes the initiative to build the nation through government programmes and communities. It is often evoked as a means to achieve a just and equal society and to suppress violence, and to encourage nation unity (Abrahams, 2016). Symbols of nation-building include national flags, national anthems, and a national constitution. In this study, the South African Constitution is viewed as the main tool for nation-building and social cohesion in South African land complexities. Social cohesion represents a social relationship between the state and society.

A national constitution is a powerful tool for nation-building because it dictates how a nation is governed. Furthermore, all national policies and programmes of a given state are drawn from the national constitution. In the South African context, the state pledged to use its 1996 Constitution as its guide to correct the divisions and injustices of the past and to build a more inclusive society and economy, while promoting a conscious sense of being proudly South African (Constitution, 1996).

Given that the apartheid system of governance was based on a divide and rule strategy, the post-apartheid South Africa recognised the need for nation-building as a process through which a society of people, with diverse origins, backgrounds, race, ethnicities, and cultures, unite within the boundaries of a sovereign state with a unified constitutional and legal dispensation, a national public system and an integrated national economy (Department of Arts and Culture, 2013). Nation-building involves the harmonisation of a country's population or citizens in a nation, through an array of policies which are implemented with the aim of building commonality among people (Harvard & Bryony, 2012).

This chapter notes that the land question in South Africa is among the motivating factors for rethinking racial and economic debates on nation-building. The issue of food security is of particular interest because of the linkages between land distribution, access and ownership and household food insecurity; and the resultant economic inequalities.

South Africa's Responses to the Land Question: A Historical Context

South Africa has a long history of land issues, which dates back to the seventeenth century to the Dutch colonisation of the Cape of Good Hope in the present-day Cape Town. Driven by the need to grow fresh vegetables and fruit, and to facilitate the good nutrition of its crew on the long sea voyage trade route from Europe to the East, the Dutch East India Company needed land for these purposes (Hendriks, 2014). For the next two centuries, South Africa was colonised by both the Dutch and the British, whose colonial presence resulted in land invasions and even wars with some of the indigenous African tribes. Later, land dispossession became a fundamental policy of the colonial state, backed by several unjust laws from the early years of colonialisation (Rugege, 2004). Non-white South Africans' effort to counter colonial dominance proved futile, such that, by the mid-twentieth century, South Africa was politically and economically controlled by the white minority who introduced apartheid rule, which lasted for nearly 50 years.

By 1913, a most systematic and institutionalised land dispossession, characterised by racially discriminatory land policy was implemented by the apartheid state. Under this arrangement, the Native Land Act of 1913 (No. 27 of 1913) apportioned only 8% of land as use as 'reserves' the black majority (O'Regan, 1990). The resultant effect was their exclusion from land ownership of arable hectares in the country. About 23 years later, the apartheid government added a 5% increase in land use for black people, resulting in mere total of 13% of land access (O'Regan, 1990). Much of the land was state-owned through the South African Development Trust, arguably held in trust for the natives (Rugege, 2004). Following the implementation of the problematic 1913 Native Land Act, black South Africans were prohibited from buying land outside the reserves. This apportionment of land remained until 1994 and has barely changed.

Some authors argue that the main purpose of the 1913 Land Act was to make more land available to white farmers, and to impoverish black people through the dispossession and prohibition of farming arrangements that permitted some self-sufficiency (Hendriks, 2014). This resulted in black people being dependent on employment in urban and farmlands for survival, a phenomenon which benefitted white farms and mines with cheap labour. A report by *The Conversation* concurs that in the homelands, many families who lacked the means to support themselves, fled to urban areas in search of employment opportunities (Bank & Hart, 2017).

By the 1950s, South Africa's population was about 20% white and about 78% black or coloured (Chimere-Dan, 1992). Despite being the minority, the white population dominated South African governance, particularly under the National Party (of Dutch origins), which imposed segregation on the country. The apartheid regime favoured the white minority over other races and left non-whites disadvantaged in terms of land ownership, income, educational opportunities and healthcare.

The unjust land laws and other socio-economic inequalities are well documented in history. For instance, during apartheid rule, while on his trial for attempting to correct the systematic land dispossession laws by the state, Nelson Mandela, the then prominent lawyer, who later became the first black South African president and a global icon for peace, categorically stated: 'I am without land because the white minority has taken a lion's share of my country and forced me to occupy poverty-stricken reserves, over-populated and over-stocked. We are ravaged by starvation and disease!' (Department of Rural Development and Land Reform, 2017). Nelson Mandela's sentiments reflect a link between severe household food insecurity and the restrictive land access laws that prevented black South Africans from participating in the mainstream economy.

Similar notable effects of the 1913 Land Act include the prohibition of non-whites from buying land outside their reserves, a phenomenon which continued until 1994. The situation was exacerbated by the government when it consistently enforced a policy of racial segregation, which further impoverished the black people and stunted their economic development (O'Regan, 1990). This is evident in the Group Areas Act of 1950 passed by the National Party's apartheid government that enabled the state to carry out forced removals from land declared to be strictly 'white areas' and to remove coloured and Indian people from these areas. As a result, of the Group Areas Act dubbed 'a process of cleaning up the black spots', some black South African with land title deeds were forcefully removed usually from fertile and well-watered land to overcrowded, overgrazed and over cultivated reserve areas (Hendriks, 2014; Rugege, 2004).

By 1951, the Prevention of Illegal Squatting, which targeted black people without formal rights to land and other racially based laws and provisions for eviction and land, intensified the Group Areas Act. This scenario saw nearly 3.5 million people being evicted by the apartheid government, and private landlords, between 1960 and 1983 (Platzky & Walker, 1985). Platzky and Walker recount that the process of eviction was characterised by demolishing and evicting black homes without court orders or compensation or adherence to constitutional or due processes (Platzky & Walker, 1985).

Indeed, what characterised the complexity of land ownership is that in pre-colonial African societies, land was traditionally a community resource, which could not be sold. It was readily available as a form of social security for community members. African society was operating under communalism. Communalism was a social arrangement where the entire population shared property in common. Private ownership was not predominant. The system of customary land ownership promoted and empowered citizens to participate in economic activities, without restrictions, under the authority of local headsmen or chiefs who were the custodians of the land. Despite modernity, thus system is still predominant in South Africa rural areas, especially in KwaZulu-Natal province.

On the contrary, the colonial governments introduced a unique form of land tenure or individual ownership, whereby land became a commodity that could be sold or purchased like other goods or services. The result of such a policy meant that whenever individuals have titles or holders, they could sell the land to meet other economic obligation (Rugege, 2004). This resulted in such individuals depriving other members of their immediate or extended families of a source of livelihood such that some communities became increasingly vulnerable to poverty (Rugege, 2004). Due to such contradictory scenarios, critics argue that land reform is not a necessity in South Africa because the poor black 'would be' landlords, are likely to sell their farmland in exchange for financial resources, and migrate to urban areas for a 'better life style' (Hall, 2004).

However, communal access to land is not secure because individuals cannot utilise the land as a form of security to acquire a bank loan or financial resources for development. Thus, in South Africa, the struggle for liberations from the repressive apartheid regime was partly based on the necessity of correcting land injustice and restoring the 'African dignity'. Forceful land dispossession from black Africans signified a loss of their dignified lives because they could no longer fend for their families and their descendants. As highlighted earlier, Africans were forced to become servants and earned below acceptable minimum wage (Platzky & Walker, 1985). Hence, prior to 1994, black Africans were the least educated, and had lowest income resources (Seekings, 2014). This is evident in the household income percentage disparities by race which revealed that in 1995 black African households ranked the poorest in South Africa with nearly 26% of them having incomes between R0.00 and R6839.00 per annum, compared with 12% of the coloured households, and only 2% of both Indian and white households (Hirschowitz & Orkin, 1996).

On the other hand, white minority dominated politics, agriculture and the economy in general. Paradoxically, this was in operative despite the 1955 Freedom Charter which set the goal of 'sharing the land' in South Africa by stating that 'restriction on land ownership shall be ended and all the land redevised among those who work for it, to banish famine and hunger…all shall have the right to occupy land wherever they choose' (Steytler, 1992). Such contradictions in land ownership resulted in high expectations among black Africans that, the eradication of apartheid rule would usher in an inclusive government with Constitution would foster greater access to land ownership among the 'historically disadvantaged'. The term 'historically disadvantaged' refers to the South African population who are predominantly black and economically poor. More specifically, it refers to South Africans who due to the unjust apartheid policy (Act 110 of 1983 Constitution of the Republic of South Africa) had been disenfranchised. The majority of the impoverished and landless, fall into the historically disadvantaged groups.

Some authors concur with the assertion that the need for South African post-apartheid land reform resulted from the historical inequalities in 'land ownership and use' (De Villiers et al., 1991; Kloppers & Pienaar, 2014).

South Africa's Response to the Land Question: Post-1994

The Constitution

In 1993, South Africa formed an Interim Constitution which resulted from negotiations (on several issues affecting the country, including the issue of property rights) between the main interest groups: the ANC and its allies, and the National Party of the apartheid government and its allies (Rugege, 2004). The Interim Constitution ushered in a new democratic government in 1994, when the apartheid regime was replaced by a Constitutional democracy led by the ANC government, with Nelson Mandela as the first black president to rule South Africa. Two years later, South Africa adopted a nation-building strategy through a democratic Constitution which clearly spells out that 'South Africa belongs to all who live in it, united in our diversity' (Department of Rural Development and Land Reform, 2017). As an incoming government, the policy of the ANC was to effect land reform which would be significant to remedy the past injustices of both deprivation and the denial of access to land. From the public's point of view, the expectations were that land reform would alleviate poverty, especially in the rural areas, redress land injustice, eliminate land eviction, formalise many of the informal settlements and provide title deeds to those living and working on the land. Based on this view, land was the basis for the prosperity of all South Africans, particularly the vulnerable black population.

Furthermore, the 1996 Constitution was more specific about land reform and more balanced in addressing the issue of property rights compared to the previous constitutions. For instance, the land question was treated as an urgent matter of rights and imbedded in the Bill of Rights under Section 25 of the Constitution (1996). This guarantees the right of property against arbitrary deprivation and provisions for the state to expropriate private property for public purposes or in the public interest, subject to just and equitable compensation. In the Constitution, 'public interest' includes the nation's commitment to land reform and to foster equitable access to all South Africa's natural resources (Constitution, 1996). Therefore, Section 25(3) of the Constitution stipulates: the amount, timing and manner of payment of equitable balance between the public interest and the interest of those affected, including: (a) the current use of the property; (b) the history of acquisition of the property; (c) the market value of the property; (d) the extent of direct state investment and subsidy in the acquisition and beneficial capital improvement of the property; and (e) the purpose of the expropriation.

The property clause included specific provisions on land reform, which imposed obligations on the government to foster greater access to land. To actualise this, the government initiated a policy document of the Reconstruction Development Programme (RDP) in November 1994, in which it undertook various aspects as measures for a land reform programme under three major principles.

i. Restitution to restore land rights to those who were dispossessed of them under discriminatory laws.
ii. Redistribution to make land more accessible to those whose land previously been denied access.
iii. Tenure reform to give security of tenure to labour tenants, farm workers and other rural dwellers who lived on land without secure rights (Department of Rural Development & Land Reform Affairs, 1997; Repubic of South Africa, 1994).

The RDP was formed because the apartheid economy had been built on systematically enforced racial divisions and income distributions. This resulted in poverty and degradation which existed simultaneously within modern cities and underdeveloped rural areas. Towns and cities were divided into townships, with inadequate basic infrastructure for blacks, but well-resourced suburbs for whites. In a similar scenario, the rural areas were divided into underdeveloped 'Bantustans' (reserves) for black people as opposed to the well-developed, white-owned, commercial farming areas. These disparities left deep scars of inequality and economic inefficiency, making South Africa's economy one of the most unequal in the world. Additionally, cheap labour policies and employment segregation control were concentrated in the white civil society hands (Wolpe, 1972).

To address these inequalities, the RDP instituted a policy framework and legislative programmes, such as land reform. The RDP was an integrated, coherent, socio-economic policy framework which sought to harmonise South Africans of different backgrounds and the country's resources towards the suppression of apartheid and building of a democratic and non-racist and non-sexist nation of South Africa (Repubic of South Africa, 1994).

Restitution

During apartheid rule, about 3.5 million blacks, in rural and urban areas, were forcibly dispossessed of their land and homes (Lahiff, 2001). As a result, since democracy, the restitution programme deals specifically with the historical rights of land. Its main objective is to restore land by supporting reconciliation, reconstruction, and nation-building. More specifically, it provides for the restitution of land rights to persons or communities who were disposed of rights in land ownership after 19 June 1913, in terms of the racially based laws or practices during apartheid (Hall, 2004).

The legal basis for restitution is provided by the 1993 Interim Constitution, Section 25(7) of the 1996 Constitution, and the Restitution of Land Rights Act 1994 (as amended in 1997). Thereafter, a Commission on the Restitution of Land Rights, under Chief Land Claims Commission (RLC) and the Department of Land Affairs (DLA), was established on which it depended for funds, administrative supply, and research expertise and policy direction. To ensure that more claims were settled, a Land Claims Court, which deals with land-related matters, was established.

Despite the government's efforts, the implementation stage of the restitution programme was not without challenges. Among these was the slow progress in resolving claims, such that, by December 1998, only 31 claims out of 63,455 individual and community claims, lodged in rural and urban areas, had been settled. By 2001, there were 12,314 claims or 18% of total claims lodged, with about R506 million spent on restitution process. About 59% of the land claimed has been resolved in terms of financial compensation and 302 000 ha have been restored (Lahiff, 2001; Rugege, 2004). Another challenge was the high cost of the restitution process whose 2001 budgetary level would require 150 years to complete the restitution (Lahiff, 2001).

One of the major challenges for restitution was the settlement of rural claims in a way that would contribute to the larger goal of land reform by 'redressing the racial inequalities in land holding, while reducing poverty and enhancing livelihood' (Lahiff, 2001). Ultimately, achieving the main objective of critical areas of land restitution remains largely unaddressed.

Land Redistribution

Being one of the pillars of land reform, the distribution programme aims to redress the past imbalance in land holding. Its main objective is to transfer large parcels of land from the privileged, white minority, commercial farmers to the historically disadvantaged. This makes land redistribution a constitutional responsibility of the government. As documented by the government, the main purpose of the redistribution programme, and revealed by the 1997 White Paper, was to redistribute land to the landless poor, labour tenants, farmworkers and merging farming for residential and productive use, to improve their livelihoods and quality of life (Deininger, 1999; Department of Rural Development & Land Reform Affairs, 1997, Hall, 2004).

Between 1995 and 1999, the redistribution programme made some noticeable progress, during which nearly 60,000 households were allocated grants for land acquisition, and 650,000 ha were approved for redistribution, representing less than 1% of the country's commercial farmland (Department of Rural Development & Land Reform Affairs, 1997).

Land redistribution mainly involves government's provision of a settlement or land acquisition grant of R16 000, equal to the basic housing grant, provided to quality households (Lahiff, 2001; Rugege, 2004).

The redistributive programme was also characterised by many projects involving groups of applicants pooling their grants to buy formerly white-owned farms for commercial agricultural purposes. To a lesser extent, groups of farmworkers reportedly used the grant to purchase equity shares in existing farming enterprises.

The rural and urban people were allocated separate grants for the acquisition of municipal commonage, available to municipalities wishing to provide communal land for use, such as typically for grazing (Lahiff, 2001). By the end of 1999, 77 municipal commonages had been implemented. By 2001, the redistribution programme process recorded some noticeable developments in the implementation process, such as the devolution of powers for project approval across the provinces, which resulted in the reduction of the cycle for implementing the land redistribution programme (Lahiff, 2001).

However, the programme has been criticised increasingly because it focuses too much on the technical criteria for accessing the type of land use that could be supported (Lahiff, 2001; Rugege, 2004). Another notable challenge of the programme was the lack of skilled labour in handling land transactions, leading to prolonged delays and loss of interest from the white commercial farmers as willing sellers. Additionally, the marked-based principle has undermined the government's reliance on current land owners (sellers) to determine when, where, and at what price, land is to be made available. Largely, the demand-led market mechanism is perceived to be an unfair approach whose participation requirements would favour elite South Africans, who already had a reasonably strong asset base, and exclude people who have none (Lahiff, 2001).

Central to this chapter is the question of appropriate land use, and promoting agriculture for household food security. While the current government policy emphasises farm settlement, based on the selection of suitable qualified individuals (usually males, who usually have access to capital of their own) to engage in market-oriented farming, such an approach continues to risk promoting an elite class of 'emergent farmers' and cannot benefit the millions of very poor South Africans, mostly women, farmworkers, and the unemployed (who have been excluded from such a progressive programme), who wish to expand their agricultural production as part of a wider livelihood strategy. More specifically, land redistribution should be carried out for the purpose of improving household food security. Such programmes must be designed to identify and meet the specific needs of marginalised groups (such as women and the rural population) that experience poverty and hunger.

Tenure Reform

Tenure reform was implemented to provide secure tenure for South Africans living for a long period, without secure rights, on land owned by others. Given its mechanism, tenure reform has the potential to benefit more people than all other land reform programmes in South Africa. The reform is backed by the provisions of the 1996 Constitution, Section 25, which stipulates that a person or community whose tenure of land is largely insecure due to past racially discriminatory laws or practices, is entitled to the extent provided by an Act of Parliament either to tenure, which is legally secure, or comparable to redress (Constitution, 1996).

The targeted beneficiaries are South Africans with insecure use of land, including farmworkers, former farmworkers, sharecroppers, labour tenants and people living in communal lands without secure rights (Rugege, 2004). In the South African rural context, tenure reform is largely perceived as a means of protecting or strengthening of the rights of residents of privately owned farms and state land, together with the reform of the system of communal tenure prevailing in the former homelands (Lahiff, 2001). More specifically, the tenure reform policy was introduced due to past the racialised apartheid policies of segregation that denied black people access land, such that many migrated to the cities or commercial farms in search of employment for their survival (Hall, 2004).

Due to such discriminatory policies, many black South Africans never acquired ownership or secure rights to land, stayed on land due to a government permit to occupy or with consent of the landowner (Rugege, 2004). The permission or consent risked being withdrawn at any time, with the consequence that the occupier became a squatter, as evidenced by the 1951 Prevention of Illegal Squatting Act, which resulted in more than three million South African being evicted by the state and private owners, mostly white commercial farmers. This resulted in the population groups being confined to overcrowded black homelands in communal land areas or 'homelands', known as 'Bantustans' (Platzky & Walker, 1985). The Homelands or Bantustans were established by the apartheid government as areas to which the majority of the black population were moved to prevent them from living in the urban areas of South Africa. In total, ten homelands were created in South Africa. These were the Transkei, Bophuthatswana, Ciskei, Venda, Gazankulu, KaNgwane, KwaNdebele, KwaZulu, Lebowa, and QwaQwa. The homelands were designed for specific ethnic groups.

Tenants' reform should be carried out along with restitution and redistribution because achieving tenure security would require the relocation of several people who currently share rights with the others due to removals and overcrowding (Lahiff, 2001). The tenure reform policy has also come under pressure due to the complex relationship between the community-based land ownership under customary law, and a democratisation of land administration under the government. As a result, a few cases of illegal evictions have come before the courts and ultimately the Constitutional Court, and only a few permanent settlements have been approved.

Therefore, from the colonial and apartheid rule to post-1994, South Africa's successive governments have designed and implemented several land reform policies which have done very little to improve the lives of the majority as evidenced by the black South Africans, who being an overwhelming majority in South Africa, still account for 95% of the poor (Woolard, 2002). It is also clear that the ANC, as the incoming government, inherited a deeply racialised economy, with few people having property rights.

Food Security and Land Reform in South Africa

Food security is defined by the 1996 World Food Summit of the World Food Programme as a 'situation that exists when all people, at all times, have physical, 'social' and economic access to sufficient, safe and nutritious food to meet their dietary needs and food preferences for an active and healthy life' (Rome Declaration, 1996). From this perspective, ensuring food security is a fundamental socio-economic factor. In the South African context, the government's concern for food security dates back to the time of apartheid, when it equated national food security with commercial farming, a sector dominated by the white minority (Van Zyl & Kirsten, 1992). As a result, much of agriculture policy focused on national self-sufficiency through commercial productions. To improve national food security, the apartheid government's 1984 White Paper on Agricultural Policy stated:

> For any country, the provisions of sufficient food for its people is a vital priority and for this reason, it is regarded as one of the primary objectives of agricultural policy. Adequate provision of this basic need of man not only promotes but it's also an essential prerequisite for an acceptable economic, political and social order and for stability. (Republic of South Africa, 1984)

The statement from the White Paper not only shows that government's need for food security as an economic tool, but also vital for the political and social–cultural sustainability of South Africa; a reflection of an obligation to nation-building. However, the reality is that due to existing discriminatory colonial policies, such as the 1913 Land Act, this nation-building strategy was far from being realised. The majority of South Africans, mostly the black population, whose livelihood depended on small-scale farming, were excluded from this fundamental economic activity and were left in abject poverty.

Petros Nkosi sentiments exemplified that:

> The land, our purpose is the land; that is what we must achieve. The land is our whole lives: we plough it for food; we build our houses from the soil; we live on it; and we are buried in it. When the whites took our land away from us, we lost the dignity of our lives: we could no longer feed our children; we were forced to become servants; we were treated like animals. Our people have many problems; we are beaten and killed by the farmers; the wages we earn are too little to buy even a bag of mealie-meal. We must unite together to help each other and face the Boers. But in everything we do, we must remember that there is only one aim and one solution and that is the land, the soil, our world.
>
> Daniels v Scribante & Another (2017)

Mr. Petros Nkosi expressed these sentiments at an Eastern Transvaal meeting as an outcry of the consequences of unjust land dispossession by the white minority, which as explained earlier in the chapter, affected mostly the black rural population whose 'dignity' was stripped off and resulted in them being became marginalised outsiders.

Some authors argue that the recurring food insecurity among poor households is rooted in the systematic socio-economic and political disparities instituted by the apartheid government as evidenced in the creation of the impoverished Bantustans and townships across South Africa (Drimie & Ruysenaar, 2010). The fundamental argument is that in rural areas, poverty levels are higher than the national average because most of the black households do not have members who are gainfully employed, but are semi-skilled and unskilled labourers who earn very little to meet their household financial obligations (Westaway, 2012). Ultimately, this compromises their food basket budget.

In post-apartheid South Africa, the need to recognise food security as a basic human right for all South Africans is situated in the Section 27(1) of the Constitution. Being South Africa's main instrument for nation-building, the Constitution states, 'Everyone has the right to have access to (a) health care services; (b) sufficient food and water; (c) social security'. The Constitution requires the state to take reasonable legislative and other similar measures within its available resources to achieve the progressive realisation of each of these rights.

In a democratic state, reasonable programmes are capable of apable of facilitating the realisation of each constitutional right. It is also acknowledged that while the Bill of Rights makes no specific mention about food security, in relation to reclaiming dispossessed land reform, several anti-poverty policies and welfare programmes have been introduced under the RDP (Department of Agriculture, 2002). The RDP identified food security as a basic human need and food insecurity as a legacy of the apartheid government (Hendriks, 2014). The commitment for food security is stipulated in the Integrated Food Security Strategy (IFSS), which was introduced in 2002. The purpose of the IFSS was to harmonise and integrate various sub-programmes of food security under one authority (Republic of South Africa, 2009b).

In the 2010–2011 financial year, the South African government reprioritised food security, as reflected in its millennium development goal aimed at halving the proportion of hunger and poverty levels in the country over the period 2000–2015 (Du Toit, Ramonyai, & Ntushelo, 2011). Yet recently, about 13.8 million South Africans were still experiencing household food insecurity. The household food insecurity is benchmarked against the national poverty line, which is determined by household consumption and expenditure for food and non-food components per month. The most vulnerable to food insecurity are female-headed households, the unemployed youth, and the rural population. The majority of these groups are black (Statistics South Africa, 2017).

Many South Africans perceive the persistent poverty among the historically disadvantaged as a result of their exclusion from land ownership and agricultural economic activities. They blame the state's failure to respond adequately to the needs of the poor who are landless and/or unemployed in the country. From this perspective, household food insecurity is directly linked to the 'extreme' poverty line.

In rural areas, for example, food insecurity is dominant where households are net deficient food producers, because their access to food is largely reliant on household income. The implication is that low-income households are the most affected by food prices heightening (Chopra, Drimie, & Witten, 2009). On the contrary, household food poverty cannot be blamed wholly on the landlessness of the majority but, in part, to dictates of global capitalism or changes in the general cost of living which result in heightened food and fuel prices. Ultimately, low-income households become increasingly vulnerable to food 'unaffordability' or food insecurity (Akinola, 2018).

In part, household food insecurity accounts for the underutilisation of land and poor governance. This happens when the government redistributes large parcels of land to people who lack the necessary skills and financial resources for agricultural production. The under-utilisation of restituted white commercial farms allocated to black emerging farmers and poor governance can hamper food security and development. A scenario of land reform, poor governance, and food insecurity was Zimbabwe's accelerated land redistribution programme, which, despite achieving its fundamental objective of restituting fertile tracks of land to the landless blacks and redressing colonial land dispossession by white minority rule, resulted in the recurrent political and economic turmoil characterised by massive unemployment, food shortages and hunger.

Similarly, the unproductive use of commercial land claim through restitution measures can hamper agricultural investment, as was the case with the ≠khomani San of the Southern Kalahari, who had been forcibly removed from the Kalahari Gemsbok area in the 1930s. The land was restored (65,000 thousand ha farmland) between 1999 and 2001. However, they abandoned the farms due to a lack of capital, resulting in aggravated poverty (Robins, 2001).

Land Expropriation Without Compensation

Due to delayed responses in resolving the land issue, post-apartheid South Africa has witnessed increasing incidents of land conflict through invasions of white farmlands by landless black people in rural and urban areas. Illegal land seizures in areas like the KwaZulu-Natal province are characterised by encroaching white commercial farmlands, establishing shelters and engaging in peasant farming (Stoddard, 2016). These recurring land conflicts have deepened the wounds of racial tension, resulting in approximately 160 cases of racial-related violence in January 2016, the highest monthly rate since 1994 (Sieff, 2016). Those cases of land hunger and violence have been attributed to the increasing unemployment and poverty levels in the country.

The continuous endeavours for accelerating land reform and racial balance in ownership resulted in the first national land audit in 2013, which revealed that very little progress had been made towards increasing access to land ownership among the disadvantaged groups in South Africa (Department of Rural Development and Land Reform, 2017). It was reiterated in the 2018 land summit in Boksburg and 2017 White Paper on Land, that the aim of the reform was to restore and reimburse the victims of apartheid and the colonial oppression of their land and as part of its strategy to strengthen the agricultural sector as part of the RDP. Subsequently, during their 54th elective conference, the ANC ruling party pledged to pursue land expropriation without compensation as an option to end the inequality in land ownership. However, this is based on the condition that land expropriation would not harm food security or aggravate a national economic crisis.

By the end of 2017, a report by the Department of Rural Development and Land Reforms also revealed that, regarding individual land ownership, that the white minority had the largest share of land (72%, more than 26 million ha farms), while black South Africans, who constituted the majority of South Africans, had the least share of less than 5% of farms. The effect of such report motivated the ANC to officially call on the government to maximise its powers of expropriation, as reflected Section 25 of the Constitution under the guidance of a 'just and equitable' democratic South Africa (Sachs, 2017).

In February 2018, pressure mounted on the land reform debate, resulting in the motion of endorsing 'land expropriation without compensation' being adopted by parliament, as a measure to consider the social-economic historical context of land dispossession and as a strategy for uniting the 'rainbow nation' by bridging the gap of land access disparities among South Africans. However, the sensitivity of the 'land expropriation without compensation' lies in the process and implementation that will be adopted to redistribute land to 'new landlords' who are capable of ensuring a viable agricultural sector, and without dividing the nation on political and racial lines (Akinola, 2018).

Conclusions

The chapter identifies the linkages between land reform, food insecurity, and poverty. Despite the government efforts in implementating several policies to improve the performance of the economy and, land reform in particular, South Africa lacks a comprehensive law that provides for effective mechanisms for addressing the needs of the poor who are most desperate for equitable land access. As a result, the land question remains a very emotive and sensitive topic to many South Africans, especially the poor and the vulnerable who were dispossessed and whose livelihood depended on agriculture.

While acknowledging that there is there is a genuine need for land reform in South Africa, it presents a dilemma to white commercial farmers who are likely to lose much of their productive land once the radical policy framework of 'expropriation without compensation' takes effect. From this scenario, the chapter recommends that if implemented within the confines of the law, well-designed and sustainably managed land reform policies, regardless of whether it is expropriation without compensation, can provide sustainable contributions to nation-building, and reduce socio-economic disparities and food poverty among South African poor.

Furthermore, the current South African land reform policy lacks a focus on enhancing household food security through small-scale farming. Therefore, the agricultural production of beneficiaries of land reform is insufficient to raise the poor from general poverty and food insecurity. The government's principle objective should be to promote the agricultural sector and to safeguard household food security. The chapter also recommend that a well-designed monitoring and evaluation system should accompany each implementation stage of the new land reform policy.

References

Abrahams, C. (2016). Twenty years of social cohesion and nation-building in South Africa. *Journal of Southern African Studies, 42*(1), 95–107.

Akinola, A. O. (2018). Land reform in South Africa: An appraisal. *Africa Review, 10*(1), 1–16.

Appalachian Land Ownership Task Force. (2015). *Who Owns Appalachia?* Lexington: University of Kentucky Press.

Bank, L. J., & Hart, T. G. B. (2017). *How land reform and rural development can help reduce poverty in South Africa September 2017*. Available https://theconversation.com/how-land-reform-and-rural-development-can-help-reduce-poverty-in-south-africa-84146.

Chimere-Dan, O. (1992). Apartheid and demography in South Africa. *African Population Studies, 7*.

Chopra, M., Drimie, S., & Witten, C. (2009). *Combating malnutrition in South Africa* (Global alliance for improved nutrition (GAIN) Working Paper, 2009(1)).

Constitutional Court. (2016). *C.C.o.S. Case CCT 50/16*. Available http://www.saflii.org/za/cases/ZACC/2017/13.pdf.

Currie-Alder, B., Kanbur, R., Malone, D. M., & Medhora, R. (2014). *International development: Ideas, experience, and prospects*. Oxford: Oxford University Press.

Chaddad, F. R., & Cook, M. L. (2004). Understanding new cooperative models: An ownership–control rights typology. *Applied Economic Perspectives and Policy, 26*(3), 348–360.

Deininger, K. (1999). *Making negotiated land reform work: Initial experience from Brazil, Colombia, and South Africa*. Washington, DC: The World Bank.

Department of Agriculture. (2002). *The Integrated Food Security Strategy for South Africa Agriculture*. Pretoria: Government Printers.

Department of Arts and Culture. (2013). *What is nation-building?* Available http://www.dac.gov.za/content/5-what-nation-building. Accessed 14 September 2018.

Department of Land Affairs. (1997). *White Paper on South African land policy*. Pretoria: DLA.

Department of Rural Development and Land Reform. (2017). *Land audit report: Version 2: Phase II: Private land ownership by race, gender and nationality*. Pretoria: Government Printers. Available http://www.ruraldevelopment.gov.za/publications/land-audit-report/file/6126.

Derman, B. (2006). *After Zimbabwe's fast track land reform: Preliminary observations on the near future of Zimbabwe's efforts to resist globalization*. Available http://citeseerx.ist.psu.edu/viewdoc/summary?doi=10.1.1.571.2696.

De Villiers, B. (2003). *Land reform: Issues and challenges. A comparative overview of experiences in Zimbabwe, Namibia, South Africa and Australia*. Johannesburg: Konrad-Adenauer-Stiftung.

De Villiers, Z., et al. (1991). A harvest of discontent: The land question in South Africa, In M. de Klerk (Ed.), Idasa, *Development Southern Africa, 8*(4), 555–557.

Drimie, S., & Ruysenaar, S. (2010). The integrated food security strategy of South Africa: An institutional analysis. *Agrekon, 49*(3), 316–337.

Du Toit, D., Ramonyai, M. D., & Ntushelo, V. (2011). *Food security*. Directorate Economic Services Production Economics Unit. Department of Agriculture, Forestry and Fisheries. Available https://www.nda.agric.za/docs/genreports/foodsecurity.pdf.

Hall, R. (2004). A political economy of land reform in South Africa. *Review of African Political Economy, 31*(100), 213–227.

Harvard, A. A., & Bryony, I. B. (2012). *Nation-building*. Harvard: Harvard Press.

Hendriks, S. (2014). Food security in South Africa: Status quo and policy imperatives. *Agrekon, 53*(2), 1–24.

Hirschowitz, R., & Orkin, M. (1996). *Living in South Africa: Selected findings of the 1995 October household survey*. Central Statistical Service.

Kariuki, J. (2009). *Agrarian reform, rural development and governance in Africa: A case of Eastern and Southern Africa*. Available https://www.africaportal.org/publications/agrarian-reform-rural-development-and-governance-in-africa-a-case-of-eastern-and-southern-africa/.

Kloppers, H. J., & Pienaar, G. J. (2014). The historical context of land reform in South Africa and early policies. *Potchefstroom Electronic Law Journal/Potchefstroomse Elektroniese Regsblad, 17*(2), 676–706.

Lahiff, E. (2001). *Land reform in South Africa: Is it meeting the challenge? Debating Land Reform and Rural Development Policy Brief 1*. Programme for Land and Agrarian Studies, University of the Western Cape: Cape Town.

Mutasa, C. (2015). *Focus of land in Africa. A brief history of land in Zimbabwe-1890–1990*. Available http://www.focusonland.com/countries/zimbabwe/a-brief-history-of-land-in-zimbabwe1890today.

O'Regan, C. (1990). *The prevention of Illegal Squatting Act. No Place to Rest: Forced removals and the law in South Africa*. Cape Town: Oxford University Press.

Platzky, L., & Walker, C. (1985). *The surplus people: Forced removals in South Africa*. Johannesburg: Raven Press at 10.

Republic of South Africa. (1984). *White Paper on the Agricultural Policy of the Republic of South Africa*. Pretoria: Government Printer.

Republic of South Africa. (1994). *White Paper on reconstruction and development: Government's strategy for fundamental transformation*. Pretoria: Government Press.

Republic of South Africa. (1996). *The Bill of Rights of the Constitution*. Pretoria: Government Printer.

Republic of South Africa. (2009a). *Land Audit, Department of Rural Development and Land Reform*. Pretoria: Government Printers.

Republic of South Africa. (2009b). *Together doing more and better: Medium Term Strategic Framework for (MTSF, 2009 – 2014)*. Pretoria: Government Printers.

Republic of South Africa. (2017). *Poverty Trends in South Africa: An examination of absolute poverty between 2006 and 2015.* Government Printers: Pretoria.
Robins, S. (2001). 'Bushmen' and double vision: The p khomani San Land claim and the cultural politics of 'community' and 'development' in the Kalahari. *Journal of Southern African Studies, 27*(4), 833–853.
Rome Declaration. (1996). *Rome Declaration on world food security and world food summit plan of action.* Available http://www.fao.org/3/w3613e/w3613e00.htm.
Rugege, S. (2004). Land reform in South Africa: An overview. *International Journal of Legal Information, 32,* 283–312.
Sachs, J. (2017). *No need to change land clauses.* Available https://www.iol.co.za/news/politics/no-need-to-change-land-clauses-8290617.
Seekings, J. (2014). South Africa: Democracy, poverty and inclusive growth since 1994. In *Democracy Works–Conference Paper.* Centre for Development and Enterprise (CDE).
Shulika, L. S., & Sabi, S. C. (2018). Zimbabwe and the quest for development: Rethinking the xeno-ethnophobia tint and the land reform question. In *The political economy of xenophobia in Africa* (pp. 153–167). New York: Springer.
Sieff, K. (2016, February 17). South Africa: Trial of four white farmers and a policeman for the murder of two black men highlights the racial divisions still haunting the rainbow nation. *Independent.*
South Africa History Online. (2018). *The homelands.* Available http://www.sahistory.org.za/article/homelands. Accessed 8 July 2018.
Statistics South Africa. (2017). *Poverty trends in south arica: An examination of absolute poverty between 2006 and 2015.* Pretoria: Government Printers.
Steytler, N. (1992). The freedom Carter and beyond: Founding principles for a democratic South African legal order. *Journal of South African Law,* 753.
Stoddard, Ed. (2016). South Africa to limit farm sizes to speed land redistribution. *Reuters.* Available https://www.reuters.com/article/us-safrica-landrightsreform/south-africa-to-limit-farm-sizes-to-speed-land-redistribution-idUSKCN0YC0GJ.
Van Zyl, J., & Kirsten, J. (1992). Food security in South Africa. *Agrekon, 31*(4), 170–184.
Westaway, A. (2012). Rural poverty in the Eastern Cape province: Legacy of apartheid or consequence of contemporary segregationism? *Development Southern Africa, 29*(1), 115–125.
Wolpe, H. (1972). Capitalism and cheap labour-power in South Africa: From segregation to apartheid. *Economy and Society, 1*(4), 425–456.
Woolard, I. (2002). *An overview of poverty and inequality in South Africa* (Unpublished briefing paper). HSRC.

CHAPTER 8

Motivations for Land Reform in Contemporary South Africa: The Case of Balobedu in Tzaneen, Province of Limpopo

Listen Yingi

Introduction

Land reform, and its impact on poverty alleviation, is an issue riddled with controversy in many countries. It is established that not having access to land or only limited access to land and its resources perpetuates poverty (Akinola, 2018; Yingi, 2019). This limited access to resources (land, for example) and the opportunities that resources give, generate conflict between classes and races in all communities. The communities and individuals who have access to land and adequate services in any given country prove to have lower poverty levels compared to those communities without access to land (Biney, 2018; More, 2011; Yingi, 2019).

The history of land conflicts is as old as the human race itself and power relations are at the centre of accessing land. Weaker groups are displaced by stronger ones and this causes conflict between races, interest

L. Yingi (✉)
University of Limpopo, Mankweng, South Africa

A. O. Akinola et al. (eds.), *The New Political Economy of Land Reform in South Africa*,
https://doi.org/10.1007/978-3-030-51129-6_8

and ethnic groups. The native Canadians, the Australian Aborigines, and the natives of the USA were displaced and forcibly removed, respectively by the powerful immigrant groups (Huxley, 1870). The same applies in South Africa, where the Khoisan tribe was displaced from their tribal land by the more powerful white settlers (Huxley, 1870; Pardoe, 2006).

The conflict over land has always been, and remains, at the core of many countries' political, economic and social development, of which South Africa is not an exception. It is indeed one of the root causes of the political tensions within sundry economies and with the former colonial powers, as was the case in Zimbabwe (Chitanga, 2018; Moyo, 2005). This explains the incessant calls to revisit the historical injustice of land dispossession by the apartheid regime.

Land Ownership and the Locality of the Balobedu Community

Land was communally owned in many parts of Balobedu before the land policy of 1913 and the legalised apartheid regime in 1948 (Biney, 2018), which reinforced land domination. The Balobedu community was forcibly removed from the area where a farming conglomerate is presently situated. The Balobedu community stays close to the large, white-run commercial farms, which are owned by ZZ2. Most of the community members are not employed, except a few who are employed on part-time basis by the giant tomato farming enterprise (ZZ2). Like other South African communities, during colonial rule, the local population was dispossessed of their land, while the small-scale farming that helped rural households to survive was also undermined in favour of white commercial farming. The unequal treatment between black and white farmers has undermined the livelihoods of the local community and, hence, the effect of these relations is reflected in the consistent land conflict evident in South Africa.

South Africa's land hunger and conflict is not a new phenomenon; it began around 1652, during foreign domination of African natives through colonialism. When the Europeans moved inland, they faced resistance from the native inhabitants of the land (South African History Online, 2018). Africans were displaced and had their land taken away and their culture destroyed and replaced by western values (Makhado, 2012). The unresolved historical marginalisation, oppression and land dispossession continue to threaten the peace and stability of South Africa in the democratic era. The persistent inequality and wealth gap between black and white people in the country constitute one of the motivations for land reform in contemporary South Africa.

Given the fact that land reform is a basic need for rural and semi-rural communities, the failure to address access to it engenders dissent within the dispossessed communities. The inability of the African National Congress (ANC) government to effectively address the injustices and inequalities fuelled by dispossession of the natives' land and property explains the need of land by the local population in the twenty-first century. With the decrease in gainful employment in the urban areas and other failed expectations, the rural-urban movement has drastically reduced, resulting in an accelerated demand for land by the black population.

Discriminatory Laws and Land Ownership in South Africa

The need for the current land reform programme arose from the racially discriminatory laws and practices which were in place for the largest part of the twentieth century, especially those related to land ownership (More, 2011). The application of these discriminatory laws and practices (Native Land Act of 1913 - Act No. 27 of 1913) resulted in extreme inequalities in relation to land ownership and use.

As a result of the constitutional obligations, the post-apartheid government embarked on an ambitious land reform programme which was aimed at settling all claims for redistribution by 2005 and redistributing 30% of white-owned commercial agricultural land to black South Africans by 2014. However, more than 13 years after that initial target, there are still many unsettled land claims and less than 10% of the redistribution target has been achieved. One of the reasons for the failures was the adoption of the willing buyer, willing seller approach, which subjected land to market forces (Akinola, 2018).

Expectedly, land reform would bring the restoration of land to its rightful owners. However, after more than two decades of democracy, South African land and agrarian reform (which was guided by the willing buyer, willing seller approach) has failed, as evidenced by the very few claims that have been settled since they were lodged in 1998. An example of this is the Venda community (Madimbo Corridor) where, year after year, the claimants are called to assemble so that they can sign papers:

"We have signed settlement agreements several times but they continue to come to us for further verifications. Now we have signed a settlement agreement based on the last financial year budget of 2015/2016 but now it is 2016/2017. That thing is not going on well" (SA Links, 2016).

This puts land redistribution and land restoration at the centre of social, economic, and political tensions and it is closely linked to socio-economic development (SA Links, 2016). Land reform in South Africa stands on the three pillars of land tenure, land restoration and land redistribution. Land redistribution and land restoration are applicable to this area of study. It is important to note that the slow pace of these two land reform programmes is not the only challenge faced by the programmes. It has been reported that more than 90% of agricultural land, transferred in terms of these two programmes, is not being used productively (Denene, 2018). This situation not only contributes to increasing levels of poverty and unemployment among these land reform beneficiaries, but also threatens food security. A factor that further compounds the crisis is the recent calls by some politicians inciting landless South Africans to illegally occupy land belonging to white farmers, creating a potentially explosive situation (SA Links, 2016).

It is evident that the challenges faced by the land reform programmes are in urgent need of attention (Valente, 2008). Valente (2008) alludes to the fact that the willing buyer, willing seller approach denies native Africans access to land, thereby deepening poverty and inequality and aggravating the pressures on the state to accelerate the reform agenda.

One of the earliest challenges faced by the first democratically elected government was how to address the unequal distribution of land in the country. The South African government has shown a commitment to eradicate, or at least alleviate for now, the inequalities and injustices of the past and has initiated a comprehensive land reform programme, addressing restitution, land redistribution and tenure security, with a strong constitutional basis. The Constitution is clear on the land restitution programme, stating in Section 25(7) that:

> A person or community dispossessed of property after 19 June 1913 as a result of past racially discriminatory laws or practices is entitled, to the extent provided by an Act of Parliament, either to restitution of that property or to equitable redress. This is one of the major motivations for land reform in the present South Africa. The South African government is

> bound to provide land to the dispossessed communities. (Constitution of South Africa, 1996)

Section 25(5) explains that in the land redistribution programme, which is the second pillar of land reform, the state is obliged to take "reasonable legislative and other measures, within its available resources, to foster conditions which enable citizens to gain access to land on an equitable basis".

Thirdly, tenure security is addressed in Section 25(6) of the Constitution, which points out that:

> A person or community whose tenure of land is legally insecure as a result of past racially discriminatory laws or practices is entitled, to the extent provided by an Act of Parliament, either to tenure which is legally secure or to comparable redress. In other words, the constitution of South Africa is pro land reform and it strongly supports the abolition and extinction of inequality and racially based injustices.

This chapter examines the decisive factors responsible for rethinking the land question and the land reform programmes of the government. The first section presents the background to the chapter, while the subsequent section locates the study in historical discourse.

Research Methodology

The study is concerned with interpreting the subjective experiences, that is, the perspectives of individuals being studied. Qualitative research involves an in-depth interrogation of a given topic, hence the choice of this research design (Grix, 2010). Qualitative research is deemed appropriate for its ability to produce descriptive information in the analysis of people's individual and collective social actions, thoughts, and perceptions. Through a purposive sampling technique, the study adopts face-to-face unstructured interviews.

Participants (22) were selected out of the 255 households under study. A criterion for selection was the availability of participants who are either beneficiaries of land, land claimants or other stakeholders in the land reform programmes. The research was carried out from January 2017 to April 2017. The participants were located in Kga Modjadji in Modjadjisloof. The research was guided by the principle of anonymity.

The table below shows the participants' profiles:

Access to land	*Educational qualifications*	*Age*	*No. of participants*	*Employment status*
Yes	One degreed participant and the other one is a matriculate	45–49	2	Employed
None	Standard 4	50–65	5	Not employed
None	Diploma level	40–45	6	Not employed
Small garden	Matric to Master's degree level	25–40	7	Part-time employment

Source Author's Compilation

Most of the participants fall in the economically active bracket but are not employed despite their educational attainment. The few who are employed are engaged on a contract basis.

Apartheid Regime and Land Issue

The struggle for liberation against apartheid in South Africa is intimately integrated into calls for the abolition of skewed access to land. The three liberation movements against apartheid (African National Congress Pan African Congress and Black Conscious Movement) in South Africa had a land policy in their manifestos. This is a clear indication that land reform is the major point of contention in the apartheid era and in democratic South Africa. The legacy of apartheid continues to define post-apartheid South Africa to the extent that black South Africans are still disadvantaged economically. More than 80% of the viable and productive land is in the hands of the minority white race (Biney, 2018). This makes the issue of land to be racial and segregatory. This situation drives black South Africans to demand what they believe was stolen from them.

The most prominent instrument used by the apartheid regime to establish and enforce its policy of racial segregation was through legislation. Through its limitation on land ownership, the government confined the majority of the population to a few homelands, in which ownership was permitted (Hall, 2014). Generally, this generated extremely skewed land ownership and land use patterns where historically disadvantaged South Africans did not own the majority of the productive agricultural land.

The enactment of the apartheid Natives Land Act of 1913 led to the eviction and dispossession of many black people from their productive ancestral lands to less productive lands, as was the case in Tzaneen (Bolobedu Community) (Hall, 2014; Moyo, 2000). The eviction and dispossession of people resulted in millions of black people being peasants and farm labourers with no land rights. It is estimated that over 3,5 million blacks in South African's urban and rural areas lost their land and rights in property through forceful evictions during the apartheid era (Makhado, 2012). The Land Act gave the government the power and authority to specifically prohibit Africans from buying land after June 19, 1913.

The apartheid system and policies caused most blacks to be landless in the country of their birth and hence there is now the struggle to reclaim their lost identity as landowners (Moyo & Mohammed, 2009). The Bantustan areas included land granted to black South Africans by the South African Republic government, previously created locations and reserves, and land owned under the informal or formal trusteeship system. The land reserved for blacks was not fertile for agricultural production and could not meet the needs of the growing black population who require land for food production and small-scale agriculture. Cousins and Mahenehene (2013) assert that many blacks were forced to work as mere labourers at the white commercial farms, factories and mining industries. Land dispossession has put the land question at the centre of a struggle in South Africa, leading to black resistance and has become a focus of liberation movements.

Forced removals in support of racial segregation have caused enormous pains, trauma and hardship in South Africa, and no settlement of land issues can be reached without addressing such historical injustices. Many segregatory developments happened in South Africa; of most importance was the dispossession of black communities such as the Khomani San of Southern Kalahari, from their lands. Many communities, for example, the Ndebele in Mpumalanga, and Pedi in Limpopo, around the then Pietersburg areas, were also forcibly removed to 'homelands'.

On the restoration of the land in 1994, only some of the original inhabitants decided to return, and tensions emerged between the different groups (Gordillo, 1999). The conflicts within and between the people who were once dispossessed of their land illustrate the continuing relevance of racial, ethnic and class identities in land restitution. The foreign powers destroyed these identities and regarded them as primitive. The clash of African and European identities was reinforced through the complex and ambivalent relationships that developed between leaders and community members, and between the community and the state.

Analysis of the Land Discourse in South Africa

Land reform in South Africa has become a controversial topic in political, national and international discourses and crucial to South Africa's economic survival (Hall, 2013). Such concerns are not unique to South Africa. The motivations for land reform in most African states are due to frustrations which grew out of the models which denied people of African descent of their land. The Balobedu people were forcibly removed from their ancestral land and they were relocated to barren and mountainous lands (South African History, 2012). The land crisis in Zimbabwe grew out of frustrations over the government's land reform programme and resulted in white-owned farms being seized. President Mugabe drew international attention to Zimbabwe's land crisis by failing to react to the widespread violence, or even, as some interpret his actions, endorsing such attacks (Scoones et al., 2010).

The challenge of land restitution highlights South African land reform struggles. Land restitution aims at providing land to the victims of forced removals that began with the implementation of the Native Land Act in 1913 (Act No. 27 of 1913). Okumbor (2010) states that land restitution is based on rights and it is restorative in nature and, as such, constitutes the South African state's attempt to redress unequal access to land through the reversal, when possible, of land rights to communities and individuals who have experienced land dispossession during foreign domination.

In South Africa, the need for land has reached unprecedented levels, especially with the emergence of the forceful Economic Freedom Fighters (EFF) party in political mainstream politics, interrogating the national questions and calling for the adoption and implementation of expropriation of land without compensation. Post-apartheid South Africa is facing serious challenges on how to settle the contentious issue of land. The land question in South Africa is also being derailed by international capitalist interests, which do not favour the expropriation of land without compensation policy that has been adopted by the ANC-led administration.

Although the land expropriation without compensation was approved by parliament, the challenge is in its effective implementation. International powers have vested interest in the land policy in the country and are trying to influence the government towards abandoning LEWC. This is evidenced by the response of the American President, Donald Trump, advising the South Africa government (Denene, 2018) to exercise caution in its adoption and possible implementation of LEWC.

Willing Buyer, Willing Seller Approach

The main instrument through which land restitution and redistribution would be attained is through the willing buyer, willing buyer approach to land reform. This involves the government buying land from 'willing sellers', which are predominantly white landowners or farm owners, and allocating the land to chosen beneficiaries. The high cost involved with this approach and the 'unwillingness' of the white landowners to sell productive land or farms remains a huge challenge for the success of the reform model (Moyo, 2000).

The proponents of the willing buyer, willing seller approach postulate that the cooperation of landlords is the most important factor for any successful implementation of land reform. The guiding principle for the willing buyer, willing seller approach is that it is a voluntary programme, and only the land of owners who voluntarily sell will be touched; landowners, who do not want to sell, will not be compelled to do so.

According to Binswanger (1999), this approach aims to replace the confrontational atmosphere that has characterised land reforms. The willing sellers, in turn, are paid 100% cash, based on the full market value of their lands. Binswanger claims that "this will provide a strong incentive for landowners to sell land". Aliber (2013) opines that the failure of the willing buyer, willing seller approach in South Africa, Zimbabwe and Namibia has denied the landless and many people access to land. The South African government has had to abandon the willing buyer, willing seller approach due to its inherent complications. Its failure constitutes one of the reasons for adopting LEWC as the more appropriate instrument for effective land reform programmes. Nel (2015) notes that land reform failure may lead to a situation similar to that of Zimbabwe, where the government forcefully expropriated white-owned farms to redistribute to the landless black people without compensation.

The Balobedu community has waited for far too long after lodging their claim to the land. The government is too slow to deliver land to the landless Balobedu community. While LEWC has been staunchly resisted by the white population, in particular, addressing the historical dispossession should be at the top of the agenda of any responsive government in South Africa. The black majority should be given access to productive land for ownership or use. Moyo and Mohamed (2009) assert that the chaotic land reform programme which happened in Zimbabwe was due to the prolonged oppression of the landless. A land reform programme has to deal with redressing the inequalities between races and ethnicities that came about because of unequal power relations between the colonisers and the colonised. Apparent inequalities in most societies and access to land and other services trigger conflicts, and result in social and economic instability and redundant growth (Hall, 2013; Moyo & Mohamed, 2009; Nel, 2015).

The Balobedu Community and Their Land Claim

The Pan Africanist Congress (PAC) leader, Luthando Mbinda, criticised the government for being slow in the land restitution and redistribution process (SA Links, 2016). On the 16th of April 2016, Mbinda addressed the National Assembly during the debate on the Rural Development and Land Reform Budget Vote and maintained that the land question was at the centre of the struggle for liberation and said he could not understand the reasons behind unsettled claims (Co-Pierre, 2016; More, 2011; SA Links, 2016). Expectations were high that the post-apartheid government would accelerate the restoration of land to its rightful owners/communities who were disposed of their right to land, like the Balobedu community. However, after more than two decades of democracy, the South African government has failed, as evidenced by the few claims that have been settled since they were lodged in 1998.

The Balobedu, like many other communities, has waited for too long for their claim to land to be finalised. It is unfortunate that their claim to land is still to be considered. The delays involved in the land redistribution and restitution are frustrating those who have been waiting for a long time to repossess land that they termed as 'stolen' land. Like Zimbabwe, the target population for land reform is the historically disadvantaged, peasants, who have been denied access to land and were made poor due to the denial of their land rights. The ANC government should seriously consider embarking on a comprehensive land reform to empower these disadvantaged individuals, groups and communities. Land is an asset and a resource, and the restriction of access to land aggravates poverty, particularly for those in the rural areas who depend on land as vital sources of survival and improved livelihood (Akinola, 2018).

Perennial strikes in the mining sector are an indication of a restive population. Calls for resource redistribution have been made in some political circles and have found expression in the ANC's former Youth League president, Julius Malema, who now leads the opposition party, the EFF, which vehemently calls for land expropriation without compensation. It is evident that the ANC accepted the implementation LEWC to score political points due to the ruling party's present loss of popularity across the country.

Major Empirical Findings and Discussion

This study has discussed several social, economic, political and psychological motivations for land reform in contemporary South Africa. The following are the findings on this investigation:

The Need to Reclaim Lost Identity and Culture Due to Land Dispossession

The participants indicated that what pushes them to claim their land was the need to restore their lost identity. One of the participants indicated that:

> We feel useless and not important to be a community without land. Our land is being used by someone to make a living and huge profits yet we are overcrowded here. Our sedentary agriculture way of life has been destroyed. In order to preserve our culture and rebuild our identities, we need to get our land back.

The community feel that they are still to realise the benefits of democracy two decades after its advent. Fanon predicted African governments' failure to give land and other key resources after independence. Fanon (1963) contends that the independent African states will continue to suppress the land needs of poor people, just like the former colonial masters.

Pressure on the Small Residential Pieces of Land

A participant stated:

> Our pieces of land are very small and very skeletal. Due to the size of the land, we only use the land for residential purposes instead of farming.

The participants indicated that it is very difficult to eke out a living from the limited spaces available to them as a community. Much of the land is in the hands of the white minority, mostly in the rural areas, which are underdeveloped. This pushes the communities to demand their land back in their quest for survival.

The Need to Cultivate Crops and Rear Animals

The Balobedu community indicated that they need land so they may cultivate crops and rear animals. As one of the participants indicated:

> We grow maize, rapoko, sorghum, groundnuts, roundnuts and millet. We grow crops and rear animals at the same time but the small portions of land limit us. We survive on subsistence agriculture. At times we produce enough for our families and some for sale like vegetables and small grains like finger millet, sorghum, and nuts (Ditlogo). Some of the crops which we cultivate included tomatoes, bananas, pawpaw, chillies, beans, spinach, mealies, and water melons. These crops give us quick cash for sale or by the roadside for passersby.

The biggest challenge is that the best portions of land are owned by ZZ2, while the community resides in areas of steep slopes and barren soils.

Exclusion of the Locals in the Socio-Economic Spheres

The community in question is completely excluded as far as developing themselves through land is concerned. Land has the potential to alleviate poverty and other social ills in society, hence limited access means stunted development. The community is yet to realise the benefits of democracy more than two decades later (More, 2011), which represents socio-economic exclusion.

The Increase in Poverty Levels Among the Rural Population

The high levels of poverty in the rural areas push people to demand for their land also in order to increase their employment opportunities. Participants indicated that they were completely dispossessed by the apartheid government and have been marginalised by the post-apartheid successive government since 1994, as explained by More (2011). According to the participants, the colonial and apartheid government crafted laws which denied them their land rights, and the opportunity to access productive land. They also strongly hold that the influence of white people is predominant in the post-1994 policies on land and land-related matters. The respondents also decry the manipulative tactics of the political elites that continue to use the land question as instrument of political mobilisation and electoral campaigns.

Some urban dwellers, who have experienced unemployment and hostile city life, returned to the rural areas but found themselves redundant due to a lack of land or productive land to access for farming purposes. Most participants indicated that they were not employed in the cities due to the retrenchments necessitated by the current economic instability confronting South Africa. They indicated that the only way they could survive would be to ensure the return of their ancestral land. However, they are sceptical of the possibility of that happening under the current land reform scheme. A small section of the participants in Balobedu community posits that tenure security is of paramount importance if land beneficiaries are to make productive use of the allocated land or farms. One participant queried, "*How can I invest and care for the land if there are no title deeds?*"

The biggest challenge of the South African land reform programme is the lack of a proper land ownership policy. Government has failed to grant proof of ownerships to those who have been allocated land and others who have laid claim to land in South Africa. The viewpoints of participants are reiterated by Mawoe (2018), who asserts that in pre-colonial African communities, land tenure systems in Africa were shaped by traditions of ancestral lineage. In contemporary Africa, the traditional value system of the indigenous population has been distorted by centuries of colonialism and foreign dominations through modernisation. African culture and traditional practises continue to evolve and change due to cultural interactions, demographic pressures, socio-economic change, and political processes adopted by the African states in their bid to be modern or western.

Conclusion

Land reform is an instrument adopted by the South African government to redress the injustices of apartheid, redistribute land to black South Africans and transform the structural basis of racial inequality. That land reform issue is entrenched in the Constitution and in government policy is a victory for a transformative agenda in South Africa. During the last two decades of democracy, land reform has fallen far short of both public expectations and official targets. Land reform performs an important symbolic function in post-apartheid South Africa, as tangible evidence of a nation addressing historical injustice as part of a wider process of nation-building. It also has the potential to form the centre-piece of a programme of rural restructuring: to transform social and economic relations and provide a structural basis for broad-based pro-poor development initiatives.

The chapter has shown the limitations of the present land policy to achieve the set objectives. This is most obvious in the low hectares of land transferred, land occupations in urban and rural areas, failure to restructure the agricultural economy, which remains dominated by relatively few commercial white-owned farming enterprises alongside millions of small and poorly-funded black farms. There is also evidence of an under-utilisation of land that has been transferred, the continuing abuse and eviction of farm dwellers, the high proportion of non-functioning communal property institutions and the lack of any firm evidence of job creation or poverty alleviation through existing land reform schemes.

Despite the rhetoric of comprehensive land reform programme through the RDP and different White Papers and constitutional provisions for land reform, the land reform programme has had limited success and further legislative interventions, such as forced expropriations, might become necessary. However, in order to legitimise forced expropriations, an amendment to the Constitution is very important. Based on the nature of the state, it remains to be seen whether the current regime will demonstrate the will power to implement the provisions of the reviewed

Constitution and effectively enforce LEWC. Another concern is about the place of the masses and dispossessed in the LEWC programmes.

As expected, there is resistance to the proposed LEWC. Politically, the forces hostile to land reform—within business circles, the agricultural 'establishments' dominated by white commercial farmer organisations, agri-business, conservative academics and even some government officials—have been effective in keeping the radical restructuring of land policy, landholding and the agricultural economy off the policy agenda since 1994. Recent shifts in the perspectives of the ruling party, inspired by the EFF, and the reality of reform failures, have impacted the calls for LEWC. The policy, if implemented, will be a dramatic change from the liberalisation of land reform to the radicalisation of land policy. Current legislation, as indicated earlier, does allow for expropriation without compensation. Already this is a tool that the government could utilise.

As already provided for in the Constitution, various elements of the land reform programme aim at addressing poverty and unemployment, as well as resolving land inequalities and injustices inherited from the past. Despite these, progress, especially in areas such as redistribution and tenure reform, has been generally slow and ineffective, which justifies the demand for policy change. Indeed, the main challenge has been the lack of state capacity to deliver on the policy, as stated in the Constitution. The state therefore has to develop its capacity to deliver on the promise of land reform as provided in the current Constitution and, if eventually adopted, should demonstrate the capacity to implement LEWC. This is required to avoid the Zimbabwean experience.

References

Akinola, A. O. (2018). South African land reform: An appraisal. *Africa Review, 10*(1), 1 16.

Aliber, M. (2013). *Land reform in South Africa and its emerging challenges*. Pretoria: HSRC Press.

Biney, A. (2018). Fanonist 'pitfalls' in the Pan African movement since 1945. *Africa Insight, 48*(3), 1–17.

Binswanger, H. P. (1999). Reflection on land reform and farm size. In C. Eicher & J. Straatz (Eds.), *International agricultural development*. Baltimore, MD: Johns Hopkins University Press.

Chitanga, D. (2018). Land reform and the calculus for power in Zimbabwe's democratic transition. In A. O. Akinola & H. Wissink (Eds.), *Trajectory of land reform in post-colonial African states: The quest for sustainable development and utilization*. Cham: Springer International Publishing.

Co-Pierre, G. (2016). *Why nations fail: The origins of power, prosperity, and poverty*. African Institute for Financial Markets and Risk Management. Cape Town: University of Cape Town.

Cousins, B., & Mahenehene, P. (2013). Land rights conflicts. *Journal of Agrarian Change, 12*(1), 43–59.

Denene, E. (2018, September 22). Land: Access versus ownership. *Farmers Weekly*. Available https://www.farmersweekly.co.za/opinion/blog/letter-from-the-editor/land-access-vs-ownership/.

Fanon, F. (1963). *The wretched of the earth* (Philcox, R., Trans., 2004). Paris: François Maspero édituer.

Gordillo, G. B. F. (1999, May). *Latin American land reforms in the 1990s*. Paper presented at the Workshop on Land: New Context, New Claims, New Concepts, organized by CEDLA, Amsterdam.

Grix, J. (2010). *The foundations of research*. New York: Palgrave Macmillan.

Hall, R. (2013). Farm workers and farm dwellers in Limpopo province, South Africa. *Journal of Agrarian Change, 13*(1), 47–70.

Hall, R. (2014). Land reform and its aftermath in South Africa. *Journal of Agrarian Change, 14*(1), 121–137.

Huxley, T. (1870). On the geographical distribution of the chief modifications of mankind. *Journal of the Ethnological Society of London, 4*, 124–165.

Makhado, R. A. (2012, November). South Africa's land reform debate: Progress and challenges. *SSRN Electronic Journal*.

Mawoe, M. (2018). Land policies in Africa: A case study of Nigeria and Zambia. In A. O. Akinola & H. Wissink (Eds.), *Trajectory of lang reform in post-colonial African states: The quest for sustainable development and utilization*. New York: Springer International Publishing.

More, M. P. (2011). Fanon and the land question in (post) apartheid South Africa. In N. C. Gibson (Ed.), *Living Fanon: Global perspectives*. New York: Palgrave MacMillan.

Moyo, S. (2000). *The political economy of Zimbabwe: Land acquisition and redistribution in Zimbabwe*. Harare: Sapes Books.

Moyo, S. (2005). *Land reform under structural adjustment in Zimbabwe: Land use challenge*. Harare: Sapes Books.

Moyo, S., & Mohamed, F. K. (2009). *Scoping Mission Report: Key tenure issues and reform processes for Sierra Leone*. Report commissioned for the Ministry of Land, Country Planning and the Environment, by the United Nations Development Programme.

Nel, Y. (2015). Land grabs to take off in South Africa. *The Observer*, Polokwane.

Okumbor, J. C. (2010). *Land reform and development. A case study of Manavhela Ben Lavin Nature Reserve, Limpopo province* (Unpublished MA dissertation). University of Limpopo, Turfloop, South Africa.

Pardoe, C. (2006). *Becoming Australian. Before farming and claiming*. Kow Swamp, southern Australia: Correl.

SA Links. (2016) *Land claims in South Africa. The past, present and future*. Cape Town.

Scoones, I., Marongwe, N., Mavedzenge, B., Mahenehene, J., Murimbarimba, F., & Sukume, C. (2010). *Zimbabwe's land reform: Myths and realities*. Cape Town: James Currey.

South African History Online. (2018). *Grade 11 - Apartheid South Africa 1940s to 1960s*. Available https://www.sahistory.org.za/article/grade-11-apartheid south-africa-1940s-1960s.

Valente, C. (2008). *Land redistribution in South Africa: A Q2 analysis of its impact on beneficiaries' welfare*. Bristol, UK: University of Bristol.

Yingi, L. (2019). The chasm between sexes in accessing land and its produce: The case of rural women in Zimbabwe. In A. O. Akinola & H. Wissink (Eds.), *The trajectory of land reform in post-Cclonial African states: The quest for sustainable development and utilization*. Cham: Springer International Publishing.

CHAPTER 9

Small-Scale Farming, Fourth Industrial Revolution and the Quest for Agriculture Development

Luyanda Mtshali and Adeoye O. Akinola

Introduction

South Africa has a dual agricultural economy, with both well-developed commercial farming and small-scale communal or individual farming. Agriculture contributes a relatively small share of the total Gross Domestic Product (GDP). Moreover, it is important to note that it provides employment and earning foreign exchange. According to the South African Yearbook 2008/9, the commercial agricultural sector has grown by approximately 14% per year since 1970, and the total economy has grown by 14.5% over the same period, but, by 2008, agriculture's share of the GDP has declined to 2.5% (Burger, 2019). In 2017, the sector's contribution to the GDP was 2.4%, and the South African economy grew by 1.3% (South African Government, 2019).

L. Mtshali · A. O. Akinola (✉)
University of Zululand, Kwadlangezwa, South Africa
e-mail: AkinolaA@unizulu.ac.za; aoakinola@uj.ac.za

A. O. Akinola et al. (eds.), *The New Political Economy of Land Reform in South Africa*,
https://doi.org/10.1007/978-3-030-51129-6_9

Over the past few years, smallholders' involvement in food production and their contribution to economic stability and social security has become important. The government, which has invested in small-scale farming, believes that food security depends on smallholder agricultural development, which is vital for economic sustainability. Aside from the efforts to empower small-scale farmers, it is important to ensure the long-term efficiency of the land, such as effective cultivation of land, crops profitability and the well-being of farmworkers, as well as security for farmers.

During the first industrial revolution, agriculture and other industries used coal, water and steam engine, mechanical products equipment. The second revolution involved a division of labour, evolution of electricity and mass production; and the development of machines did enhance productivity and effective processing of agricultural by-products at a faster rate. With more demand for food due to population growth, the Third Industrial Revolution advanced into electronics, Information Technology (IT) and automated products. While this altered the economic foundation of developing countries, the Fourth Industrial Revolution (4IR), characterized by cyber-physical system and use of Infrared Receivers (IR) will have more of an impact on the agricultural sector in developing countries like South Africa.

Before the introduction of 4IR, the agricultural and land sector has been confronted with the challenge of meeting the target of transferring 30% of land, under the control of white people, through the apartheid's system of land dispossession, back to black people. This is to be achieved through the three elements of land reform: land restitution, land redistribution and land tenure. Up to the present, only 3% of that land has been redistributed. Based on the historical disempowerment of the black people, emerging farmers solely depend on the government for the provision of land or farms, through the willing buyer, willing seller approach, and other supporting structures required for land productivity.

Farms, however, are struggling, and many have been abandoned due to the absence of support systems and a lack of the required skills to manage big farms. Many of the black beneficiaries who have been granted land, and/or farms have no title deeds. The black farmers are operating under dire financial constraints and they have limited access to bank loans. Thus, how such groups will effectively be a participant in the 4IR remains a great concern.

Questions continue to be raised about the continued inability of the state to address the prevailing violence and socio-economic inequality in South African society. Land reform, which was conceived as an instrument for the development of the rural poor, has not significantly improved household poverty among black people. Effective land reform is one of the best ways to close the inequality gap and enhance the productivity of small-scale farming. Therefore, the chapter examines the implication of 4IR on black farmers and the feasibility of embracing 4IR in the agricultural sector amidst the prevalent challenges associated with land reform failures.

Understanding Concepts: Emerging Farmers and Fourth Industrial Revolution (4IR)

In literature, there is no consensus concerning the definition of 'emerging farmers', therefore, the terms 'smallholder', 'emerging', 'small-scale' and 'family', 'peasant' farmers are used interchangeably. The National Department of Agriculture (NDA) and Department Agriculture, Forestry and Fisheries (DAFF) observed emerging farmers as the previously underprivileged farmers who were anticipated to become commercial farmers (Lee, 2017). Many of them have become farm workers under the employment of commercial farmers, proving the inequality in the sector.

The Department of Agriculture, Forestry and Fisheries (DAFF, 2012: 1) conceptualizes "smallholder" farmers as those with limited resource support relative to commercial farmers. Additionally, smallholder farmers are well defined as those farmers owning limited plots of land, compared to the commercial farmers, on which they grow crop for their own consumption and one or two cash crops, and depending completely on family labour (DAFF, 2012: 1). There are other explanations of small-scale farmers and the definition varies depending on the understanding of the writer.

AgriSETA (2010) defines 'emerging farmers' as those who may be striving to move from subsistence farming to a more commercial model, those who have benefited from land reform processes and want to establish an agricultural enterprise on the land that has been allocated to them, and those who have benefitted from the Black Economic Empowerment (BEE) funding to acquire a stake in a farm and are trying to achieve profitability.

The Fourth Industrial Revolution reflects the overwhelming coming together of technology, namely artificial intelligence (AI), robotics, the 'Internet of Things' (IoT), 3D printing, biotechnology, nanotechnology, autonomous vehicles, quantum computing and energy storage, among others. The cyber-physical systems, vital fundamental features of the 4IR, are not limited to the unification of employees working on their delegated duties using software, hardware and additional tools, including AI (Baldassari & Roux, 2017).

Globalization and its attendant development of information and communication technology (ICT) become the foundation upon which 4IR is erected. The 4IR is aimed at drastically increasing farm and industrial productivity and agricultural efficiency by producing more, at a shorter period of time. However, there are concerns that 4IR will result in job losses in vital sectors, including the agricultural industry, and black South Africans will be the great losers. Furthermore, the integration of emerging farmers into the industrial revolution will be very challenging.

The eruption of internet-centric data flow, global competitiveness and digital tools has been well discovered by different authors, such as Klaus Schwab, who is a well-known economist (Hwang, 2016). Schwab explicitly grouped together all these features of technology into physical autonomous vehicles, and advanced robotics, and 3D printing as digitalization technicalities. Moreover, the IoT, for storage of data, would be useful to keep up with daily updates about each mechanism.

The 4IR is not limited to help with improving the quality of health, such as genetic trends and sequencing, synthetic biology, genetic engineering and editing of genes to prevent diseases. The abstractness of these gigantic transformation is obvious, but the 4IR gives rise to practical preparation and application of developments and enhancing of the existing technology.

The 4IR is characterized by the following farm management software:

> Precision agriculture and predictive data analytics; Sensors that help farmers to collect data and to monitor crop health, weather and soil quality; Animal data (software and hardware aimed at better understanding livestock, from breeding patterns to genomics); Robotics and drones; Smart irrigation; Next-generation farms, where technology is used to provide alternative farming methods to enable farming in locations that previously could not support traditional agriculture; and Marketplaces (technological platforms

that connect farmers directly to suppliers or consumers). (WCDoA & USB, 2018: 10)

Although the 4IR is observed as being determined by extreme computerization and extreme connectivity, this has shown more progress and evidence that the upheaval consequential from the 4IR is not only from technology. This has also to do with demographic shifts, macroeconomic trends and globalization (Baweja, Donovan, Haefele, Siddiqi, & Smiles, 2016). Furthermore, the World Economic Forum (2016: v) notes that the "technological revolution are sets of broader socio-economic, geopolitical and demographic drivers of change, each interacting in multiple directions and intensifying one another".

Background to the Study

In contemporary South Africa, agriculture is facing major and various challenges, such as droughts, policy uncertainty, consumer trends and activism, competitiveness of merchandisers and value chains. Furthermore, there is a fall in investment and financial support from government, which negatively impacts the quest of the black small-scale farmers to embrace mechanised farming and be technological advanced as required by 4IR. The increased regulation of agro-food systems has aggravated policy uncertainty, while natural disasters, as a result of climatic change, have manifested in water shortages and droughts, such as in agriculturally buoyant are like Cape Town and the Western Cape province, in general (CDKN, 2012). Moreover, the issues of skills acquisition or the lack thereof have limited the output of black farmers, who are predominantly uneducated.

Public and policy discourse in the country have been dominated by the prospects of using the 4IR to achieve agricultural sustainability through the transformation of small-scale farming systems. The notion of sustainability has been elucidated by various authors with different interpretations. However, sustainable development is the progress established to meet the present needs without compromising the capability of future generations to meet their own needs, depending on their differences and essentials at that time (IISD, 2020). Moreover, Groenewald (2002: 4) observes that, besides the setting and the nature of sustainability, the most important objective of sustainable agriculture and rural development is most based on food production increases, and sustainable manners to enhance food production for the unforeseeable future. Food security in the country also depends on the growth of small-scale farming, which is one of the targets of the 4IR.

The Department of Agriculture introduced the Comprehensive Agricultural Support Programme (CASP) to facilitate the growth of smallholder farmers. CASP is a post-apartheid settlement support programme for the beneficiaries of land reform in South Africa and the 'previously disadvantaged' who acquired land through private means. The programme aimed at information and knowledge management in the farming industry, the use of technical and advisory assistance, responding well to the financial mechanisms and investing more on the training and capacity building, expanding the marketing and business development in rural areas and lastly improving farming infrastructures required to produce quality product. In reality,

> Emerging and small farmers often lack economies of scale. Their production prospects are negatively influenced by insufficient access to land, which in turn affects their access to credit, technology and other resources. Lower production volumes translate to lower bargaining power with large buyers, and the ability to compete for a better price. (Malan, 2018)

Small-scale farmers may lack the required skills needed for packaging of their products and this could cause mechanical damages and food to spoil. It also limits the quality of their products and their marketability. Indeed, the majority of consumers are mindful of the appearance of farm produce before buying it, which is why there are so many retailers selling the same products but of different quality (Raleting, 2011: 68). Therefore, without access to modern technology (which many new farmers cannot afford because of its high cost), small-scale farmers will struggle to benefit from 4IR. A report rightly notes that while

> the cost of technology is decreasing worldwide, yet South Africa remains a net importer of most technologies. Cultivars and seed are often protected by patents and plant breeders' rights owned by large global companies, making local access more expensive. (WCDoA & USB, 2018: 3)

There is also a concern over disaster management between the government and Department of Agriculture, especially when it comes to drought and funds to support small-scale farmers. The full embrace of 4IR will result in more demand for electricity and extensive use of machines and robots.[1] Therefore, the issue of energy security needs to be improved through renewable energy sources. Over the years, South Africa has experienced power outages nationwide, tagged 'load-shedding'. These energy issues are even worse in the rural areas. Electricity outages are a common occurrence because municipalities are unable to pay the national power agency, Eskom, while cases of stolen cables exacerbate the issue. On the other hand, in some areas, drought has threatened the farming industry in the past few years, particularly in Cape Town. Small-scale farmers are most vulnerable to climatic changes, lack of finance and access to land and depleting farm infrastructures. Without government intervention, small-scale farmers will battle to survive in a 4IR-driven agriculture industry (Wolfert et.al., 2017).

Fourth Industrial Revolution and Agriculture Development

Literature reveals that agricultural production plays an important role in rural development, particularly with respect to household food and nutrition security (Aliber & Hart, 2009). Agriculture has a multiplier effect that stimulates national and rural economy. Over the decades, farmers have played an essential role in addressing challenges across the world. Many countries rely on commercial farming, but the place of small-scale farming cannot be undermined. Indeed, the smallholder farming sector is the backbone and precondition for political and socio-economic development, if adequately supported by effective policy.

The Agricultural Research Council (1990: 3) was established through the Agricultural Research Act (Act no. 86 of 1990) to: Promote sustainability and equitable economic participation in the agricultural sector; promote agriculture development and growth in related industries; facilitate sector skills development and knowledge management; facilitate and ensure natural conservation; promote national food security, and contribute to a better quality of life. Evaluating the existing policies in relation to agricultural productivity, it was found that emerging black farmers are confronted by challenges that are outside the purview of the

[1] According to Sung (2018: 11), robots can be defined as "intelligent agricultural production systems that can minimize human intervention, control themselves, and maximize efficiency".

government. There are spaces for non-state actors to occupy, which could lead to a bridge of the gap between white and black farmers. However, both have always accused the government of favouring one group over the other. Therefore, available literature holds that the implementation of government has led to an uneven spatial supply of agricultural products by both white (majorly commercial farmers) and black farmers (predominantly emerging farmers). The 4IR is expected to bridge this gap through public-private partnerships.

South Africa's agricultural economy can be enhanced by accommodating 4IR in the sector, particularly the use of robots to drive performance. Robots and Artificial Intelligence (AI) can be engaged for improved productivity in different areas of the farming industry. The three aim at improving productivity through computerization (otherwise known as automation), which would involve unmanned farming systems, leading to the promotion of eco-friendly farming (Sung, 2018). The advancement of technology has to be securitized and well-organized to accommodate deserving farmers and integrate emerging farmers through agriculture policies.

Research and innovation organizations (both public and private) are essential to deliver the required support by covering agro-processing, knowledge management, biotechnology, engineering, natural resources (soil, water, climate), and biometry services agricultural information. The research output is passed on to farmers (commercial and small-scale) through a number of trainings and extension to enhance their skills and supports probability to compete.

The 4IR will have a major impact on the agricultural sector and this will be through the rationalization of the current problems and resolving many challenges of agriculture. Agriculture is a representative industry in which inputs and outputs are unpredictable due to its nature its shortcomings, such as drought. Farming, in a modern era, requires expertise. Some chemicals are harmful when they are not well-monitored, managed and used accordingly, which is very common among untrained farmers. Even though training for the farmers in preparation for 4IR will be available, it is unclear how emerging farmers will be integrated into this process. Through 4IR, problems concerning constructing an optimized agricultural associate end production can be eliminated, while distribution and consumption will be enhanced.

Whilst it is challenging to give a precise picture of what the agriculture sector will look like in the next 20–35 years, one thing is clear: the global population explosion will trigger unprecedented technological development of the agricultural sector. This will engender fervent competition among farmers. Small-scale farmers will find it challenging to compete with commercial farmers.

Population growth has contributed to climate change, which has negatively affected the quality of soil, in its richness and fertility. Furthermore, water degradation is a challenge to farmers. While seawater is being utilized presently by some farmers, many do not have access to such resources. This further calls for new agricultural technologies to tackle these problems.

According to BBrief (2019), there is a need to increase government performances on agriculture and resolve existing challenges before embracing 4IR, which requires more commitments from all stakeholders, particularly from the government. The government must demonstrate the political will to make small-scale farmers benefit from 4IR. The first call for the South African government is how to resolve the land question and accelerate the pace of land reform. Despite the implementation of the three elements of land reform (restitution, redistribution and land tenure) in the country, the spatial distribution of farms and land distribution remained unchanged, without benefiting rural farmers, while land inequalities continue unabated.

Apart from the general inequality between the white and black people, in respect of land relations, there are also discriminating practises against women. Thus, South Africa's land and agricultural sector is characterized by both racial and gender inequality. To curtail these, the national and provincial Department of Agriculture (DOA) is trying to develop policies and programmes to support those who were previously disadvantaged. Gender and gender dynamics inherent in agricultural production need to be taken into account if women farmers are not to continue being marginalized members of the rural development community. The government has made provisions for the development of agriculture in the Constitution and other document policies on land such as the 1997 White Paper on Land Reform. These policy templates addressed the plights of small-scale farmers. Also, the policies have expanded their scope to helping commercially oriented black farmers grow their business by partnering with foreign countries in the area of products' exchange and other means of engagement in progressive agricultural sectors.

Developed countries, such as the United States and Japan, are trying to resolve issues in agricultural through mechanization, automation, and the modernization of farming practises (Sung, 2018). They lead in the 4IR, which has developed the scale and commercialization of agriculture in their countries. In response to this movement, future agriculture is predicted to evolve into features of 4IR, like high-tech businesses where systems are joined with artificial intelligence and data (Lee, 2017). The systems will congregate into a single unit in which farm machinery, farm management, production forecasting, seeding the soil and irrigation are combined (Lee, 2017). The use of the core technology of the 4IR namely, big data, artificial intelligence (AI) and robots will be integrated with agriculture to make a new era of superfusion in the farming industry. The era will advance multifaceted social, economic and ethical values combined with various industries and expressed in business models. The introduction of the 4IR to agriculture will serve different levels of farmers and also address their existing challenges before attempting to implement transformation and change (Lee, 2017).

Hart and Aliber (2010) maintained that the support provided by the South African government to smallholder farmers promotes the acceptance of new technologies, but has failed to pay attention to the variety of farmers in a range of the circumstances they face every day. In order for new technology to be integrated into a farming system, there must be a profound consideration for the implication of the new technology and how it will affect black farmers. To fully utilize the technology, the farmers need access not only to land, but to education, funding and training. Furthermore, the technologies should align with their farming needs and cover appropriate agricultural extension support.

In general, black farmers, including men and women, are confronted with a range of cultural and socio-economic factors that limits their economic opportunities. For instance, low levels of education have limited their ability to take advantage of modern technology. Therefore, simply including women as beneficiaries of land-related projects or agricultural endeavours will not redress the inequality they experience; there is a need to remove all obstacles impeding their quest for viable farming enterprises. For example, women have restricted access to agricultural funding, which could have empowered them for land productivity. The 2009 General Household Survey (GHS) revealed the diverse challenges women farmers encounter in accessing the relevant supports from government and non-state organizations (Hart & Aliber, 2010).

Access to Land

The impact of policy application in South Africa has been mostly similar to that of many other countries worldwide, although one feature differentiates South Africa from others. This is the widespread racialization of land ownership and the inability of the reform agenda to redress this inequality. During the apartheid dispensation, white people owned 87% of land and only 13% was owned by black people (Akinola, 2018). Despite the fact that land is an important resource for agricultural development, access to land is dominated by white commercial farmers.

The South African government has only given small areas, like two hectares or less, to smallholder farmers, which accounts for their unequal access to land and low agricultural productivity. Despite government's implementation of market-led agrarian reform, the white farmers' dominance of land still persists. Evidently, land redistribution, through the willing buyer, willing seller approach, has proven to be ineffective, due to the inadequate financial allocation to the land, and non-involvement of alternative assistance from non-state agencies and institutions (Lahiff, 2008). According to BFAP BASELINE (2018), the access to land in South Africa is a burning political, development and emotional issue. Policy uncertainty is one of the greatest challenges facing South African agriculture at present, in relation to the implementation of land reform policies. In particular, the prospect of expropriation without compensation has raised many questions among stakeholders in the field of agriculture and land reform. Overall, the implementation of strategies and programmes on land reform has been poor and farmers (both small-scale and commercial) and other targets of the reform are becoming pessimistic because of poor government performance (Akinola, 2018).

Even though agriculture supports more than 530 million people in Africa, majority continue to face diverse challenges, limiting their productivity (AU-NEPAD, 2013). During apartheid, the white commercial farmers occupied fertile agricultural lands with appropriate resources, while black farmers who were alienated to former homelands possessed infertile and fallow land; this situation still persists more than two decades after majority rule.

Resolving the issue of land, and adopting 4IR without proper procedure during the formulation and implementation processes of land reform policy framework, which supports growth and food security, can generate negative consequences. As discussed, the prevailing land reforms are the product of the discriminatory land policies of the past. It is important that land reform supports the core of the commercial agricultural sector, which is a key driving force of the economy and food security in the country. The current political rhetoric regarding land expropriation without compensation has affected investment in the agricultural sector significantly and impeded the development of the agricultural sector. The decline in exports is a result of voluminous imports to South Africa, and with this the jobs in high-value export positioned crops could be lost in the short-term and result in female and male farmworkers losing their jobs (BFAP BASELINE, 2018).

Education

As expounded by Hart and Aliber (2010), there are low levels of education among black South Africans, both male and female. This is a concern for the advancement of science and technology in the agricultural industry. The government's plans to train uneducated farmers on how to use modern machines and apply technology to growing plants will be a huge challenge. Some commercial farmers, especially in KwaZulu-Natal are well-disposed to developing skills and technology training to emerging black farmers, but the unstable relationship between the two groups has negatively impacted on the success of such engagement. Furthermore, the new technologies, including genetically modified input and biotechnology that are useful for emerging commercial farmers, require new management skills, which are mostly lacking. The small-scale farmers seem to be competing, without success, with the commercial farmers when it comes to product quality and access to bank loans, let alone the process of transporting their harvest to market points. As a result, education and training of small-scale black farmers will be needed to boost their coping skills, especially as 4IR prepares farmers to engage in the more sophisticated world of technology, through the input and output markets.

Tripp (2001) argued that based on the variety of rural households, the development and delivery of technology and innovation programmes (4IR) is not a certain answer to rural development to change the agriculture sectors.

The Question of Extension Services and Support System

Both government and non-governmental organizations have failed to deliver adequate support for farming and to provide the required resources to develop the agricultural sector. The most affected are the emerging farmers who are still struggling financially and unable to market their farm produce. Farmers' competence and productivity can be facilitated mostly by the effectiveness and efficiency of the strategies to combat the challenges experienced by emerging farmers in the rural areas.

According to Makhura and Mokoena (2001: 455), agriculture industries are challenged by vast threats, such as black farmers encounter difficulties when they attempt to access agricultural markets, and, as a result, product quality is affected, produce is damaged or rotten. Resolutions to such challenges require thorough review and systems that will be workable to change the lives of black farmers. Moreover, emerging farmers in the underdeveloped rural areas in South Africa struggle to participate in commercial markets because of a variety of constraints, such as farming skills, lack of equipment and access to credit (Wynne & Lyne, 2003: 566). The author notes that the primary problems emanate the information irregularities in business contracts and proceed to farm markets, which influences the effectiveness of small-scale farmers to engage in the production in food. However, the complicity involved in maintaining transparency in contracts related to joint-ventures engenders high transactional expenditures that negatively affected small-scale farmers (Mbatha & Antrobus, 2008). Government supports of commercial farming and undermining of small-scale farming continue to express itself in unequal access to resources and gaps in agricultural efficiency.

Exploring joint-ventures may be the future practice for empowering black farmers but, it is important to study its usefulness under the 4IR and its reality in South Africa. Both small-scale and commercial farmers may have similar interests in agricultural business, but they face different realities. Therefore, the adoption of joint-ventures should not be taken as a universal approach but subjected to specific cases.

Agriculture uses 70% of the world's freshwater resources (FAO, 2017: 1). In most developing countries, including South Africa, with less water investment, new technologies, techniques and methods are required. Without government intervention and support, only the commercial farmers have the capacity to access these opportunities, while emerging farmers have no financial wherewithal and logistic capacity to benefit from the utilization of new technology that creates access to water resources. With proper planning and government supports, rural farmers stand to benefits from 4IR.

Smallholders, Value Chains and Markets

The adoption of diverse farming methods to grow different crops will involve new marketing strategies. Thus, it might be difficult to copy foreign practises without an attempt to domesticate the process. The commercial agriculture industry has existed for centuries, with about 90% of global population engaged in agriculture. Additional, more than 80% of the populations of OECD main countries are involved in the farming industry (Lee, 2017). However, presently, only 2–3% of the global population are involved in agriculture. In South Africa, the majority of the youth are engaged in other productive activities and not willing to engage in land-related endeavours or agriculture (Akinola, 2018). According to Lee (2017), in the Republic of Korea, for example, more than 50% of the population of farmers in some households are over 60 years old, and over 40% are over 65. Also, the global working population, comprising mostly of youth, has diverted from agriculture to manufacturing business and manufacturing service industries. Thus, in the present world economy, only 5% of the world's population are workings in agriculture, yet it supplies for more than 60% of the world's business.

Conclusion

The chapter has located the land and agriculture discourse in the broader spectrum of the fourth industrial revolution in South Africa. Indeed, there are policy gaps in the land and agricultural sector, which must be addressed before the implementation of 4IR in the agricultural sector. Land reform expert, locally and internationally, should re-engage towards resolving the complexity around the land question. The viability of the agricultural sector depends of the success of a land reform scheme. Therefore, a comprehensive land reform programme, that specifically enhances small-scale farming and also protects commercial farming, has to be formulated and implemented. The government should strengthen public-private partnerships (PPP), specifically in the interests of smaller-scale producers. This may become necessary to bridge the gap between African emerging farmers and their privileged white commercial farmers, who have strategically positioned themselves as the beneficiaries of 4IR.

Before extending 4IR to the agriculture sector, there should be concerted efforts to support and develop small-scale farmers towards focusing on all subdivisions of business activities in the agriculture sector. Small-scale farmers must be trained in the value chain and market analysis, storage, transportation, commercialization, production and sales (including online platforms), market access, partnership formation, business and financial management before any effort to join the 4IR. Moreover, farmers should be allowed to participate in decision-making processes that affect their daily activities on the farms. Part of the problem in South Africa is the changes in reform agenda and policy implementation due to the ruling elite's different perspective about agriculture and the place of small-scale farming in the broad agenda for agricultural development. The apartheid policy triggered the imbalanced spatial distribution of farms by different farmers, while post-apartheid has failed to significantly restructure the divided agricultural landscapes that delivered resources based on racial considerations. The result is the prevailing domination of the white people over black people.

Therefore, the government has a responsibility to revisit the land reform programmes, and empower all the stakeholders in the agricultural sector, before introducing 4IR as the assured path to sustainable agricultural development. Some farmers are not familiar with the concept of the 4IR and they do not have full knowledge on the impact of the 4IR in the agricultural ecosystem. It is necessary to engage in mass enlightenment of farmers and analyse the impacts of 4IR on all aspects of agriculture, and on rural and agricultural life as a whole. The government should create a synergy between existing practises and 4IR towards building a sustainable farming community driven by state-of-the-art technology. Thus, agricultural technology and farming skills will be advanced and there will be new, sustainable opportunities for farmers.

References

Agricultural Research Council. (1990). *Agricultural Research Act 86 of 1990*. Available https://www.arc.agric.za/Documents/Agricultural%20Research%20Act%20%2086%20of%201990.pdf.

AgriSETA. (2010). *Sectoral analysis agriculture*. Available https://www.agriseta.co.za/downloads/news/AGRISETA_Sector_Analysis_290610-version_2.pdf.

Akinola, A. O. (2018). South African land reform: An appraisal. *Africa Review, 10*(1), 1–16.

Aliber, M., & Hart, T. G. B. (2009). Should subsistence agriculture be supported as a strategy to address rural food insecurity? *Agrekon, 48*(4), 434–458.

AU-NEPAD. (2013). *Agriculture in Africa: Transformation and outlook*. Johannesburg: New Partnership for Africa Development.

Baldassari, P., & Roux, J. D. (2017). Industry 4.0: Preparing for the future of work. *People & Strategy, 40*(3), 20–23.

Baweja, B., Donovan, P., Haefele, M., Siddiqi, L., & Smiles, S. (2016). *Extreme automation and connectivity: The global, regional, and investment implications of the fourth industrial revolution*. UBS White Paper for the World Economic Forum Annual Meeting 2016. Available https://www.ubs.com/global/en/about_ubs/follow_ubs/highlights/davos-2016.html.

BFAP BASELINE. (2018). *Agricultural Outlook 2018–2027*. Available http://www.bfap.co.za/wp-content/uploads/2018/08/FAPBaseline-2018.pdf.

Burger, D. (Ed.). (2019). *South African Yearbook 2008/9*. Available http://www.gcis.gov.za/resource_centre/sa_info/yearbook/2008-09.html.

CDKN. (2012). *Managing climate extremes and disasters in the agriculture sector: Lessons from the IPCC SREX report*. Climate and Development Knowledge Network. Available www.cdkn.org/srex.

Department of Agriculture, Forestry and Fisheries (DAFF). (2012). *The framework of the zero hunger programme*. Pretoria: Department of Agriculture, Forestry and Fisheries.

FAO. (2017). *Water for sustainable food and agriculture: A report produced for the G 20 presidency of Germany*. Rome: Food and Agricultural Organisation.

Hart, T., & Aliber, M. (2010). The need for an engendered approach to agricultural technology. *Agenda: Empowering Women for Gender Equity, 84*, 75–90.

Hwang, J. S. (2016, July). The Fourth Industrial Revolution (industry 4.0): Intelligent manufacturing. *SMT Magazine*, pp. 10–15. Available http://www.magazines007.com/pdf/SMTJuly201.

International Institute for Sustainable Development (IISD). (2020). *Sustainable development*. Available https://www.iisd.org/topic/sustainable-development.

Lahiff, E. (2008). *Land reform in South Africa: A status report 2008* (Programme for Land and Agrarian Studies, Research Report No. 38, pp. 1–49).

Lee, J. R. (2017). *The Fourth Industrial Revolution and future agriculture* (200 ed.). Science and Technology Policy Institute.

Lee, Y. B. (2017). *Convergence of agriculture R&D and 4th Industrial Revolution* (1st ed). Jeonju, Republic of Korea: SY Ra.

Makhura, M., & Mokoena, M. (2001). *Market access for small-scale farmers in South Africa*. Pietermaritzburg: University of Natal Press.

Malan, N. (2018, December 9). The new agriculture and developing emerging farmers: Harnessing the Fourth Industrial Revolution. *Daily Maverick*. Available https://www.dailymaverick.co.za/article/2018-12-09-the-new-agriculture-and-developing-emerging-farmers-harnessing-the-fourth-industrial-revolution/.

Mbatha, C. N., & Antrobus, G. G. (2008). Institutions and economic research: A case of location externalities on agricultural resource allocation in the Kat River basin, South Africa. *Agrekon, 47*(4), 470–491.

Raleting, P. M. (2011). An investigation of institutional factors influencing vegetable production amongst small-scale farmers in Central Eastern Cape: A case of six vegetable projects in the Nkonkobe Local Municipality. *Doctoral Dissertation*. University of Fort Hare.

Republic of South Africa. (2019). *Agriculture*. Available www.gov.za/about-sa/agriculture.

South African Government. (2019). *Agriculture, land reform and rural development*. Available https://www.gov.za/about-sa/agriculture.

Sung, J. (2018). The Fourth Industrial Revolution and precision agriculture. In S. Hussmann (Ed.), *Automation in agriculture—Securing food supplies for future generations*. Available http://dx.doi.org/10.5772/intechopen.71582.

The Western Cape Department of Agriculture and University of Stellenbosch Business School (WCDoA and USB). (2018). *The future of the Western Cape agricultural sector in the context of the Fourth Industrial Revolution* (Synthesis report). Available https://www.usb.ac.za/wp-content/uploads/2018/07/THE-FUTURE-OF-THE-WC-AGRICULTURAL-SECTOR-IN-THE-CONTEXT-OF-4IR-FINAL-REP.pdf.

Tripp, R. (2001). Agricultural technology policies for rural development. *Development Policy Review, 19*(4), 479–489.

Wolfert, S., Ge, L., Lan, G., Verdouw, C., & Bogaardt, M. (2017). Big data in smart farming—A review. *Agricultural Systems, 153*, 69–80.

World Economic Forum. (2016). *The future of jobs: Employment, skills and workforce strategy for the Fourth Industrial Revolution*. Available http://www3.weforum.org/docs/WEF_Future_of_Jobs.

Wynne, A. T., & Lyne, M. C. (2003). An empirical analysis of factors affecting the growth of small-scale poultry enterprises in KwaZulu-Natal. *Development Southern Africa, 20*(5), 563–578.

CHAPTER 10

Rural Land Reform and Local Economic Development Through Agri-Parks: A Case Study of Harry Gwala Municipality in KwaZulu-Natal

Sultan Khan

Introduction

Rural land reform and local economic development (LED) are inextricable concepts linked to the post-apartheid South African land debacle. It is at the centre of most contemporary political debates on the issue of land reform without compensation. Colonialism, and later apartheid, supported the dispossession of large tracks of rural land to promote white privilege in the agricultural sector. Over the years, it has caused deep emotional wounds, which continue to manifest more than two decades after democracy. As a consequence of past land dispossession, it has been

S. Khan (✉)
University of KwaZulu-Natal, Durban, South Africa
e-mail: Khans@ukzn.ac.za

A. O. Akinola et al. (eds.), *The New Political Economy of Land Reform in South Africa*,
https://doi.org/10.1007/978-3-030-51129-6_10

a source of inequality, poverty and unemployment, which is most prevalent in the rural areas of the country, wherein most of these agricultural sectors are located.

In the wake of contemporary debates on land expropriation without compensation (LEWC), white people in the rural agricultural sector are concerned about their future and the viability of sustaining their agri-businesses should expropriation of land without compensation be implemented (Gerber, 2018). Nevertheless, white privilege in the agri-business sector has, over many years, provided thousands of jobs, been a catalyst in promoting the commercial sector allied to agri-business and, above all, been the foremost 'breadbasket' of the nation and the region. Given the uncertainty confronting rural agri-businesses and the concomitant exodus of white farmers from the country, there is an aura of food insecurity surrounding LEWC, especially considering its failure elsewhere on the African continent. The most cited case in contemporary times is Zimbabwe, where rural land reform failed, resulting in a national economic catastrophe (Gumede, 2018; Sedumedi, 2012: 10–11).

One of the foremost questions that can be asked in the South African context is whether rural land reform can be used as a positive measure to stimulate LED. What international models can be adapted to stimulate the industrialisation of the South African rural areas? Can these international models stimulate LED amongst emerging rural farmers? These are some of the questions that need to be answered in examining rural land reform and the opportunity it presents for LED. The chapter focuses on the Harry Gwala Development Agency (HGDA) located in the province of KwaZulu-Natal, wherein rural land reforms are underway and LED is being promoted through Agri-parks.

LED and Land Reform as Catalyst to Stimulate Rural Development

Rural areas, by their very nature, are endowed with natural resources (vegetation, flora, minerals, precious stones and fauna amongst others). Aside from their low population density, this does not mean that natural resources are not subjected to degradation through uncontrolled, informal and unmanaged economic activities. Due to poor service delivery in the rural areas, there has been increased pressure on the natural resources, leading to severe deforestation and overgrazing, soil erosion and surface water degradation (Nkomo, 2013: ii). In order to reduce pressure on natural resources, it becomes imperative that service delivery to rural communities is provided. Although rural inhabitants place pressure on natural resources, big enterprises such as mining use technologically advanced methods to harvest resources from these areas. Often it is characterised by untold and irreversible damage to the environment.

Notwithstanding such practices, the availability and preservation of natural resources in different forms present an opportunity for LED through industrialisation. Considering that rural areas are endowed with valuable natural resources, it is not surprising that the urban centres and national entrepreneurs play a parasitic role by extracting raw material through commercial means. Living in an era of globalisation, even multinational companies are complicit in exploiting the vast natural resources available in rural areas.

There is comprehensive literature about the state of development in rural areas. Poverty, diseases, homelessness, lack of basic infrastructure and unemployment are a few of the social ills prevalent in rural areas. In many underdeveloped and developing countries, arresting rural social and economic ills are beyond the fiscal capability of nation states. One way of coping with the development impasse is by stimulating rural development through LED programmes and projects. In many respects, rural areas are known to be the food basket for locals, big cities and the globe, although the remittances filtering back into its economy may be negligible.

LED in recent times has gained much popularity amongst policy makers and practitioners engaged in rural development. It has been widely practised in several nations, such as India, Brazil, Puerto Rico, Kenya and the Philippines, to mention a few, with marked degree of success. As a concept, it is known to be elusive, with multiple definitions depending on the context, area of focus and locality. However, when applied to a rural context, it is more than just a group of networks and interaction that involves both the state and the private sector. LED refers to a participatory process which encourages social dialogue and public-private partnerships in a defined geographical area. It enables local stakeholders to jointly design and implement a development strategy which fully exploits local resources and capacities, and makes best use of the area's comparative advantages (ILO, 2003, in South African LED Network, n.d.).

According to the World Bank (2003: 7), LED is the "process by which public, business and the non-governmental sector partners work collectively to create better conditions for economic growth and employment generation with the aim of improving the quality of life for all". Similarly, the UNHABITAT (2003: 1) defines LED as,

> A participatory process where local people from all sectors work together to stimulate local commercial activity resulting in a resilient and sustainable economy. It is a tool to help create decent jobs and improve the quality of life for everyone, including the poor and marginalized.

This is achievable through various strategies, such as the municipality having their own business support centres, and through initiatives like cooperatives (small business often owned by the public) that are encouraged by government, and through a development agency (Mthimkhulu, 2015: 11).

LED differs from traditional development strategies. While traditional development strategies tend to adopt sector-wide approaches to development, LED focuses on a territorial approach, targeting the development of a region or locality, rather than an industrial sector. In traditional forms, the development strategy is often known to be top-down, characterised by centralised control by the state. The central government decides where local economic intervention is needed. Inputs from local people and communities in LED programmes and projects are driven from below and advocate the need for promoting economic development in all areas.

In essence, LED allows for equal and active participation of local stakeholders in the formulation of development strategies, making them better tailored to local needs. Fundamentally, LED becomes a process in which partnerships between local governments, community-based groups and the private sector are established to manage existing resources to create jobs and stimulate the economy of a well-defined territory (Zikhali et al., 2014: 27). While LED has at its core an economic focus, its goal is ultimately to achieve a sustainable pattern of development, inclusive of economic, social and environmental issues (Ariatti, 2013: 12).

In the rural context, LED programmes and projects are known to provide great potential for economic development to the extent that it can stimulate the industrial sector. Central to the success of LED is land reform programmes that provide opportunities for poverty alleviation. This position is informed by the understanding that access to land —especially agricultural land—contributes to household incomes and therefore contributes to improved rural livelihoods (Dlamini, 2016: 117). As one of the world's leading development agencies, the World Bank has consistently viewed agriculture as a vital economic sector in the rural context. Manona (cited in Dlamini, 2016: 119) argued that a large aspect of the development discourse regarding agriculture has mainly focused on commercial agriculture, at the expense of smallholder agriculture.

The debate on the specific contribution of the smallholder agriculturalist on LED remains much debated. It is unclear whether development strategies should depend on smallholder farms to make a significant contribution to development, employment creation and poverty reduction. In this respect Aliber (2005: 10) contended that there is no consensus on whether agriculture is the appropriate method to rural poverty alleviation, notwithstanding the role agriculture plays in the economies of developing countries. On whether smallholder farms can contribute to LED, Gollin (2014: 5) observed that many smallholder farms, which are crop farms, cover less than five hectares of land. This questions their abilities to make a significant contribution to the local economy. However, he also contended that these farms provide employment to some people and they are certainly a source of food and sustenance for many rural poor households. Most of the output from these smallholder farms are mainly for household consumption. The National Institute of Statistics in Rwanda, for instance, conducted a household survey which suggests that only half the grain production by smallholder farms enters the market channels, while the rest is consumed within the producing households (Gollin, 2014: 6). Likewise, Dlamini (2016: 123) noted a similar pattern in the production and consumption of produce in household farming activities in Uganda. In Uganda, about two-thirds of bananas are consumed within the producing households, while in northern Ghana, the households which produce maize consume about 80% of their output.

There is contrary evidence that smallholder farms within LED projects and programmes provide significant levels of employment. Gollin (2014: 6) noted that over the period from 2001 to 2010, only 1.2% of the agricultural workforce in Benin consisted of employees, as defined by the International Labour Organization (12,000 out of nearly one million). Similar low proportions (less than 2% of the agricultural workforce) worked as employees in Guinea, Ethiopia, Tanzania and Sierra Leone. The exceptions to this rule were countries with large-scale plantations for export crops, in which large fractions of the agricultural workforce consisted of employees in countries such as Botswana (11.2%) and with even larger fractions in South Africa (59.1%) and Mauritius (55.3%)

(Gollin, 2014: 6). What this trend suggests is that in the African agricultural economy, there are very few employees in the smallholder farming community, except for those engaged in large-scale commercial farming. The majority of workers in the agricultural sector are self-employed in smallholder farms located within the household.

Concept of Agri-Parks and Rural Development

Globally, the concept of Agri-park is not new. It has been widely practised over decades in countries such as China, India, Brazil, Mexico, Chile, United States, Malawi, Egypt and Kenya. In the South African context, this concept has gained momentum in the past three or more years as a panacea to arrest poverty through stimulating LED in the rural areas.

Since the twentieth century, agriculture has undergone massive transformation as compared to the past where it was viewed as a subsistence activity amongst farmers around crop and livestock production. In present times, agriculture has rapidly turned to technology and the market-oriented industry. It extends itself from agricultural production, to technologically advanced agri-science and agri-business. As a localised business activity, it strongly interfaces with the national and global economy. People working in the agricultural sector no longer just work on farms but are connected to the businesses of seed, fertiliser, agro-chemical, farm machinery, food processing, marketing and trade. Work in the financial, research, food processing, marketing and trade has made agriculture a huge business enterprise (Gandhi, 2014: 44).

As a business enterprise, it is better known as agri-business in the agricultural community. The pioneers of the field of agri-business at the Harvard Business School, Davis and Goldberg (cited in Gandhi, 2014: 44), defined agri-business as the sum total of all operations involved in the manufacture and distribution of farm supplies; production operations on the farm; and the storage, processing and distribution of the resulting farm commodities and items. These agricultural activities are located in one region, which is commonly referred to as an Agri-park. Agri-parks basically comprise of all activities undertaken by agri-business. The concept refers to a networked innovation system of agro-production, processing, logistics, marketing, training and extension services, located in a rural area (Department of Rural Development and Land Reform, 2017a: 2). As a network, it promotes a market-driven mixture and combination of various agricultural activities and rural transformation services.

It is a well-defined industrial platform, where agro-industries and other companies engage in agro-processing and related activities, in a concentrated locality. Agri-parks facilitate localised competitiveness and growth, help farmers gain competitiveness in the markets and facilitate the creation of backward and forward commercial linkages (Food and Agricultural Organisation of the United Nations, n.d.).

Agri-parks can be seen as a combination and interaction of both agriculture and industry. Agri-based economies need agricultural land and industries, which can make the agricultural output more profitable through products. Industrialisation is the major source of economic development and is known to be the key for reconstructing the rural economy (Sutcliffe, 1971: 16). They play a vital role in providing enormous opportunities to value addition to not only the main produce, but also, the bi-products and wastes. Advancement in agro-based industries curbs rural-urban migration by opening up job opportunities in allied sectors such as transport, marketing and related agricultural activities. It integrates both rural and urban economies by eliminating social and economic imbalances (Verma & Kesavan, 1986: 213). Agro-based industries, through mutual development of agriculture and industry, pave the way for rural development, which helps promote decentralisation of development in the local economy and empowers local communities (Sahoo, 2001: 5–6).

Since agro-based industries are the source of indigenous raw materials, finished products become cost effective which is further advantaged by mechanisation resulting in mass production. Access to indigenous material and the skill to process it, reduces the dependency on external technical skills. Hence, Agri-parks act as a catalytic agent and a forerunner to accelerate agriculture and the economy, as a whole, through industrialisation (Bagalkoti, 1996: 19).

The very nature of the location in the rural areas creates opportunities to absorb surplus labour in a variety of agricultural related activities. Agro-based industries are instrumental in harnessing the potentials of agriculture, as well as industry, through their mutual integration; they accelerate the rate of rural and economic development (Yadav & Rana, 2005: 10). Since Agri-parks are dependent on a variety of service delivery requirements, they act as an agent for the development of infrastructure in rural areas, which often is lacking (Sahoo, 2001: 12–14).

Although Agri-parks are lauded to provide numerous advantages to stimulate the industrial economy in rural areas, there is reason to believe that there are certain drawbacks to this concept. India's Green Revolution in the past 30 decades has experienced certain setbacks due to various challenges (Reddy, 2016: 2). Reddy (2016) asserted that the kind of agro-industries that developed failed miserably because of outdated technology, poor management and an inability to meet the dynamic, expanding demand for quality goods, from a rapidly growing population, with rising incomes.

Insufficient capital; loans from non-institutional agencies at exorbitant rates of interest; the seasonality of agro-based industries; and the comparatively lower number of working days in these industries caused unemployment in many times of the year. In addition, corrupt practices of government officials; lack of young people participating in agro-based activities; a higher proportion of old-aged and middle-aged entrepreneurs; women and child labour in the agro-sector; low level of education amongst entrepreneurs; caste of the entrepreneurs and the nature of agro-based industries, chosen by agri-entrepreneurs, have been identified as some of the challenges experienced during the Green Revolution in India (Reddy, 2016: 191–198).

Added to the constraint experienced by agri-entrepreneurs, Sahoo (2001) identifies a multitude of factors that affected them in the state of Orissa, India. Political pressure and activities of vested interest groups mostly guided and influenced the selection of beneficiaries for government subsidies. Most of the agro-industrial units were located in entrepreneurs' houses in order to avoid transport costs and other recurring costs. The entrepreneurs of agro-industries mostly had small resources at their disposal and were unable to build a stock of raw materials to last a financial year, even for that matter, a considerable part of the year. The non-availability of raw materials in adequate quantity, and in time, also affected production schedules resulting in financial losses. Most agri-businesses sold their produce mainly on the local markets, as these businesses lacked both physical and financial resources and manpower to market their produce outside the local markets. Supply of power to production units was irregular and fluctuated, leading to material losses and delays in productivity. The use of the most advanced technology for agri-businesses was lacking due to poor finances, ignorance and lack of awareness on how to adopt new technologies in the production process. Dishonesty was rife as many did not engage professional managers in their businesses, resulting in improper accounts and records being maintained for audit and inspection purposes, and not preparing balance sheet accounts, as an indicator of the profit and loss of the enterprise (Sahoo, 2001: 220–239).

Agri-Parks as a Form of LED Amongst Emerging Rural Farmers in South Africa

The agricultural sector in South Africa is bifurcated in form. It is dualistic in nature and consists of a well-integrated, highly capitalised commercial sector, with approximately 35,000 white farmers, producing around 95% of agricultural output on 87% of total agricultural land. In contrast, 4 million black farmers in the smallholder sector are located on 13% of land in the former homelands created under apartheid (Pienaar & Traub, 2015: 4). This contrast between commercial and smallholder farmers is a direct result of the historical dispossession of land which has come to haunt the new democracy in the last 24 years. More recently, the issue of redistributing white-owned agricultural land through LEWC is being challenged in the Constitutional Court, which outcome is being awaited.

Notwithstanding the protracted controversy surrounding land redistribution, the need for rural development and transformation is a pressing issue, especially in the light of rising levels of poverty. The National Development Plan (NDP), launched in 2012, views agriculture central to promoting employment and creating food security opportunities. It estimates that agriculture would potentially create a million jobs by 2030 (Department of Rural Development and Land Reform, 2016: 19). In order to achieve this goal, the NDP identifies Agri-parks as an important mechanism and strategy for supporting small-scale agricultural production and stimulating agro-processing in rural areas. It is considered to be a catalyst for economic transformation that aims to improve access for smallholder farmers to the agricultural value chain.

An Agri-park is a networked innovation system of agro-production, processing, logistics, marketing, and training and extension services located in district municipalities. As a network, it enables the growth of market-driven commodity value chains and contributes to the achievement of rural economic transformation (Department of Rural Development and Rural Reform, 2016: 6). It is founded on the 'one household one hectare' principle as a key apparatus to promote agrarian transformation and provide landless people with access to land. The Agri-parks programme targets smallholder producers in the country's poorest districts. Support for smallholder farmers are provided through capacity building, mentorship programmes, setting up farm infrastructure, promoting extension services and making available production and mechanisation resources. It is envisaged that smallholder farmers will eventually own 70% of Agri-parks, while the remaining 30% will comprise government and commercial farmers (National Treasury, 2018: 4).

Given the expectations surrounding Agri-parks as an apparatus for stimulating LED in rural areas, the concept has been launched in all of South Africa's District Municipalities with the expectation that it will stimulate the rural economy and promote transformation. Agri-parks are supported by the government. A total of 44 Agri-parks have been set up in the different districts of the country. These parks are, and will be, supported by government over a period of ten years to ensure economic sustainability. Thus far in the 2015/2016 budget of the Department of Rural Development and Land Reform, it disbursed R2 billion to establish Agri-parks in the different district municipalities of the country, each valued at R45 million (Ngwenya-Mabila, 2015: 2).

The Department of Rural Development and Land Reform (2017a: 14) envisages major national outcomes through investment in Agri-parks. In keeping with the NDP, it hopes to create one million additional jobs in the agricultural sector by 2030 and ensure that one million hectares of rural land are under cultivation. As far as employment is concerned, 145,000 new jobs are anticipated in the agro-processing sector by 2020, while at the same time 300,000 smallholder farmers would have emerged. It hopes to reduce rural unemployment from 49% to under 40% by 2030. Agri-parks, it is hoped, will be the catalyst around which rural industrialisation will take place (Ngwenya-Mabila, 2015: 2).

In an annual report (2016/2017) to the Financial and Fiscal Committee (FFC), the Department of Rural Development and Land Reform and Commission on Land Restitution reported successes that have been achieved through Agri-parks to date. In this period, three Agri-hubs became operational. These are Ncora in the Eastern Cape, Springbokpan in North West and Brandvlei in Gauteng. A total of 53 infrastructure projects has been completed at the level of farmer production support units and on farms, to support smallholder farmers. In the coming financial year, it is anticipated that delivery would be scaled up across the country and significant focus would be placed on farmer mobilisation and organisation to enhance farmer participation in the value chain and the ownership model of the districts' Agri-parks (Department of Rural Development and Land Reform, 2017b: 6).

The FFC was further informed on job creation opportunities that emerged out of the Agri-park projects. It facilitated 6169 jobs from its rural development initiative and 2742 jobs from its land reform projects. However, youth unemployment still remains a challenge. However, through the National Rural Youth Service Corps (NARYSEC) Programme, 2711 youth were enrolled to pursue training in different vocations in the agricultural sector and were seconded to Agri-parks across the country. In addition, to promote community participation and integrated governance, district land reform committees and district Agri-park management councils have been established and are functioning across the country. These serve as platforms for participatory development and enhanced service delivery (Department of Rural Development and Land Reform, 2017b: 6).

From the above exposition, it would appear that Agri-parks, despite being a very new and innovative concept, over a short period of time, are showing signs of positive advancement. However, it should be noted that it is competing against persistent challenges inherited from the past, which needs to be considered as possible threats to its implementation and success. Pienaar and Traub (2015) suggested the importance of understanding the socio-economic context of the smallholder farmer in South Africa, if they are going to be empowered towards sustainable livelihoods through agricultural activity. The classification of smallholder farmers is nearly homogenous and their history, culture and characteristics are very similar. The smallholder farming community is known for its small farms that are labour-intensive, use traditional production techniques and often lack institutional capacity and support. The average age of the household head is 56 years, with an average of only 5 years of education, of an equivalent of grade 5 education. In so far as the farming of produce is concerned, 80% of the smallholders' farm food for household consumption, with the remaining 20% farming to market their produce (Pienaar & Traub, 2015: 5).

Pienaar and Traub (2015: 6–7) further observed that the majority of these rural farming households comprise women, children and the elderly. The majority (55%) of these households were headed by females and the average household consisted of 5 individuals. Furthermore, in terms of income, the main sources of income are social welfare grants from the government, specifically old age grants and child support grants, with monthly incomes of R522 and R282, respectively. Expenditure on farm inputs was approximately R36 per month, indicative of the relatively small investment and production systems. In essence, these characteristic of the smallholder farmer needs to be factored into the establishment of technologically advanced Agri-parks.

LED Prospects and Challenges in the Harry Gwala District Municipality Land Reform

The Sisonke District Municipality changed its name to the Harry Gwala District Municipality (HGDM) in 2015. It is named after the prominent late African National Congress (ANC) stalwart, Harry Themba Gwala. The district municipality is predominantly rural in composition with small urban centres. These small urban areas serve as economic and administrative hubs for the region. It represents four local municipalities, namely Nkosazana Dlamini Zuma, uMzimkhulu, Greater Kokstad and Ubuhlebezwe. It is characterised by large agricultural activities, plantations, natural vegetation and traditional authority-owned land (Integrated Development Plan, 2017a: 46).

In 2014, the Department of Cooperative Governance and Traditional Affairs (COGTA) undertook a comprehensive study towards a growth and development plan for the district municipality. It noted the key demographic profiles of the municipality. The population size for the HGDM was 461,420, spread over a surface area of 10,547 km^2. Given the size of the physical landscape of the district, the population density per kilometre is low. It equates to approximately 43 people per square kilometre. The racial composition of the area comprises predominantly black people (94%) with whites and coloureds making up 2 and 3%, respectively. Female-headed households make up 55.1% of the population (Department of Economic Development, Tourism and Environmental Affairs, 2018: 161). The most likely explanation for more than 50% of the households being represented by females may be attributed to the large-scale migration of males to the urban centres for employment or due to attrition as a result of the HIV/Aids pandemic, which is known to be high in the area.

The area is characterised by high levels of informal housing. Only 41.5% of households live in formal dwellings (COGTA, 2014: 7). The population is a youthful one with 37.9% being under the age of 15 years and 57.2% between the ages 15 and 64 years. A third (33.4%) of the population are in a state of poverty (COGTA, 2014: 8–9), with 25.4% of the population being unemployed (Integrated Development

Plan, 2018: 123) and with a large section belonging to the youth category. The number of households in the area is 112,287 and of this, the number of agricultural households amounts to 54,411 (Department of Economic Development, Tourism and Environmental Affairs, 2018: 161). This trend suggests that 48.4% of the households derive their livelihood through engagement with some form of agricultural activity.

A critical factor with which the Harry Gwala District Municipality is faced is the skills deficit in the region. In the period 2001–2011, there has been an improvement in education across all the municipalities, but, the level of people with a Matriculation (grade 12) or higher qualification is still very low (less than 15% across the district). People with no education accounted for 11% of the population (Sisonke District Municipality, 2011: 27). Even though those who have a Matric and higher education qualification do not have the necessary skills required in the district, as the skills required are primarily related to agriculture and tourism. This situation is worsened since agriculturally oriented businesses which may require low-level skills are becoming increasingly mechanised and technologically oriented (COGTA, 2014: 12). With such low educational and skills' levels, it is not surprising to note that 29% of those that are employed earn between R1 and R400 monthly and 44.1% have no income at all (Integrated Development Plan, 2018: 140).

A huge development issue facing the district is the lack of easy access to the region due to poor road conditions. Unreliable electrical supply is also problematic, especially for businesses engaged in processing value added products, which require refrigeration. There is a huge backlog in service delivery. The lack of potable water, the wide prevalence of informal human settlements, absence of solid waste collection, management and sanitation disposal amenities are some of the challenges confronting the district (COGTA, 2014: 12). This lack of even basic infrastructure is attributed to the limited capital budget that the district has access to in order to implement acceptable levels of service delivery and maintenance programmes.

The low municipal rates base to service its residents and limited operational budget to employ staff to improve public sector capacity adds to the state of low-level infrastructure (COGTA, 2014: 15). This is illustrated by examining the 2015/2016 financial year income. In this period, revenue from within the municipality amounted to R67.6 million, with capital grants and subsidies from the central government for capital and operational costs amounting to R249.8 million and R270.7

million, respectively (Medium Term Revenue and Expenditure Framework, 2015/2016: 10). The municipality is the least contributing district to the national Gross Domestic Product (GDP) at an estimated rate of 1.7% (Integrated Development Plan, 2017b: 102). Clearly, the district is too financially impoverished to progress with any extensive infrastructure and service delivery programmes.

Notwithstanding the unsatisfactory socio-economic status of the district municipality, the availability of large tracks of agricultural land has been and is the mainstay of the region. It is well known for its high agro-ecological potential due to an abundance of high-quality soils, high altitude and abundant water supply. Commercial farms and, to a large extent, commercial plantations, form the foundation of the economy of the region. Climatic conditions make the area suitable for a variety of products, including crops and vegetables, livestock and sugar cane. The agricultural sector is one of the main drivers of the regional economy. In total, 73% of the land is utilised for agricultural purposes. It produces 25% of the Gross Value Added (GVA) products, which is critical to the economy of the district (Department of Rural Development and Land Reform, 2016: 54). In 2010, the forestry sector contributed approximately over R331 million to the district's GDP and constituted more than 8% of the district's economy, while agriculture produces 11% of GDP in the region and manufacturing produces 18% (Department of Economic Development, Tourism and Environmental Affairs, 2018: 162).

In terms of a variety of agricultural produce in the area, animal husbandry is also a lucrative agri-business. For instance, Clover Dairies harvests 30% of the total Clover production in the country and it is estimated that this constitutes 15% of the national milk production from the region (SDA Project Management Unit, 2013: 4). However, it must be noted that while the land coverage assessment shows the highest land utilisation for agricultural purposes for the district and realising high productive yields, it has not produced enough employment, despite the extensiveness of the sector and the land used for cultivation purposes (COGTA, 2014: 16).

Land ownership in the region is shared by many stakeholders. These are the government, small-scale farmers, white and black commercial farmers, tribal authorities, private households and the municipality. The largest proportion (42.5%) of land is owned by white commercial farmers, followed by the state (19.8%). Tribal authorities own 9.2% of the land

and conservation and eco-tourism comprising 11.5%. Commercial black-owned land is made up of 7.4%, while the unknown land ownership category amount to 9.4%. A small percent (0.3%) of land is owned by the municipality (Sisonke Development Agency Project Management Unit, 2013: 6). There are pending land claims in the municipality, of some three thousand claims that were outstanding to be finalised, in 2013 (Sisonke Development Agency Project Management Unit, 2013: 10).

This uncertainty in land claims impact both locally based black and white farmers, as well as national and international corporations who have invested in the different agricultural sectors. In addition, it has undermined existing and potential agro-business confidence in investing in the region and has impeded the economic viability of both commercial and smallholder farmers. Even in instances were land reform has been implemented, beneficiaries do not necessarily have the skills to adequately utilise the land (COGTA, 2014: 17). Agriculture is a complicated, expensive and demanding task, which in the twenty-first century is dependent on scientific technology and skills.

Although land restitution and redistribution claims are slow and protracted, different stakeholders in the region are making concerted efforts to work together in the development of the region through a social compact, were all stakeholders support and engage with the broad principles of development that will benefit the region. For instance, new and emerging black farmers in the agri-business sector are seeking economic empowerment through development and are positively disposed to partnering with private sector white farm-owners. Traditional leaders are committed to overseeing the process of land claims within their jurisdiction and ensure that land is appropriately used for development. White farmers are amenable to retaining their lands which are currently productive and their unfarmed land could be expropriated without compensation. Stakeholders believe that such an approach will ensure that the pressing social issues which were created in the past—poverty, inequality and landlessness—are redressed (Sisonke Development Agency Project Management Unit, 2013: 12). Given the positive disposition of key stakeholders on matters concerning land and the agricultural economy in the region, in 2016, the Final Master Agri-park Business Plan for the Harry Gwala District was created.

Conclusion

Land reform in all forms in South Africa evokes emotional responses from those that have been made landless and historically excluded from ownership. Since the emergence of democracy, much debate has been directed at the pace of land reform. Given the slow pace of reform, expropriating land without compensation is currently being contested in the Constitutional Court, in particular white-owned farmlands in the rural areas, where large tracks of land have been developed for commercial agricultural purposes. These disputed rural agricultural lands are known to be the breadbasket of the nation and contribute enormously to the local and national economy, but at the same time it is a source of hunger and poverty for local communities. While the debate on the form of land reform is continuing, there is increasing agreement that agricultural land in the rural areas can be the gateway for economic development and a solution to the poverty woes that plague local communities. Land reform, simultaneously combined with LED programmes and projects, can serve as a panacea to stimulate rural development.

In this context, the concept of rural Agri-parks is being experimented with where smallholder farmers and those emerging are provided an opportunity to not only to market their produce but also to add value through modern processing mechanisms. It is envisaged that through Agri-parks, rural agriculture can serve as a catalyst for industrialisation, as witnessed in other developing parts of the world.

The case study of Harry Gwala District Municipality illustrates the nature and extent of rural poverty and the extent to which the local community is excluded from participating in the economy due to landlessness and socio-economic challenges. It highlights how when value is accorded to natural resources in people's livelihood, they come to appreciate its importance and become motivated to participate in rural economic reform. Notwithstanding the socio-economic challenges prevalent in the district, a social agreement and commitment amongst all stakeholders (government and public sector; private sector and civil society; associations and organisations) set the foundation to drive economic reform in the Harry Gwala District Municipality. In testimony of this, the Final Master Agri-park Business Plan for the Harry Gwala District was ascended to in 2016 as a blueprint for the district and this plan is currently being actioned.

References

Aliber, M. (2005). *Overcoming underdevelopment in South Africa's second economy, synthesis of the 2005 development report in UNDP*. Human Sciences Research Council, Development Bank South Africa.

Ariatti, C. A. (2013). *Agriculture and local economic development: A case study of the uMshwathi Local Municipality*. A dissertation submitted in partial fulfilment of the requirements for the degree of Master of Business Administration. Graduate School of Business and Leadership, College of Law and Management Studies, University of KwaZulu-Natal.

Bagalkoti, S. T. (1996). Non-farm activities in rural areas: A case for agro-processing. In M. V. Gowda & S. Subrahmanya (Eds.), *Studies in agricultural development* (p. 179). Delhi: Deep and Deep Publication.

Department of Cooperative Governance and Traditional Leaders (COGTA). (2014). *Annual report*. Available: http://www.cogta.gov.za/cgta_2016/wp-content/uploads/2016/06/COGTA-Annual-Report-2014-2015.pdf.

Department of Economic Development, Tourism and Environmental Affairs. (2018). *Harry Gwala District Municipality environmental management framework* (Draft Status Quo Report). Available: https://www.nemai.co.za/documents/HGM-EMF/10627-20181130-HGDM-EMF-DS-Report-Draft.pdf.

Department of Rural Development and Land Reform. (2016). *Final master Agri-park master plan for the Harry Gwala District Republic of South Africa*. Available: http://www.ruraldevelopment.gov.za/phocadownload/Agri-parks/Business-Plans/KwaZulu-Natal/Harry%20Gwala%20DM%20Final%20Master%20Agri-Park%20Business%20Plan.pdf.

Department of Rural Development and Land Reform. (2017a). *Your Agri-park, your future*. Republic of South Africa. Available: http://www.ruraldevelopment.gov.za/phocadownload/Agri-parks/Cammisa/29-02-2016-FBDM-Agri-Park-MBP.pdf.

Department of Rural Development and Land Reform. (2017b). *Commission on land reform 2016–2017 annual report*. DRDLR.

Department of Rural Development and Rural Reform. (2016). *Agri-park master plan version 1 Overburg District Municipality Western Cape*. Republic of South Africa. Available: http://www.drdlr.gov.za/phocadownload/Agri-parks/Cammisa/15-04-2016-Agri-Park-Master-Business-Plan-Overberg-DM.pdf.

Dlamini, S. I. (2016). *Transforming local economies through land reform: Political dilemmas and rural development realities in South Africa*. Degree of Doctor of Philosophy in Political Science, University of KwaZulu-Natal, School of Social Sciences, Pietermaritzburg, South Africa.

Food and Agricultural Organisation of the United Nations. (n.d.). *Territorial investment tools—Agro-industrial parks and special economic zones*. Agricultural Economics Division. http://www.fao.org/economic/esa (Accessed 8 October 2018).

Gandhi, V. P. (2014). Growth and transformation of the agribusiness sector: Drivers, models and challenges. *Indian Journal of Agricultural Economics, 69*(1), 44–74.

Gerber, J. (2018). Land: The people speak—"My white brothers and sisters, don't worry, man tells hearing". *News24*. https://www.news24.com/SouthAfrica/News/land-the-people-speak-my-white-brothers-and-sisters-dont-worry-man-tells-hearing-20180803 (Accessed 24 August 2018).

Gollin, D. (2014). *Smallholder agriculture in Africa: An overview and implications for policy* (Working Paper). International Institute for Environment and Development, Oxford University.

Gumede, W. (2018). Lessons from Zimbabwe's failed land reforms. *News24*. https://www.wits.ac.za/news/latest-news/in-their-own-words/2018/2018-10/lessons-from-zimbabwes-failed-land-reforms.html (Accessed 12 September 2018).

Harry Gwala Municipality. (2015/2016). *Annual budget and supporting documentation of the Harry Gwala District Municipality*. Medium Term Revenue and Expenditure Framework.

Harry Gwala Municipality. (2018). *District growth and development plan*. Harry Gwala District Municipality Draft Integrated Development Plan.

Integrated Development Plan. (2017a). *Final Integrated Development Plan 2017/2018*. Harry Gwala District Municipality, KwaZulu-Natal.

Integrated Development Plan. (2017b). *Final Integrated Development Plan 2017–2022*. Harry Gwala District Municipality, KwaZulu-Natal.

Mthimkhulu, S. N. (2015). *An examination of business perspectives on the role of Umhlosinga Development Agency as economic development agency*. Dissertation submitted in fulfilment of the requirements for the degree of Master of Commerce, Graduate School of Business and Leadership, College of Law and Management, University of KwaZulu-Natal.

National Treasury. (2018). *Vote 39 rural development and land reform*. Estimates of National Expenditure, Republic of South Africa.

Ngwenya-Mabila. (2015). *One District-One Agri-Park implementation in context of rural economic transformation model*.

Nkomo, S. L. (2013). *Developing key success criteria for rural development initiatives in the context of sustainable land management*. Submitted in fulfilment of the academic requirements for the degree of Master of Science in the Discipline of Geography, School of Agricultural, Earth and Environmental Sciences, College of Agriculture, Engineering and Science, University of KwaZulu-Natal, Pietermaritzburg Campus.

Pienaar, L., & Traub, L. N. (2015, August 8–14). *Understanding the smallholder farmer in South Africa: Towards a sustainable livelihoods classification*. Paper Delivered at the International Conference of Agricultural Economist, Milan Universita Degli Studi Di Milano.

Reddy, G. L. K. (2016). *Problems and prospects of agro-based industries in Kurnool district* (Unpublished dissertation). Sri Department of Economics, Venkateswara University, India. http://shodhganga.inflibnet.ac.in/jspui/browse?type=author&value=S.Hatna+kumari (Accessed 9 October 2018).

Sahoo, S. K. (2001). *Role of agro industries in the economic development of Orissa: A case study of the un-divided Cuttack district* (PhD thesis). Utkal University, Bhubaneswar, India.

Sedumedi, E. (2012). *Impact of lands restitution on local economic development*. Master of Commerce, College of Law and Management Studies, University of KwaZulu-Natal.

Sisonke Development Agency Project Management Unit. (2013). *Fast-tracking of land claims in Sisonke district and land reform support and enhancement of agribusiness productiveness in Sisonke district*. Framework Document.

Sisonke District Municipality. (2011). *The state of the district economy: A local economic review*. Sisonke Socio-Economic Profile.

South African Local Economic Development Network. (n.d.). South African Local Government Association. http://www.led.co.za/what-is-led (Accessed 25 September 2018).

Sutcliffe, R. B. (1971). *Industry and underdevelopment*. London: Addison-Wesley Publishing Company.

UNHABITAT. (2003). *The local economic development series. Promoting local economic development through strategic planning* (Trainer's Guide). United Nations Human Settlements Programme (UN-HABITAT), Nairobi, Kenya.

Verma, N. K., & Kesavan, V. K. (1986). Agro-based industries in Haryana—Growth in output and employment. *Agricultural Situation in India, 41*(4), 213–215.

World Bank. (2003). *Local economic development: A primer developing and implementing local economic development strategies and action plans*. Washington, DC: World Bank.

Yadav, B. S., & Rana, S. (2005). *Rural empowerment through agro-based industries*. New Delhi: Shree Publishers and Distributors.

Zikhali, W., Ncube, G., & Tshuma, N. (2014). From economic development to local economic growth: Income generating projects in Nkayi district, Zimbabwe. *The International Journal of Humanities and Social Studies, 2*(2), 27–33.

CHAPTER 11

Balancing Land Restitution and Public Interest in South African Socio-Economic Development: A Critical Appraisal of the Restitution of Land Rights Act

Tumo Maloka

Introduction

The question whether the unjust dispossessions of land perpetrated on whole peoples in the past should be corrected by restitution in kind is a constitutional and political minefield. Granting reparations in the form of returning land to the dispossessed former owners or their present-day successors is forbiddingly more complex than the questions posed by other forms of reparations. Regardless of which part of the world is under review, restitution cases are often painful (Alexander, 2012; Cavanagh, 2013; Ronen, 2008; Van Ho, 2016). Restitution throw into focus South Africa's history of racial discrimination and land dispossession. The South African Constitution rightly acknowledges that the past is one of deep societal division, characterised by "strife, conflict, untold suffering and

T. Maloka (✉)
University of Limpopo, Limpopo, South Africa

A. O. Akinola et al. (eds.), *The New Political Economy of Land Reform in South Africa*,
https://doi.org/10.1007/978-3-030-51129-6_11

injustice" (*Minister of Finance v Van Heerden* 2004 (6) SA 121 (CC) para 116). Accordingly, land reform is conceived as a prerequisite for the attainment of social justice, and by implication, social cohesion. The importance of the second objective, however, overshadows the first one. Promoting social cohesion is one of the most difficult, yet one of the most important, challenges facing South Africa (Burns, Hull, Lefko-Everett, & Njozela, 2018; Palmary, 2015).

Indeed, a claim for the restoration of dispossessed rights in land is a pre-eminent constitutional and socio-economic issue. As revealed:

> Undeniably, the umbilical cord that joins any particular community and its ancestral land is strong and it has a highly emotional element that has to be respected. That does not, however, mean that all other public interest considerations should be ignored. Land is finite and there are millions out there who also wish to have their share. All claims and aspirations cannot be satisfied. A balance must be struck and the limited resources of the country must be considered. (*Khosis, Community, Lohatla v Minister of Defence* 2004 (5) SA 494 (SCA) para 31)

The restitution of land rights is a vital part of the constitutional quest to heal the divisions and exclusions of the past (Klug, 2018). It is foreshadowed in Section 25(7) of the 1996 Constitution which proclaims that,

> a person or community dispossessed of property after 19 June 1913 as a result of past racially discriminatory laws or practices is entitled to the extent provided by an Act of Parliament, either to restitution of that property or equitable redress.

Simply put, land reform is laden with complexity and controversy. The willing seller-willing buyer principle adopted by the government has proved to be ineffective in accelerating land reform (Makhado, 2012). Ardent resistance to land expropriation without compensation (LEWC) by traditional authorities triggered a "secessionist threat", thereby posing a severe challenge to constitutional sovereignty and social unity (Nicolson, 2018). Like the tense period before 27 April 1994, when the country was on the edge of possible civil disruption, the discourse on LEWC has also created a volatile sociopolitical atmosphere.

The controversy concerning LEWC in no way undermines the fact that what informs land reform remains the Restitution of Land Rights Act 22 of 1994. A discerning grasp of the objectives and implementation of the Restitution Act are necessary in order to answer the focal questions that have arisen concerning two decades of land reform processes in South Africa. A primary answer to the question of expropriation emerges clearly from exposition of selected cases on Section 34 of the Act. The aspects of Section 34 which balance land restitution and public interest in socio-economic development inquiry are consequential. Appraisal of Section 34 raises more fundamental questions about the trajectory of land reform and equitable access to land in South Africa.

The Three Elements of the South African Land Reform Programme

To fully engage with Section 34 of the Act, it is important that the framework of the land reform in South Africa be briefly outlined. After the successful democratic transition from apartheid, the ruling party, the African National Congress, stated in the Reconstruction and Development Programme (RDP) that land reform was to redress the injustices of forced removals and the historical denial of access to land (Kloppers & Pienaar, 2014; Mostert, 2014). It included a commitment to redistribute 30% of agricultural land within five years and to make land reform the central pillar of rural development. RDP was to ensure security of tenure for rural dwellers, eliminate overcrowding and to supply residential and productive land to the poorest section of the rural population.

The elements of the government's land reform programme, outlined in the 1997 White Paper on Land Policy, are provided for in the Constitution. The three dimensions of the programme are as follows: land restitution, land redistribution and land tenure reform.

Land Restitution Programme

This programme pivots around the Restitution of Land Rights Act in terms of which a person or community dispossessed of property after 19 June 1913 (the date of the Natives Land Act), as a result of racially discriminatory laws or practices, is entitled to lodge a claim for restitution of that property or comparable redress. It thus is directed at addressing the wrongs of apartheid (Atuahene, 2010, 2014).

Land Redistribution Programme

The primary objective of the land redistribution programme is to provide the disadvantaged and the poor with land for residential and productive purposes. Land redistribution takes several forms (e.g. group settlement with some production; group production; commonage schemes; on-farm settlement of farm workers and farm worker equity (Sibanda, 2001).

Land Tenure Reform Programme

This programme aims to provide people with secure tenure where they live, to prevent arbitrary evictions and fulfil the constitutional requirement that all South Africans have access to land and legally secure tenure of the land. This is probably the most neglected aspect of land reform but has the potential to impact on more people than all other land reform programmes combined (Lahiff, 2001). The Land Reform (Labour Tenants) Act 3 of 1996 provides for the protection of the rights of labour tenants and gives them the right to claim land.

The Interim Protection of Informal Land Rights Act 31 of 1996 was passed as an interim measure to protect people in the former "homelands" against abuses of their land rights by traditional authorities, administrative measures or property developers who fail to consult the occupiers of affected land.

The Extension of Security of Tenure Act 62 of 1997 (ESTA) further bolsters security of tenure of farm workers and labour tenants. ESTA aims to protect the people who live on land with the consent of the owner or person in charge against unfair eviction and create long-term tenure security through on-or-off-site settlement assisted by a government grant and the landowner.

Statutory Context

In terms of the Restitution Act, persons and communities who are entitled to restitution of a right in land are defined (S2) and "restitution of a right in land" is said to mean either (a) the restoration of a right in land, or (b) equitable redress (S1). There is a restitution statute that is meant to give effect to the overarching constitutional priority of land restitution and reform required by Sections 25(5) to (7) of the Constitution. These provisions were inserted in the Constitution in recognition of the country's racial history of widespread dispossession of land from individuals and communities because of discriminatory laws and practices (*Concerned Land Claimants' Organisation of Port Elizabeth v Port Elizabeth & Community Restoration* 2017 (2) SA 531 (CC) para 26).

It bears mentioning that Section 25(7) confers a right to restitution or equitable redress but leaves the form and manner of redress to legislation. Neither a claimant nor a community may insist on original land dispossessed (In *Kranspoort Community* 2000 (2) SA 124 (LCC) para 82). Similarly, what is appropriate property restitution or equitable redress in response to historical dispossession is bound to vary and be subject to the specific context (*Blaauwberg Municipality v Bekker* 1998 (1) All SA 88 (LC) para 34).

While a claimant of land rights is not always entitled to restoration in the land claimed (*Baphalane Ba Ramokoka Community v Mphela Family* 2011 (9) BCLR 891 (CC)), the restoration of the land claimed must enjoy primacy when feasible. That is much clear from the scheme of the Act and relevant case law (*Department of Land Affairs v Goedelegen Tropical Fruits (Pty)* 2007 6 SA 199 (CC)). On its face, a non-restoration order subverts and defeats the primary objective of restoring land to the dispossessed majority. Foremost, Section 34 of the Restitution Act pre-empts land restoration. Naturally, there is discontent about granting of non-restoration orders. Yet, the answering refrain is that Section 34 accords with the statute's objective to achieve equitable redress, while avoiding major social disruptions, which might substantially prejudice the public interest. To that end, the Restitution Act makes it plain that when a court decides a matter under this legislation, it must bring to account "the desirability of avoiding major social disruption" (S33(d)). In short, Section 34 warrants a closer inspection.

The Importance of Section 34(1) of the Restitution Act

The pivotal provisions of Section 34(1) of the Restitution Act permit a national, provincial or local government body, in respect of land owned by it, or which falls within its jurisdiction, to apply to the Land Claims Court for an order that the land in question, or any part of the land, or certain rights in the land, shall not be restored to a claimant. If an order for non-restoration were made, a successful claimant would be entitled only to monetary or other equitable redress but not to the actual restoration of the land. Section 34(6) prevents a court from making a non-restoration order unless the twin threshold requirements of *public interests* and *substantial prejudice* are satisfied. It is hard to envisage a restoration that seriously prejudices the public could be in the public interest.

It is important to note that a court must be satisfied that a non-restoration order is justified by the applicable legal principles and facts. It must make a value judgement on what is in the public interest and what is substantially prejudicial. The outcome of the value judgement will depend on an assessment of all the facts. This means that a public body seeking non-restoration order must adduce the facts necessary to enable a court to exercise a value judgement of where the public interest lies, in relation to particular land sought to be restored (*Nkomazi Municipality v Ngomane of Lugedlane Community* 2010 3 All SA 563 (LCC) para 9.3). Without question, a non-restoration order is invasive of restitution rights, and for that reason, the statute requires that it may be made only when the threshold requirements have been met.

When determining public interest, a court must carefully weigh all the relevant factors on how public interest will be prejudiced. The factors are listed in Section 33 of the Restitution Act. Not all of them are necessarily applicable in any given case. Factors such as the feasibility of restoration (S33(c)(A)), social upheaval (S33(d)) and the current use of the land are closely related to the public interest considerations in Section 34(6)(b). What is involved in determining the question of public interest, is a weighing or balancing of private interests on the one hand and the public interests on the other (*Khosis Community, Lohatla v Minister of Defence* 2004 (5) SA 494 (SCA) para 38). The court must also keep in mind that the truncation of the claimant's right may be limited to non-restoration only since a claimant would still be entitled to other forms of equitable redress, provided the curtailment passes the *public interest* and *substantial prejudice* tests.

Section 34(5) confers the power only on the Land Claims Court to choose from a range of options, which range from a dismissal of an application, granting an order insulating the land in question from a restoration order to any other order deemed necessary. The choice of the order will always depend on the facts established. If those facts justify an order excluding restoration, the court may not grant a dismissal, simply because it is one of the options listed. It must grant only the order justified by the facts.

Section 34(5)(b) requires that a non-restoration order must be made in respect of "land in question or part of the land". It is indeed the duty of the government body seeking a non-restoration order to identify with reasonable certainty the land in question. If this did not happen, the Land Claims Court would be unable to fashion an order that precisely targets the land in question. After all, a non-restoration order is invasive of the constitutional right of a claimant to possible restoration. Therefore, the order must be made with sufficient particularity to ensure that the possible redress that would result in a successful claim that is not unduly curtailed.

Pitching Restoration Against the Public Interest Considerations

The Battle School

The case of *Khosis* shows, better than any other case, the fight between the claimant communities and the government. The *casus belli* for this litigation was the area upon which the Lohatla Army Battle School of the SA National Defence Force ("SANDF") is situated in the province of the Northern Cape. The parties were in dispute since 1993, when the defence force applied for the eviction of the Free group (a portion of the Khosis people) from the Khosis area. The respective stances of these parties have not been affected by the reference of the land claim to the Land Claims Court or the numerous attempts to settle the matter.

The battle school plays an important role in the economy of the Northern Cape—one of the poorer provinces—in general and, more particularly, in the immediate vicinity (*Khosis* para 25). The permanent personnel amounts to 2400, of which 500 are civilians. In the surrounding towns, 423 state-owned houses are occupied by staff. Official spending involved the formal business sector, including industry, farming and the Regional Services Council. Many towns and villages, as far away as Kimberley and Upington, were likely to be adversely affected. It could also not be overlooked that the battle school area was heavily contaminated with unexploded ordnances and was, as such, not fit for human or animal use (*Khosis* para 27). It could not be cleared cost effectively.

In order to forestall restoration, pursuant to Section 34, the Minister of Defence and the Premier of the Northern Cape applied to the Land Claims Court for an order declaring that no part of the battle school area will eventually be restored to any of the communities, in spite of vigorous opposition by the Free Khosis community, joined somewhat faint-heartedly by the other two communities, namely the Gatlhose and Maremane. Unlike the Khosis community, the attitude of the two communities was different. The other two communities had accepted monetary compensation equal to the land value of the reserves, ignoring the "compensatory" land which they already possessed.

The Minister argued that it was in the public interest that SANDF should be entitled to the exclusive use of the whole of the Lohatla area. The Free group insisted though that the reserves should be restored to the three communities and, in the alternative, also intractably, that the Khosis area should be allocated to the communities.

The First Threshold Requirement: Public Interest

The first tier question the Supreme Court Appeal had to decide whether it was in the public interest that the reserves should not be restored (S34(6)(a)). The finding of the Land Claims Court that it was in the public interest that the reserves should not be restored to the Gatlhose and Maremane communities was not challenged on appeal. The Khosis Free area still remained for consideration. Precisely, it is not clear whether the Khosis area, right in the middle of the school, could be excised from the battle school and whether it was in the public interest that a small community should live within the midst of the school.

In considering its decision in this regard, a court has to take into account the factors listed in Section 33. All of them are not necessarily applicable in any given case. However, in a case such as the present, the general approach ought to be that the dispossessed community is entitled to restoration of the land unless restoration is trumped by public interest considerations. In support of restoration of the Khosis area, the appellants stressed the desirability of remedying past human rights' violations, the history of the dispossession and the hardship caused to the community.

There were insuperable obstacles against restoring the Khosis area to the claimant group. They stemmed mainly from the fact that the SANDF requires the whole area for training purposes, including the Khosis area, otherwise, training at brigade level would be impossible. Certain manoeuvres, which are essential for training, would be impossible to execute. Soldiers, who have to be prepared for any eventuality, would know that—because of the limitation on the use of the Khosis area—attacks cannot come from the east or west. New weapons systems would not have been tested fully. The range and rate of fire of modern weapons demand safety arcs. The Khosis area fell within the danger zone (*Khosis* para 34). The access road crosses the battle area. Exercises can only be conducted by crossing the area and that is the reason why the area has not been fenced. During exercises, access and egress would have to be restricted.

It was inevitable that the Khosis, in due course, had to leave Lohatla. The allocation of the south eastern part of the battle school to the communities was also mooted but, as mentioned, the Free group later rejected this proposal (*Khosis* para 36). Another decisive factor relating to public interest is that the Khosis area could not simply be allocated to the Free group. It follows that the prospects of restoration of the land were effectively obliterated.

This, then, leads to the second threshold requirement.

The Second Threshold Requirement: Substantial Prejudice

The main thrust of the appellants was directed at the second threshold requirement. Put simply, whether the applicants established that the public or any substantial part thereof would suffer substantial prejudice unless the order was made in advance (S34(6)(b)). Counsel posed the question: "Why now?". The occupation of the Khosis had been in contention since the late 1970s and the battle school had all along been able to operate (*Khosis* para 39). To answer the question, the court pointed out that it was important to consider the situation of the Free Khosis group, apart from that of the Gatlhose and Maremane.

The issues that had to be resolved in order for the early settlement of the land claims were caused by the Free group. The Maremane and Gatlhose communities, consisting of many thousands of people who could not return to the land, remained in an indeterminate state. They lived on land that is insufficient for their needs. A large amount of money had been set aside by the State to enable them to purchase additional land. That could not happen because the small Free group refused to accept the inevitable judgement against them. Every delay in finalising their claim must, by the very nature of their displacement, amount to substantial prejudice (*Khosis* para 41).

Counsel for the Minister presented a detailed and vigorous submission to the effect that the safety of the Free group was at stake. According to the Minister, although the Khosis area is the least contaminated, it is a total anachronism to maintain a totally isolated, small, civilian population in the middle of a battle school, more so because the danger to life where live ammunition is used during training is obvious (*Khosis* para 43). The court agreed with the Land Claims Court that the Free community has suffered substantial prejudice because of the absence of education, health, social services and personal security. The ultimate conclusion was that "the Free group should have left Lohatla before those persons died and before social conditions deteriorated to an extent where children have to suffer because of the ideals of their parents" (*Khosis* para 46).

Nkomazi Land Claim

Nkomazi, located in Nelspruit, in the province of Mpumalanga, is extremely rich in natural resources, with some of the most valuable agricultural land in South Africa and consisting of intensive and large-scale farming activities. The farming activities in the area make a significant contribution to the economy of the region and the agricultural requirements of the whole country. In addition, the area makes a substantial contribution to the development of tourism in the region and country because of its unique location adjacent to the Kruger National Park.

The land which was sought to be excluded from restoration fell within the delineated urban edges of the towns of Malelane, Hectorspruit and Komatipoort and Marloth Park. The four towns have many tourist facilities catering to the national and international market. The N4 highway to Mozambique runs through the land within the four towns. It is an extremely important and busy route, through normal towns, while Marloth Park is a holiday town. The towns are centres of business, making a considerable contribution to the creation of the income and wealth in the area, with educational and health facilities for the thousands of private owners of residential sites.

With regard to the public interest requirement, it was submitted that it would be in the interest of the public at large, the communities occupying the four towns, and indeed the claimants themselves, that the integrity and functioning of the towns be maintained. It would not be feasible nor in the public interest for the state to buy out four towns and dislodge the current owners, businesses and other enterprises for the purpose of restoration to claimant communities (*Nkomazi* para 19). It is germane to note that the claimants, in their own versions, were not dispossessed of urban properties, but of rural land. The major social disruption that would ensue in the wake of restoration speaks for itself.

Furthermore, land expropriation within the urban edges of the towns would be prohibitively expensive and counterproductive. Restoration was neither physically nor economically possible, nor realistic. Accordingly, the public at large would be better served by an order for financial compensation or other equitable relief.

In resisting the granting of non-restoration order, it was argued by one of the claimant communities that the use of the land in the four towns, if restored, would be consistent with their current use and could therefore not be said to be inimical to the public interest, and/or detrimental to the public, or substantial part thereof, as contended by the municipality (*Nkomazi* para 21). The municipality, it was submitted, could still remain in control of the properties within the town, either on the basis of servitude, lease or ad hoc agreements with claimants in a manner that would preserve their rights on the restored land. The claimants also maintained that an order in terms of Section 34 would constrain and prejudice settlement ongoing negotiations with the owners of the Komatipoort Golf Club.

An assessment of the public interest required a comparison of the deprivation of some private convenience or resource, in this case properties within the delineated urban edges of the four towns, with the benefit that was likely to result from such deprivation for the general public or part thereof. A balancing of private, as against public, interests was called for.

The court concluded that the practical effect of the restoration of the land within the delineated urban edges of the four towns would entail the expropriation of that land by the government for the purpose of restoration thereof to the claimant communities (*Khosis* para 27). The government would have to pay just and equitable compensation to the owners of the expropriated properties, taking into account *inter alia* the market values of the such properties (S42 E(3) of the Restitution read with S25(3) of the Constitution).

Properties in the four towns would have to be expropriated at huge and prohibitive financial cost to the government and restored to the claimants who were dispossessed of rural land, the value whereof by any standard would have been significantly less than the expropriated built up land, restored. There was also the fact that the land already been restored to the claimants, paid for by the government, with no regard to compensatory land received upon dispossession, and the benefits of restoration to the claimants' private interest, not only far outweighed but toppled the benefit to the public interest (*Nkomazi* para 27). Had this scenario prevailed, the claimants would have been substantially overcompensated, contrary to the interests of justice and equity, factors which have to be taken into account in terms of Section 33(c) of the Act (*Mphela v Haakdoornbult Boerdery CC* 2007 (5) SA 596 (SCA) paras 48-61).

The factors listed under Section 33(e)(B), namely the history of the dispossession, current use of the land and the history of acquisition and use of the land, as well as specified in Section 33(3)(A), the amount of compensation or any other consideration received in respect of the dispossession, and the circumstances prevailing at the time of the dispossession, would also militate against overcompensation and the restoration of land within the urban edges of the four towns. Endorsing the proposition that the restoration of entire townships was unthinkable, economically impossible and contrary to equity and justice, the court alluded to the prohibitive expense of expropriating land within the urban edges of the towns.

Kwalindile Land Claim

The events giving rise to the proceedings in *Kwalindile Community v King Sabata Dalindyebo Municipality* 2013 6 SA 193 (CC) had their genesis in *King Sabata Dalindyebo Municipality v Landmark Holdings (Pty) Ltd* 2013 3 All SA 251 (SCA) (KSD). The facts in the latter case, *KSD*, were simple enough. The municipality granted a long-term lease to Landmark for the purposes of building a mall on the remainder of Erf 912, in the town Umtata. The remainder of Erf 912 Umtata was the property donated by the national government to the provincial government of the Eastern Cape in April 1997, and the provincial government, in turn, donated it to the King Sabata Dalindyebo Municipality in December 1997. At the time the municipality took over the land, it was alerted that the land could be subject to land claims. It is noteworthy that the land claims of the KwaLindile and Zimbane communities enjoyed the support of the Land Claims Commissioner and the Minister for Agriculture and Land Affairs.

While land claims were lodged with the Regional Land Claims Commissioner in respect of Erf 912, construction commenced on the disputed land. This prompted the claimant communities to approach the Regional Land Claims Commissioner for relief. The Land Claims Court granted an interim interdict prohibiting developments on Erf 912, "pending the finalization of serious and consultative negotiations with all parties concerned". The Regional Land Claims Commissioner also threatened to approach the Land Claims Court in terms of Section 14(2)(d) of the Act to recommend that the court set aside the leases and that the land be restored to the claimants.

Landmark Holdings, engaged by the municipality to provide infrastructure and services like undertaken bulk earthworks, sued the municipality for breach of contract. The municipality's defence to Landmark's claim of breach of contract was that it became impossible for it to give vacant possession to Landmark, due to the gazetting of the KwaLindile community's land claim and the commissioner's steadfast threat of interdict to the development of the property in the event of it continuing. The defence was, therefore, one of supervening impossibility of performance. In other words, the supervening impossibility set it when the Land Claims Court granted the interim interdict. Landmark was bound to comply with the interim interdict and not continue with the development.

The High Court rejected the municipality's defence of supervening impossibility, reasoning, among other things, that it had been aware of the land claims (prior to the conclusion of the lease agreement) and "could or should have clarified the situation irrespective of whether it believed the claims to be valid or not" (*KSD* para 23). The municipality failed to act, and this was contrary to public expectations. It could have brought a Section 34 application prior to developing the property, that if indeed there was supervening impossibility, the High Court held that it has been created by the municipality's own conduct. The court also highlighted the fact that the interdict "was not an absolute legal impediment but rather precluded development pending negotiations and was for a limited period of time" (*KSD* para 23).

The KSD Municipality belatedly applied and was granted Section 34 order by the Land Claims Court. The granting of the application indicated that if municipality had taken the course timeously, the impossibility would have been removed. In the end, the Supreme Court Appeal granted R300 million as damages in favour of Landmark for breach of contract.

The granting of the non-restoration order by the Land Claims Court during the proceedings in *KSD* galvanised the KwaLindile and Zimbane communities to approach the Constitutional Court after their earlier setback in the Supreme Court Appeal. Mindful of the insuperable obstacles to the full restoration of the entire Erf 912, both applicant communities were careful to emphasise the limits of the claim to restoration of the undeveloped and vacant land within the remainder of Erf 912. To be precise, the Zimbane community had made its position quite clear that, "it is not seeking restoration to itself of the city of Mthatha and properties in private hands" (*KwaLindile* para 53).

In *Kwalindile*, the main area of contention between the two claimant communities and the municipality was whether it would be in the public interest that the communities claim not be restored to them, or whether the *public interest* would suffer *substantial prejudice* should a court refuse to make a non-restoration order ahead of the final determination of the claim. Put in another manner, the Constitutional Court had to probe whether the Land Claims Court had correctly determined the public interest and the substantial prejudice threshold requirements imposed by Section 34(6)(a) and (b) in the light of the facts.

The likelihood that if a non-restoration order was not made would chaos and social disruption occur in the city of Mthatha was the overriding consideration for the Land Claims Court. In the word of the Land Claims Court—"to avert the chaos that would follow were established cities and settlements suddenly carved up piecemeal into as many separate and disparate piece and portions as these were claims" (*King Sabata Dalindyebo Municipality v Kwalindile Community* [2010] ZALCC 33 para 28). Similarly, the Supreme Court Appeal also premised its decision that all land in Mthatha is urbanised and developed or has been properly earmarked for future development. The Supreme Court Appeal was influenced by the possible destruction of the "urban fabric" of the Mthatha community that is "completely urbanised" and "continually engaged in the development of the city in various directions" (*King Sabata Dalindyebo Municipality v Kwalindile Community* [2012] 3 All SA 479 (SCA) para 28).

The Constitution Court noted that the Supreme Court Appeal findings were based on incorrect assumptions. As already stated, the applicant communities did not seek restoration of urbanised and developed parts of Remainder of Erf 912 or any other part of Mthatha for that matter. Therefore, the Supreme Court Appeal erred in upholding the order made by the Land Claims Court under Section 34(6) of the Restitution Act:

> Nothing on the facts justifies the conclusion that it is in the public interest for rights on vacant and undeveloped land not to be restored. Similarly, there is no evidence that restoration will cause social upheaval and disruption, or that the public will suffer substantial prejudice simply because vacant and undeveloped land on the fringes of the town may be restored to the applicants when their claim over the Remainder of Erf 912 is finally determined. (*KwaLindile* para 58)

The Supreme Court Appeal could have tailored its order to exclude undeveloped land within the Remainder of Erf 912. For instance, it could have immunised the actual restoration of the land on which the commercial development stood. In other words, where the shopping complex and other commercial properties are located within the urban environs of the City of Mthatha.

The Constitutional Court also addressed the contention by the property developer that the restoration of its developed property to any other claimant is neither feasible nor in the public interest. In simple terms, the development was *a fait accompli*. The shopping complex was in daily use providing the public access to facilities and amenities that were otherwise unavailable to them. However, the stance of the communities was that they did not seek the restoration of developed and privately owned land (*KwaLindile* para 70).

In granting an order in terms of Section 34(6), the Land Claims Court should have tailored its order only in respect of the land on which the property developer held a registered long lease. It should have held, as the Constitutional Court did, that it would not be in the public interest and would be substantially prejudicial to the public to order restoration of the land of Erf 18647 (*KwaLindile* para 71). The order should have been limited to the cadastral description of Erf 18647, as described on the surveyed diagrams attached to the written lease.

Similarly, the Supreme Court Appeal's findings that the communities had no sentimental or ancestral attachment to the land claimed were unfounded. The fact is that the Zimbane community has lived for nearly two centuries on the land, as borne out by the ancestral graves located in the vicinity of the land claimed, which the municipality had, at its ordinary council meeting in 2002, resolved to respect and fence off (*KwaLindile* para 59).

Conclusion

The unresolved, perennial, national question of the restoration of land to the disposed majority means that it cannot be simply said, "What is past is past".

The reasons for the stalled transformative land reform process, envisaged in the RDP and articulated in the 1997 White Paper on South African Land Policy, are manifold. Leaving aside the problems of bureaucratic inertia and malfeasance besetting the Department Rural Development and Land Reform (DRDLR), the willing buyer, willing buyer approach has contributed to the land reform programme not succeeding in achieving its objectives.

The governing party's 2017 Nasrec Conference took a far-reaching resolution to start a process towards constitutional amendment of Section 25 of the Constitution, to make possible land redistribution without compensation. Paradoxically, the ANC resolution comes at a stage when the Zimbabwean government has made a *volte force* about its previous land seizure programme. It established a Compensation Committee under its Land Acquisition Act to allow former commercial white farmers to be compensated for land seized 18 years old.

Zimbabwe provides a cautionary tale about land expropriation without compensation (*Government of the Republic of Zimbabwe v Fick* 2013 (5) SA 325 (CC)). It must be acknowledged that Zimbabweans might have seized the land without compensation 18 years ago, but collectively paid for it through eight consecutive years of economic stagnation, job losses, de-industrialisation and a loss of agricultural export revenues (Sihlobo & Kirsten, 2018). With respect, in South Africa, the present-day clarion call for expropriation of land without compensation is a ploy to win elections and distract the populace.

What emerges out of analysis of the *Khosis/Nkomazi/Kwalindile Community* case is that the process of land restitution, with its multiple and converging claims by communities, is effectively placing a stranglehold on redistribution. This has deferred the resolution of claims. Critical areas need to be addressed in order to expedite land restitution. Uppermost is tackling the failure of the DRDLR to spend its budget, resulting in reduced funding made available by the treasury. Another is to deal with severe capacity constraints—particularly in relation to quality and quantity of staffing. In summary, there is more to land reform than the expropriation of land without compensation, and the current fixation on it risks obfuscating the importance of recognising Section 34 in emasculating land restoration.

References

Alexander, G. S. (2012). *The complexities of land reparations* (Cornell Legal Studies Research Paper No. 12-63), pp. 1–24. Available: https://ssrn.com/abstract=2171422.

Atuahene, B. (2010). *The long-term economic benefit of financial compensation distributed by the South African land restitution commission*. 5th Annual Conference on Empirical Legal Studies Paper. Available: https://ssrn.com/abstract=1619194.

Atuahene, B. (2014). The importance of conversation in transitional justice: A study of land restitution in South Africa. *Law and Social Inquiry, 39*(4), 902–937.

Baphalane Ba Ramokoka Community v Mphela Family 2011 (9) BCLR 891 (CC).

Blaauwberg Municipality v Bekker 1998 (1) All SA 88 (LC).

Burns. J., Hull, G., Lefko-Everett, K., & Njozela, L. (2018). *Defining social cohesion* (SALDRU Working Paper No. 216(1)), pp. 1–18.

Cavanagh, E. (2013). *Land rights that come with cut-off dates: A comparative reflection on restitution, aboriginal title, and historical injustice*. Available at SSRN: https://ssrn.com/abstract=2297188 or http://doi.org/10.2139/ssrn.2297188.

Concerned Land Claimants' Organisation of Port Elizabeth v Port Elizabeth & Community Restoration 2017 (2) SA 531 (CC).

Department of Land Affairs v Goedelegen Tropical Fruits (Pty) 2007 6 SA 199 (CC).

Government of the Republic of Zimbabwe v Fick 2013 (5) SA 325 (CC).

Khosis Community, Lohatla v Minister of Defence 2004 (5) SA 494 (SCA).

King Sabata Dalindyebo Municipality v Kwalindile Community 2010 ZALCC 33.

King Sabata Dalindyebo Municipality v Kwalindile Community 2012 3 All SA 479 (SCA).

King Sabata Dalindyebo Municipality v Landmark Holdings (Pty) Ltd 2013 3 All SA 251 (SCA) (KSD).

Kloppers, H. J., & Pienaar, G. J. (2014). Historical context of land reform in South Africa and early policies. *Potchefstroomse Elektroniese Regsblad/Potchefstroom Electronic Law Journal, 17*(2), 607–707.

Klug, H. (2018). Decolonization, compensation and constitutionalism: Land, wealth and the sustainability of constitutionalism in post-apartheid South

Africa. *South African Journal on Human Rights* (forthcoming). Available at SSRN: https://ssrn.com/abstract=3244000.
Kranspoort Community 2000 (2) SA 124 (LCC).
Kwalindile Community v King Sabata Dalindyebo Municipality 2013 6 SA 193 (CC).
Lahiff, E. (2001). *Land reform in South Africa: Is it meeting the challenge?* (PLAAS Policy Brief, 1), pp. 1–6.
Makhado, R. (2012). *South Africa's land reform debate: Progress and challenges*, pp. 1–6. Available at SSRN: https://ssrn.com/abstract=2181379.
Minister of Finance v Van Heerden 2004 (6) SA 121 (CC).
Mostert, H. (2014). Land as a "national asset" under the Constitution: The system change envisaged by the 2011 Green Paper on land policy and what this means for property law under the Constitution. *Potchefstroomse Elektroniese Regsblad/Potchefstroom Electronic Law Journal, 17*(2), 760–797.
Mphela v Haakdoornbult Boerdery CC 2007 (5) SA 596 (SCA).
Nicolson, G. (2018, July 5). Zulu King Goodwill Zwelithini uses expropriation bogeyman to perpetuate control of tribal land. *Daily Maverick*.
Palmary, I. (2015). Reflections on social cohesion. *Psychology in Society, 49*, 62–69.
Republic of South Africa. (1994). *Restitution of Land Rights Act 22 of 1994, as amended by Act 48 of 2003*.
Republic of South Africa. (1996). *Interim Protection of Informal Land Rights Act 31 of 1996*.
Republic of South Africa. (1996). *Land Reform (Labour Tenants) Act of 1996*.
Republic of South Africa. (1996). *South African Constitution Act 108 of 1996*.
Republic of South Africa. (1997). *Extension of Security of Tenure Act 62 of 1997*.
Ronen, Y. (2008). The dispossessed and the distressed: Conflicts in land-related rights. In E. Brems (Ed.), *Transitions from unlawful territorial regimes. Conflicts between fundamental rights* (pp. 1–42). Intersentia: Antwerpian. Hebrew University International Law Research Paper No. 13-07. Available at SSRN: https://ssrn.com/abstract=1021761.
Sibanda, R. (2001, June 4–5). *Land reform and poverty alleviation in South Africa*. Paper presented at the SARPN conference on Land Reform and Poverty Alleviation in Southern Africa held at the Human Sciences Research Council Pretoria, 1–10.
Sihlobo, W., & Kirsten, J. (2018). *A compendium of essays on land reform in South Africa*, pp. 1–36. AgriBIZ and Stellenbosch University.
Van Ho, T. (2016). Is it already too late for Colombia's land restitution process? The impact of international investment law on transitional justice initiatives. *International Human Rights Law Review, 5*(1), 60–85.

CHAPTER 12

Climate Change and Land Issues in South Africa: A Convergence

Oluwole Olutola

Introduction

Climate change is a worldwide phenomenon. It is described as 'the challenge of our generation' (UNFCCC, 2017). No single country of the world is spared, as the phenomenon shows no respect for national territorial divisions. However, Africa and, by extension, South Africa, are particularly vulnerable to climate change. There are many factors responsible for South Africa's vulnerability. These range from the country's geographical location, complex topography, proximity to world oceans (namely Indian Ocean, South Atlantic Ocean and the Southern Ocean, which extends to its shores), interaction of various climate-sensitive issues, and low adaptive capacity (Glazewski & Collier, 2012; Mambo & Faccer, 2017).

The effects of climate change in South Africa are escalating, with evidence seen in an increased number of extreme weather events such as droughts, floods, high winds and heatwaves (DEA, 2017). South Africa's vulnerability to climate change extends across virtually all sectors.

O. Olutola (✉)
University of Johannesburg, Johannesburg, South Africa

A. O. Akinola et al. (eds.), *The New Political Economy of Land Reform in South Africa*,
https://doi.org/10.1007/978-3-030-51129-6_12

Although the agro-water sector is the most affected, other key sectors such as energy, mining, health, tourism, manufacturing, trade and investment, are equally not spared from the negative consequences associated with climate change.

Another issue is that South Africa is embroiled in land issues (Atuahene, 2011; Louw, 2013). To correct the imbalances of the apartheid system and as a means of socio-economic redress, the post-1994 democratic South Africa shuttled between various land reform initiatives and agricultural restructuring programmes; of which neither of the two interventions has been able to effectively deliver the set objective (Greenberg, 2013). The issue of land in South Africa is not only cultural and socio-economically important, it is also highly political due to the country's apartheid history.

Going forward, President Cyril Ramaphosa consistently cited the planned 'land expropriation without compensation' (LEWC) as the preferred government policy direction vis-à-vis land reform in South Africa (Beinart, 2018). In its intent, the move is aimed at expropriating land without compensation, having recourse to the debatable Section 25 of the South African Constitution (Daniel, 2018). At face value, the land expropriation reform suggests a positive development in a bid to rectify the injustices of past discrimination. However, the same reform is enmeshed in controversy and its appropriateness given the South African context is also highly contested. In addition, it is not certain whether the new approach will bring about a conclusive and desired constitutional amendment, particularly with regard to Section 25 of which the South African parliament already passed a motion in February 2018 for its review and, also, held public hearings to allow for LEWC as part of the land reform process (Agri SA, 2018; PMG, 2018).

Against this background, this chapter examines the convergence of climate change and land-related issues as two critical challenges facing contemporary South Africa. Relying on political ecology as its theoretical framework and a systematic review of a range of secondary sources, this chapter appraises the link between climate change and land-based resources in light of the implications for re-balancing the historically skewed land distribution in post-apartheid South Africa.

The chapter engages the introduction as section one, while section two provides the theoretical framework in the context of political ecology within the liberal perspectives. Section three attempts a review of a range of purposely selected literature. The motivation is to further shed light on the existing knowledge with regard to the connections between climate change and land-based resources in South Africa. Section four discusses the reality of the linkages between the two concepts and how they impact on land reform in post-apartheid South Africa, while section five concludes and highlights policy recommendations.

Theoretical Framework—Political Ecology

To create a proper theoretical discourse around climate change and land matters in South Africa, this chapter adopts 'political ecology' within the broader liberal perspectives. The choice of political ecology is primarily informed by a broad view regarding the connections between political power, economy, social justice, environmental issues and land-based resources. Clearly, these are the main concentrations in this study. However, it is worth noting that there are many theoretical strands of political ecology. These range in focus from political economy, political institutions and environmental subjects.

Although this study is mainly concerned about environmental issues, especially those that focus on climate change and land matters in South Africa, the fact remains that even within the environmental strand there are at least five distinct thoughts. These, according to Perreault, Bridge and McCarthy (2015: 209) are: (1) environmental knowledge, which seeks to explain nature and how the different understandings of the environment impacts on it; (2) environmental change, which focuses on nature-society relations and how they affect various social entities differently; (3) environmental governance that focuses on the various social groupings and by which rule they manage nature, and the effect it has on them; (4) environmental identities, which deal with the question of how social constructions are formed and mirrored by way of access to nature and control over it; and (5) environmental politics, which deal with the numerous undercurrents of political mobilisation around nature.

This chapter yields to these intellectual differentials in various ways in terms of focus and analysis. However, it shows exceptional leanings towards environmental change and politics. Political ecologists generally share a common allegiance to nature-society relations, with some basic assumptions. Nevertheless, before turning to highlight these common theoretical underpinnings, it is appropriate to first address the question: What does political ecology mean?

In the opinion of Piers Blaikie (cited in Forsyth, 2008: 756), political ecology not only focuses on the link between a sound knowledge of the environment and politics, but also how environmental discourse can be reconstructed with the goal of lifting socially vulnerable people above common environmental challenges. This definition draws significant attention to the interplay between humans and the environment as well as the need to see environmental changes in social and political terms. Blaikie and Brookfield (1987: 17) opine that this human-environment linkage revolves around the constant interaction between society and land-based resources as well as within social groupings in society.

Similarly, according to Watts (2000: 257), political ecology seeks to explain the intricate connections between nature and society, but with a careful analytic approach. This is particularly important in the context of the various forms of access and control over resources and their implications for environmental health and sustainable livelihoods. Central to Watt's proposition, political ecology is sensitive to the politics around the environment and how it brings about cultural mobilisation, including how such practices are contested, fought over and negotiated (Watts, 2000: 259). It is imperative to note that climate risk and landed property rights serve to represent the ecological cultural practices in the context of this chapter.

With regard to the common basic assumptions, Bryant and Bailey (1997) point out that political ecologists more generally assume that environmental change and ecological issues are strongly linked to the political system; costs and benefits linked to environmental change in terms of social and economic impact are in most cases shared among stakeholders unevenly; the existing social and economic inequalities are amplified by such unequal distribution of costs and benefits; and there are political implications given the power relations among actors. Moreover, it is a consensus among political ecologists that local choices often result from regional actions, which are in turn functions of global politics. Hence, any strain on human-environment linkages within the global circle would affect both regional and local considerations given that the main focus of political ecology is about nature-society relations (Robbins, 2012).

By integrating political, socio-economic and ecological issues as well as advocating fundamental changes in the management of nature and the rights of people, a political ecology approach offers at least three distinct benefits as far as this study is concerned. First, it allows for critical explanations aimed not only at understanding the depth of the twin ecological challenges of climate change and land issues, but also their influences on the South African state and society. Secondly, it underscores the need for scalable solutions[1] to these challenges. Thirdly, it advocates collective action, thereby stressing the important role of various actors. These, in the context of this study, include the South African government, businesses (local and foreign), environmental nongovernmental organisations (local and international), farmers' associations and individual farmers (commercial or small-scale), and other relevant stakeholders.

Literature Review

Studies on climate change in South Africa have grown considerably in the last few years. One major underlining factor responsible for this upsurge is the unanimity among scholars that South Africa is especially vulnerable to climate change and, also, it is critically important for the government to take the issue more seriously than is currently the case. The Scenario Building Team (2007) lent credence to such intellectual harmony, considering the global perspective as far as the challenges of climate change are concerned. With regard to land reform, there is obviously a plethora of studies concerning the centrality of land issues to the socio-economic and political systems within South Africa. However, the missing point is how these two phenomena interconnect. Besides, it also remains an issue how South Africa has been affected by their intersection, even though literature on the impacts of climate change and land-based resources, especially water and agriculture, abound.

To shed more light on this and for a better approach, the review of extant literature in this section is structured under the captions: climate change: impacts and approaches in South Africa; land matters in South Africa.

Climate Change: Impacts and Approaches in South Africa

The reality of changing climate and its negative effects on socio-economic and ecological assets all over the world is no longer an issue of debate. The Intergovernmental Panel on Climate Change (IPCC, 2007, 2014) did

[1] Scalable solutions involve exploring alternative interventions with the capacity to effectively tackle climate change and land matters in post-apartheid South Africa without affecting the growth of the South African state and society.

much justice to this. However, scholars share different positions regarding the extent to which climate change is an environmental issue (Brauch et al., 2011). For instance, while Nwebaza and Kotze (cited in Olutola, 2017) hold that climate change is both an environmental as well as a development issue, Stern (2012) is more emphatic that climate change extends beyond environmental issues, as it affects almost all aspects of national economies ranging from energy, industry, transportation, water, agriculture and forests. Taylor (2014: 10) reasons that climate change represents a powerful agent of anti-development, which, if left unchecked, will roll back the already uneven achievements of the modern era.

Granted that the debates around a clear demarcation between climate change and purely environmental concern are not yet over, there is consensus that climate change is an ecological issue and its effects are multifaceted. Agriculture is one of the key sectors that suffers the most from climate change, even though it also ironically contributes to it. For instance, through the use of fossil-fuel in agriculture (the manufacture and use of agricultural inputs and farm machinery) and land management activities (such as deforestation and the burning of crops and animal waste, including bush burning), the agriculture sector significantly contributes to anthropogenic greenhouse gas (GHG) emission (Lenka et al., 2015: 38). Biofuels, as energy sourced from agricultural plants, represent one of the low carbon options to mitigate the effects of climate change. However, through biofuels, carbon dioxide is directly removed from the air and its growth sometimes produces unintended environmental impacts, considering that some crops can even generate more greenhouse gases than do fossil fuels depending on the methods used to produce the feedstock and process the fuel (FAO, 2008: 55).

Generally, the impact of climate change on agriculture is for the most part negative. This is regardless of whether it is small-scale subsistence farming or large-scale commercial farming. While the impacts on small-scale subsistence farming are generally complex and localised (IPCC, 2007: 10), the effects on large-scale mechanised farming that produces the bulk of the agricultural yields in most economies are more and result largely from unstable and extreme precipitation such as heavy rainfall, flooding and hailstorms. In Africa, where most of the agricultural practices are rain-dependent, the impact of climate change is reported to be more severe, as agricultural yields in some of the African countries could be reduced by up to 50% by 2020 (IPCC, 2007: 11). This simply implies additional strains on food security on the continent.

With specific reference to South Africa, the effects of climate change regarding the different sectors have been variously examined. For instance, the climate-energy contradiction (Amusan & Olutola, 2017a; Atteridge, 2011; Bond, 2011, 2012; Death, 2014; Menyah & Wolde-Rufael, 2010; Tyler, 2010; Winkler & Marquand, 2009); the symbiotic relationship between climate change and tourism (Amusan & Olutola, 2017b; Rogerson, 2016; Steyn & Spencer, 2012); linkages with human health, particularly how the prevalence of curable and terminal health issues such as cholera, tuberculosis and HIV/AIDS are further amplified as a result of the incidence of climate change (Chersich et al., 2018; Turpie et al., 2002); and, the untoward implications for human settlements (Van Huyssteen, Le Roux, & Van Niekerk, 2013).

Similarly, established studies on the effects of climate change with regard to the agro-water sector in South Africa are just too many to be captured here. However, the key findings of common concerns are reflected. For instance, South Africa is generally regarded as a country that is prone to water scarcity (DEA, 2017: 17). Moreover, many are also united in their opinion that South Africa is already experiencing climate-induced water stress, with regard to both surface and underground water (Dallas & Rivers-Moore, 2014; Dennis & Dennis, 2012).

As a country with high vulnerability to unstable climatic conditions and limited arable land, the effects of climate change on agriculture—being the foremost climate-sensitive sector—may be disastrous. Gbetibouo, Ringler, and Hassan (2010) found that the impacts on crop yields and production vary across the regions in South Africa. For instance, they established that the Western Cape and Gauteng provinces, which have high levels of infrastructure development, high literacy rates and low shares of agriculture in the total gross national product (GDP), are relatively low on the vulnerability index. The opposite is true with Limpopo, KwaZulu-Natal and the Eastern Cape, which are characterised by densely populated rural areas, large numbers of small-scale farmers and high dependency on rain-fed agriculture, coupled with high land degradation (Gbetibouo et al., 2010). Their findings seem to confirm the earlier prediction, according to Benhin (2006), that climate change poses significant dangers to crop farming and that the effects will not be the same given the different agro-climatic regions and agricultural systems across South Africa.

Extending the discourse beyond climate change impacts, though with a particular focus on agricultural production in Limpopo, Maponya and

Mpandeli (2012) identify a number of adaptation possibilities. These include soil fertility management through the use of fertilisers, chemicals and pesticides; water management, particularly increased irrigation systems; and the use of subsidies and insurance, as a means of accelerating farmers' failure to meet transaction costs. However, their study fails to acknowledge other common adaptation strategies such as the use of different crops or crop varieties, planting trees and changing planting dates (Di Falco, 2014). Others studies include frequently less-reported options such as seeking off-farm activities, migrating to urban areas, changing farming type, using climate-friendly technologies and water conservation (Bryan, Deressa, Gbetibouo, & Ringler, 2009).

Moreover, the National Climate Change Adaptation Strategy (NCCAS) provides for a variety of adaptation options on a wider scale (DEA, 2017). Besides, by the mere acknowledgement that South Africa contends with the challenges of inadequate water, limited arable land and environmental degradation (DEA, 2017: 2), the NCCAS seems to have captured more succinctly the country's climate scenario and the need for adaptation. The same may also be said of other measures, such as the National Climate Change Response (RSA, 2011), the Long-Term Adaptation Scenarios (DEA, 2013) and the National Climate Change Response Monitoring and Evaluation System Framework (DEA, 2015).

As observed, the White Paper on the National Climate Change Response is lacking in its capacity to ensure that adaptation planning and strategies are mainstreamed across sectoral divisions in all tiers of government (Ziervogel et al., 2014: 605). The situation is further challenged by other social issues, chief among them include unemployment, widespread poverty and informal settlements. These social dynamics put additional pressures on climate-induced weather events (Mambo and Faccer, 2017). Nevertheless, the two studies share different views in terms of what the solution could be.

While Ziervogel et al. (2014: 606) advocate the need for further research around the science, effects and vulnerability of climate change as well as the various adaptation strategies to be integrated across all sectoral divisions in terms of decision-making, Mambo and Faccer (2017) believe that the vulnerability of climate change and extreme weather events could be effectively checked by addressing inequalities as well as improving basic services.

Land Matters in South Africa

Perhaps, more than anything else, the issue of land in South Africa has received and is still receiving considerable scholarly attention. Of a total surface area estimated at 121.9 million ha, over 80% (100 million ha) is used for agriculture, out of which only 12% is considered arable and the rest is deemed suitable for livestock purposes (Lotter, 2017). These figures conflict with the figures put forward by Agri SA (2018), that of the 122.5 million hectares of total land surface, approximately 76% (93.1 million ha) is agricultural land in South Africa.

Based on the report of the Department of Agriculture, Forestry and Fisheries (DAFF, 2012: 3), approximately 82 million ha is occupied by less than 40,000 commercial farmers who are predominantly white and, apparently, responsible for more than 95% of South Africa's formal, marketed, agricultural output. As contained in the report, as of 2010, approximately 14 million ha were occupied by roughly 225,000 smallholder farmers, belonging to about 150,000 households, and are predominantly black, while approximately 22.8 million households are subsistence producers, who practice agriculture mainly for purposes of own-consumption, largely by means of gardening and small-scale animal husbandry.

This racially skewed land distribution representing one of the untoward legacies of apartheid, according to Pringle (2013), is nothing but a wrong perception. This perception, he further argues, is largely informed by the vague concept of agricultural land in South Africa and, also, underpins nearly every analysis concerning what percentage of land should be redistributed, including the target of redistributing 30% of farmlands owned by white South Africans to black citizens by 2014. His key finding is that the emphasis should be on agricultural potential, which is the real value of land and the criterion for redistribution, as against the government's fictitious approach of measuring land purely in hectares. With this approach, Pringle (2013) expounds that it is evident that black people already possess approximately 48% of the agricultural land in post-apartheid South Africa.

Pringle's position aligns more or less perfectly with that of Agri SA (2018), that no agrarian land reform process can succeed unless it is based upon relevant and accurate data. Although significant improvements have been made in this regard with specific reference to the 2018 land audit by the Department of Rural Development and Land Reform, public discourse around land reform in South Africa is still mostly affected by inaccurate and self-serving data.

Likewise, much like the view held in many other studies (Atuahene, 2011; Boudreaux, 2009; Greenberg, 2013; Jacobs et al., 2003; Lahiff & Li, 2012), it is believed that land reform projects have been generally largely unsuccessful and that agricultural productivity may be put at risk and food security threatened should these trends continue. These projects are three-pronged: restitution that has to do with amending the historical rights to land; tenure reforms which are more concerned with landholding; and redistribution, which is the most important and aimed at rectifying the racially skewed pattern of land ownership by taking white-owned lands and give them to historically disadvantaged groups, mostly black South Africans (Jacobs, Lahiff, & Hall, 2003: 1). Boudreaux (2009: 3) added that land redistribution was also meant to serve the purpose of promoting social justice as well as socio-economic equity.

There seems to be a widespread agreement that the South African agricultural sector is often faced with confusion and uncertainty resulting from the inconsistencies around land reform policy, which in effect constitutes an impediment to investment in the sector. Reference in this regard is made to interventions such as Settlement/Land Acquisition Grant, willing buyer, willing seller approach to land reform, land redistribution for agricultural development and, lately, LEWC. Yet, there is no such unanimity among scholars on the reasons why land reform projects in South Africa have been for the most part ineffectual. Generally, some of the reasons put forward include a lack of political will, inadequate budget, inappropriate project design, policy uncertainty, corruption by officials, lack of or poor communication with stakeholders, weak civil society organisations, lack of tenure security and lack of access to production finance. Others include a lack of training and capacity, inadequate necessary support services and shortages of working capital. The ultimate result is seen in the widespread underutilisation of acquired or successfully transferred land. Still, a more detailed account is rendered in both the report of the High Level Panel on the Assessment of Key Legislation and the Acceleration of Fundamental Change (RSA, 2017) and the White Paper on South African Land Policy (DLA, 1997).

With specific regard to the provisions of Section 25 of the South African Constitution, Agri SA (2018) contends that the property clause, as provided in Section 25, is not an impediment to land reform; the main challenge is a failure of implementation rather than a failure of legal framework. Therefore, the South African government needs to pay compensation for any land expropriated in the national, public interest. Clearly, this is not a general position, considering that there is no constitutional clarity regarding exactly what the clauses 'just and equitable compensation' and 'equitable balance' imply in the context of land redistribution. Moreover, it is strongly believed by the leadership of the ruling African National Congress (ANC) and the majority of parliamentarians that Section 25 requires a constitutional amendment to enable the implementation of LEWC.

This question of constitutional legitimacy also adds to the other controversies around the planned LEWC. For instance, it is interesting to note that the ANC-led government proceeds with the restitution policy despite the invalidation of the Restitution Amendment Act by the South African Constitutional Court in 2016 (Beinart, 2018). For the purpose of due acknowledgement, it is pertinent to remark that the study by Walker 2005 came close to what is intended in this study. The reason is that it extended the discourse around land issues in South Africa beyond the general questions of political aspiration, popular expectation, and the capacity of land reform to achieve stated objectives. This general thinking, according to Walker (2005), is a mismatch and, thus, points to the major flaw in land reform projects in South Africa. Of particular interest is what Walker (2005) dubbed the limits to land reform and its intersection with demographic, ecological and social constraints, even though the approach was very vague and more general than specific.

Linkages and Implications

Climate change is recognised as a major factor responsible for land degradation (Kumar & Das, 2014). Other ecological hazards linked to climate change include, *inter alia*, soil erosion and contamination, the destruction of vegetation and desertification. Generally, climate change not only impacts land-based resources in terms of depletion, but it is also intricately connected to almost all facets of human existence. South Africa's experience in this regard is not an exception, although the precise magnitude of the effects of climate change on the country's land-based resources, especially agricultural land and forestry, are not yet known and, of course, still unfolding. Besides, the sensitivity of other sectors such as water, mining, energy and tourism with regard to climate impacts on land-based resources is also worthy of note. For instance, it is needless to point out that water plays an important role in agricultural land productivity through irrigation.

Extreme and harsh climate-induced weather conditions in South Africa could obviously put more pressure on agricultural land and its values. The implication is that the agricultural value of land is importantly reduced due to climate change and variability. Aside from posing significant risks to farm productivity and, by extension, food security, which constitute a major concern to land redistribution, it again reaffirms the call for a proper evaluation of land, particularly in terms of its agricultural potential as a pre-condition for any successful land reform projects in South Africa. This is extremely important to finding any scalable solutions to the country's perennial land issues, considering that most of the effects of climate change can be viewed as impacts on land (Ingram & Hong, 2011: 78).

Beyond the question of constitutionality and, perhaps, any other legal imperatives around the implementation of LEWC, the key concern is the intricate connections between climate change and land-based resources. Obviously, such a situation could increase funding risks as well as impede efforts aimed at investment promotion within the agricultural land sector. Besides, it relinquishes the challenge of another failed policy conception regarding land reform projects in South Africa given that the majority of South Africans are still not aware of the implications of climate change in their normal daily lives.

Worst still, climate change is yet to be fully accorded its proper place in national planning in terms of its mainstreaming across all sectoral policies and strategic plans, including those affecting land reform in South Africa. Climate change is still treated more as an environmental by-product than a development issue in the South Africa's development framework. This approach shoud change by elevating climate change in the same class as other national concerns such as addressing inequalities and poverty eradication. This environmental—non-developmental—framing of climate change suggests little or no progress in terms of lessening the effects of climate change on the existing socio-economic inequalities and, by extension, poverty that is widespread in South Africa. This could also represent untoward implications for the planned LEWC in view of the critical interaction between climate change and land-based resources.

Conclusion and Policy Recommendations

Climate change and land-based resources are no doubt interlinked, with implications for development issues in any state and society. For the most part, this aspect of nature-society intersection has received little or no consideration in the conception, approach and implementation of land reform projects in post-apartheid South Africa. The policy direction in the context of the proposed LEWC is also not an exception to this oversight. Having established that the agricultural value of land has been importantly reduced by the ecological effects of climate change, any meaningful discourse around land reform projects in South Africa should be based on a sound knowledge of the intersection between climate change and land-based resources and their implications for the South African state and society.

This study reaffirms the call for a proper evaluation of land, particularly in terms of its agricultural potential as a pre-condition for any successful land reform programmes. Without which, it will be difficult (if not impossible) to bring about scalable solutions to land issues in South Africa. Therefore, this study recommends a Climate Smart Land Reform (CSLR) that not only recognises the imperative of land redistribution (with or without compensation), but which also should be accomplished based on a thorough knowledge of the changing climate and its impacts on land-based resources, especially agricultural land.

In this sense, a major shift in favour of climate-sensitive policy and management is required in the way land reform is being pursued in South Africa. More importantly, the South African government should build strong synergy and partnerships with the private sector, relevant civil society organisations and other key stakeholders in the land reform projects. The Agri SA and individual farmers as among the important stakeholders readily come to mind. Finally, more contributions of research around the important intersection between climate change and land-based resources are needed to further evaluate how land reform in post-apartheid South Africa may be affected by the nature-society interlink.

References

Agri, S. A. (2018). *Submission on expropriation without compensation*. Centurion, South Africa: Agri SA.

Amusan, L., & Olutola, O. (2017a). Paris Agreement (PA) on climate change and South Africa's coal energy complex: Issues at stake. *Africa Review, 9*(1), 43–57. https://doi.org/10.1080/09744053.2016.1239932.

Amusan, L., & Olutola, O. (2017b). Climate change and sustainable tourism: South Africa caught in-between. *African Journal of Hospitality, Tourism and Leisure, 6*(4), 1–15.

Atteridge, A. (2011). *Multiple identities: Behind South Africa's approach to climate diplomacy*. Stockholm: Stockholm Environment Institute.

Atuahene, B. (2011). South Africa's land reform crisis: Eliminating the legacy of apartheid. *Foreign Affairs, 90*(4), 121–129. https://www.jstor.org/stable/23039612.

Beinart, W. (2018, March 5). Dilemmas of land reform for the Ramaphosa era. *Business Brief*. Available: https://www.bbrief.co.za/2018/03/05/dilemmas-of-land-reform-for-the-ramaphosa-era/ (Accessed 16 October 2018).

Benhin, J. K. A. (2006). *Climate change and South African agriculture: Impacts and adaptation options* (CEEPA Discussion Paper No. 21). Centre for Environmental Economics and Policy in Africa, University of Pretoria.

Blaikie, P., & Brookfield, H. (1987). *Land degradation and society*. London: Methuen.

Bond, P. (Ed.). (2011). *Durban's climate gamble: Trading carbon betting the Earth*. Pretoria: UNISA Press.

Bond, P. (2012). *Politics of climate justice: Paralysis above, movement below*. Scottsville: University of KwaZulu-Natal Press.

Boudreaux, K. (2009). *Land reform as a social justice: The case of South Africa* (Working Paper No. 09-37). Mercatus Center, George Mason University.

Brauch, H. G., Oswald Spring, U., Mesjasz, C., Grin, J., Kameri-Mbote, P., Chourou, B., … Birkmann, J. (Eds.). (2011). *Coping with global environmental change, disasters and security: Threats, challenges, vulnerabilities and risks*. New York: Springer Nature.

Bryan, E., Deressa, T. T., Gbetibouo, G. A., & Ringler, C. (2009). Adaptation to climate change in Ethiopia and South Africa: Options and constraints. *Environmental Science & Policy, 12*(4), 413–426. https://doi.org/10.1016/j.envsci.2008.11.002.

Bryant, R. L., & Bailey, S. (1997). *Third World Political Ecology*. London and New York: Routledge.

Chersich, M. F., Wright, C. Y., Venter, F., Rees, H., Scorgie, F., & Erasmus, B. (2018). Impacts of climate change on health and wellbeing in South Africa. *International Journal of Environmental Research and Public Health, 15*, 1–14. https://doi.org/10.3390/ijerph15091884.

Dallas, H. F., & Rivers-Moore, N. (2014). Ecological consequences of global climate change for freshwater ecosystems in South Africa. *South African Journal of Science, 110*(5/6), 1–11. https://doi.org/10.1590/sajs.2014/20130274.

Daniel, L. (2018, September 16). Land expropriation without compensation: What the Constitution says. *The South African.* https://www.thesouthafrican.com/land-expropriation-constitution-september-2018/ (Accessed 18 October 2018).

Death, C. (2014). The green economy in South Africa: Global discourses and local politics. *Politikon, 41*(1), 1–22. https://doi.org/10.1080/02589346.2014.885668.

Dennis, I., & Dennis, R. (2012). Climate change vulnerability index for South African aquifers. *Water SA, 38*(3), 1–10. http://dx.doi.org/10.4314/wsa.v38i3.7.

Department of Agriculture, Forestry and Fisheries. (2012). *Integrated growth and development plan 2012.* Pretoria: DAFF. Available: https://www.daff.gov.za/docs/policy/igdp121.pdf (Accessed 22 October, 2018).

Department of Environmental Affairs (DEA). (2011). *National Climate Change Response White Paper.* Pretoria: RSA. https://www.environment.gov.za/sites/default/files/legislations/national_climatechange_response_whitepaper.pdf (Accessed 19 October, 2018).

Department of Environmental Affairs (DEA). (2013). *Long-Term Adaptation Scenarios Flagship Research Programme (LTAS) for South Africa. Summary for policy-makers.* Pretoria: DEA. https://www.environment.gov.za/sites/default/files/docs/summary_policymakers_bookV3.pdf (Accessed 22 October, 2018).

Department of Environmental Affairs (DEA). (2015). *The National Climate Change Response monitoring and evaluation system framework.* Pretoria: DEA.

Department of Environmental Affairs (DEA). (2017). *National Climate Change Adaptation Strategy.* Pretoria: DEA.

Department of Land Affairs. (1997). *White Paper on South African Land Policy.* Pretoria: DLA.

Di Falco, S. (2014). Adaptation to climate change in Sub-Saharan agriculture: Assessing the evidence and rethinking the drivers. *European Review of Agricultural Economics, 41*(3), 405–430. https://doi.org/10.1093/erae/jbu014.

Food and Agriculture Organization. (2008). *The state of food and agriculture.* Rome: FAO.

Forsyth, T. (2008). Political ecology and the epistemology of social justice. *Geoforum, 39,* 756–764. https://doi.org/10.1016/j.geoforum.2006.12.005.

Gbetibouo, G. A., Ringler, C., & Hassan, R. (2010). Vulnerability of the South African farming sector to climate change and variability: An indicator approach. *Natural Resources Forum, 34*, 175–187. https://doi.org/10.1111/j.1477-8947.2010.01302.x.

Glazewski, J., & Collier, D. (2012). South Africa's climate change. In R. Lord, S. Goldberg, L. Rajamani, & J. Brunnee (Eds.), *Climate change liability: Transnational law and practice* (pp. 319–347). New York: Cambridge University Press.

Greenberg, S. (2013). *The disjunctures of land and agricultural reform in South Africa: Implications for the agri-food system* (Working Paper 26). Bellville: PLAAS, UWC.

Ingram, G. K., & Hong, Y. (Eds.). (2011). *Climate change and land policies.* Proceedings of the 2010 Land Policy Conference, Lincoln Institute of Land Policy, Cambridge, MA.

Jacobs, P., Lahiff, E., & Hall, R. (2003). *Land redistribution.* Cape Town: PLAAS (Programme for Land and Agrarian Studies).

Kumar, R., & Das, A. J. (2014). Climate change and its impact on land degradation: Imperative need to focus. *Journal of Climatology and Weather Forecasting, 2*(1), 108. https://doi.org/10.4172/2332-2594.1000108.

Lahiff, E., & Li, G. (2012). *Land Redistribution in South Africa: A Critical Review.* Washington, DC: World Bank.

Lenka, S., Lenka, N. K., Sejian, V., & Mohanty, M. (2015). Contribution of agriculture sector to climate change. In V. Sejian et al. (Eds.), *Climate change impact on livestock: Adaptation and mitigation* (pp. 37–48). New Delhi, India: Springer. https://doi.org/10.1007/978-81-322-2265-1_3.

Lotter, D. (2017). Risk and vulnerability in the South African farming sector: Implications for sustainable agriculture and food security. In J. Mambo & K. Faccer (Eds.), *South African Risk and Vulnerability Atlas: Understanding the social and environmental implications of climate change* (2nd ed., pp. 66–73). Pretoria: Council for Scientific and Industrial Research (CSIR) and the Department of Science and Technology (DST).

Louw, L. (2013). Land distribution paradoxes and dilemmas. *The Journal of the Helen Suzman Foundation, 70*, 54–65.

Mambo, J., & Faccer, K. (Eds.). (2017). *South African Risk and Vulnerability Atlas: Understanding the social and environmental implications of climate change* (2nd ed.). Pretoria: Council for Scientific and Industrial Research (CSIR) and the Department of Science and Technology (DST).

Maponya, P., & Mpandeli, S. (2012). Climate change and agricultural production in South Africa: Impacts and adaptation options. *Journal of Agricultural Science, 4*(10), 48–60. https://doi.org/10.5539/jas.v4n10p48.

Menyah, K., & Wolde-Rufael, Y. (2010). Energy consumption, pollutant emissions and economic growth in South Africa. *Energy Economics, 32*, 1374–1382.

Olutola, O. I. (2017). *The political anatomy of South Africa's climate change policy* (PhD thesis). North-West University, South Africa.

Pachauri R. K., & Meyer, L. A. (2014). *Climate change 2014: Synthesis report*. Contribution of Working Groups I, II and III to the Fifth Assessment Report of the Intergovernmental Panel on Climate Change. Geneva, Switzerland.

Pachauri, R. K., & Reisinger, A. (Eds.). (2007). *Climate change 2007: Synthesis report*. Contribution of Working Groups I, II and III to the Fourth Assessment Report of the Intergovernmental Panel on Climate Change. Geneva, Switzerland.

Parliamentary Monitoring Group. (2018, September 4). *Section 25 review of Constitution: Public hearings day 1*. Available: https://pmg.org.za/committee-meeting/26982/ (Accessed 18 October, 2018).

Perreault, T., Bridge, G., & McCarthy, J. (Eds.). (2015). *The Routledge handbook of political ecology*. London and New York: Routledge.

Pringle, E. (2013). Land reform and white ownership of agricultural land in South Africa. *The Journal of the Helen Suzman Foundation, 1*(70), 37–42.

Republic of South Africa. (2017). *High Level Panel on the assessment of key legislation and the acceleration of fundamental change*. Pretoria: Government Press.

Robbins, P. (2012). *Political ecology: A critical introduction* (2nd ed.). West Sussex, UK: Wiley-Blackwell.

Rogerson, C. M. (2016). Climate change, tourism and local economic development in South Africa. *Lepu, 31*(1–2), 322-331. https://doi.org/10.1177/0269094215624354.

Scenario Building Team. (2007). *Long term mitigation scenarios: Scenario document*. Pretoria: Department of Environment Affairs and Tourism.

Stern, T. (2012, August 2). *Remarks at Dartmouth College*. Available: https://2009-2017.state.gov/e/oes/rls/remarks/2012/196004.html (Accessed 16 October, 2018).

Steyn, J. N., & Spencer, J. P. (2012). Climate change and tourism: Implications for South Africa. *African Journal for Physical, Health Education, Recreation and Dance, 18*(1), 1–19. https://hdl.handle.net/10520/EJC119853.

Taylor, M. (2014). *The political ecology of climate change adaptation: Livelihoods, agrarian change and the conflicts of development*. London: Routledge.

Turpie, J., Winkler, H., Spalding-Fecher, R., & Midgley, G. (2002). *Economic Impacts of Climate Change in South Africa: A Preliminary Analysis of Unmitigated Damage Costs*. Cape Town: Southern Waters Ecological Research & Consulting & Energy & Development Research Centre, University of Cape Town.

Tyler, E. (2010). Aligning South African energy and climate change mitigation policy. *Climate Policy, 10*(5), 575–588. http://hdl.handle.net/11427/16585.

United Nations Framework Convention on Climate Change. (2017). *Climate change is the challenge of our generation*. Available: https://unfccc.int/news/climate-change-is-the-challenge-of-our-generation (Accessed 13 October, 2018).

Van Huyssteen, E., Le Roux, A., & Van Niekerk, W. (2013). Analysing risk and vulnerability of South African settlements: Attempts, explorations and reflections. *Journal of Disaster Risk Studies, 5*(2), 1–8. https://doi.org/10.4102/jamba.v5i2.80.

Walker, C. (2005). The limits to land reform: Rethinking 'the land question'. *Journal of Southern African Studies, 31* (4), 805–824. https://www.jstor.org/stable/25065048.

Watts, M. (2000). Political ecology. In E. Sheppard & T. J. Barnes (Eds.), *A companion to economic geography* (pp. 257–274). Oxford, UK: Blackwell.

Winkler, H., & Marquand, A. (2009). Changing development paths: From an energy-intensive to low-carbon economy in South Africa. *Climate and Development, 1,* 47–65. http://hdl.handle.net/11427/16928.

Ziervogel, G., New, M., Archer van Garderen, E., Midgley, G., Taylor, A., Hamann, R., … Warburton, M. (2014). Climate change impacts and adaptation in South Africa. *WIREs Climate Change, 5,* 605–620. https://doi.org/10.1002/wcc.295.

CHAPTER 13

Urbanization, Poverty and the Paradox of Land Reform in South Africa

Adeoye O. Akinola

Introduction

A decisive impact of globalization and the subsequent exportation of civilization to Africa were the emergence of cities, followed by the massive emigration of rural dwellers into urban centres. This has engendered contradictions in the use of land and land-related issues in South Africa. Across Africa, the complexity in the urban land use and ownership persists because of the rate at which African states are urbanizing, the 'distortionist' legacy of colonialism, as well the inability of post-colonial states to resolve the land conflict (Mandisa, 2015). Urbanization continues to be on the rise in both developed and developing countries, and the percentage of the global urban population is projected to increase to about 57% by 2050, from the 47% that was recorded in 2000 (AFDB, 2012). Furthermore, Africa has the highest urban growth rate since the 2000s at 3.5% per annum, which will continue at the same rate till 2050.

A. O. Akinola (✉)
University of Zululand, KwaDlangezwa, South Africa
e-mail: AkinolaA@unizulu.ac.za; aoakinola@uj.ac.za

A. O. Akinola et al. (eds.), *The New Political Economy of Land Reform in South Africa*,
https://doi.org/10.1007/978-3-030-51129-6_13

By 2010, the entire Asia-Pacific region's urban population was estimated at 754 million people, while 45.5% of the population lives in the urban centres (ESCAP, 2013). Indeed, urbanization rate in the region is expected to rise to about 50% in 2026. Instead of the expected growth associated with urbanization in the developed countries,

> Urbanization in Africa has failed to bring about inclusive growth which, in turn, has resulted in proliferation of slums, urban poverty and rising inequality. Inequality in African cities remains the second highest in the world with an average Gini coefficient of about 0.58, well above the average of 0.4. (AFDB, 2012)

South Africa is noted for abject urban poverty and inequality, which has its root in the foreign domination of the local population and the associated distortion of its socio-environmental landscape. The realities of apartheid policies, which underdeveloped the rural areas and appropriated arable lands for a minority, further broadened the gap between the urban centres and rural areas. This ultimately engendered the impoverishment of more than 13 million black South Africans, who were largely restricted to 'reserves', and consistently experienced denials of land use and ownership.

South Africa remains the most urbanized country in the southern African region. Indeed, urbanization leaves hundreds of millions of children in cities and towns, excluded from vital services, as infrastructure and services have failed to keep up with urban growth in many regions. The abolition of the apartheid regime, and tremendous infrastructural and industrial development of the urban centres, enhanced massive rural-urban migration. Studies reveal that more than half of South African population resides in urban centres. Two years after the end of apartheid, 1994, the inhabitants of cities rose from 55.1 to 57.5%, by 2001 (Todes, Kok, Wentzel, Zyl, & Cross, 2008).

South Africa continues to undergo rapid urbanization, with more than 60% of the population residing in urban areas (Campbell, 2016). The urban eruption soon generated many social and economic issues such as poverty, unemployment, food scarcity, land hunger and illegal occupation of land and erection of informal settlements, abuse of urban space, depletion of infrastructures and ineffective service delivery.

The land dispossession and forced removal of the black population, under the 1913 Native Land Act, resulted in skewed land arrangements, and insecurity of tenure for the larger part of the population. In both apartheid and post-apartheid dispensations, access to land constitutes one of the country's most socially and politically sensitive concerns (Department of Environmental Affairs, 2007a). Agitation over land and land resources continue to dominate the South African polity; hence, the imperativeness of changes in prevailing national land policy (Akinola, 2016). Land reform aims at generating expansive employment, increasing rural incomes and curtailing the overcrowding in South African cities. Furthermore, South African land reform focuses on the attainment of justice, agricultural improvement and agrarian reform. However, within the broad theme of land reform, "the questions of urban land, its use, and its ownership, are either ignored or constructed in terms of the provision of housing or urban economic development" (Mandisa, 2015: 1)

In the post-apartheid era, land-related matters are more profound in public discourse during political transition. Indeed, the political upheaval that led to the exit of President Zuma in 2017, and the ascension of the then Vice President, Cyril Ramaphosa, as President, and the incoming general election, brought renewed activism to the land reform agenda. There have been calls, initiated by Julius Malema's Economic Freedom Fighter (EFF) party, for a revisit of the existing land policy, and the immediate radicalization of the reform agenda based on 'land expropriation without compensation'. This was borne out of the failure of land reform programmes, the reinforcement of the pre-1994 land inequality, the inability to use land reform as instrument of agrarian reform and the human capacity of the grass-root population (Akinola, 2018a). Furthermore, the evident illegal land occupations in major cities, poor service delivery in city suburbs and lack of housing facility, as well as dwindling infrastructural developments in the cities have led to a revision of the prevailing land policy.

This study evaluates the influence of South African land reform on rural-urban migration and explores the convergence between poverty and urbanization within the land reform framework. The chapter is divided into four sections. The introductory section provides the background to the study, which is followed by the reality of urbanization in South Africa. Section three presents the link between urbanization and land reform, and the last section concludes.

Methodology of Study

A qualitative research method, through unstructured interviews, was adopted to grasp the perceptions of the participants in the urbanization-land reform convergence in South Africa. In all, ten respondents were purposively drawn[1] from the following sets of individuals: officials of non-governmental organizations (KwaZulu-Natal Christian Council and Association for Rural Advancement involved in land reform and rural development); two South African government agencies that deal with land reform; legal practitioners on property rights; academic experts in land reform; women community leaders; and others involved in land-related issues in their respective communities and countries (land-owners and the landless). The interviews were conducted in the provinces of KwaZulu-Natal and the Northern Cape from September 2017 to October 2019. The research was sponsored by the University of Zululand Research Ethics Committee.

South Africa and the Urbanization Question: The Reality

A very decisive result of modernization was the evolution and spread of urban centres across the world. It changed the socio-economic and demographic configurations of traditional African societies and dislocated their communal lifestyles. Globally, urbanization is often linked with industrial and economic growth, but in Africa, it is characterized by lower levels of income, inadequate infrastructure investments and poor service delivery (Plaatjies, 2015). South Africa's urban explosion corresponds with that of other African countries. Studies have projected that by 2030, half (50%) of Africa's population will be residing in urban areas. In the case of South Africa, as of 2010, about 62% of the population lived in urban centres, which constituted an increase from 52% in 1990 (Mandisa, 2015: 1; Ruhiiga, 2014). In 2001, 57.5% of South Africans resided in cities, while 42.5% lived in rural areas (Department of Environmental Affairs, 2007b).

Historically, South African urbanization was founded on a need to control the migration and settlement of the black population, in a bid

[1] The University of Zululand Research Ethics Committee approved the conduct of the research, and written informed consent was presented to the participants. The research was guided by the principle of anonymity.

to restrict their access to cities, and condemn many to 'homelands', located in the rural areas without basic infrastructures and poor economic prospects (Todes et al., 2008). As consistently revealed in literature, during apartheid, the urban policy was mainly driven by four major values, which benefited the minority white inhabitants (Ruhiiga, 2014). These were directed at curtailing the rural-urban migration of the black population, a ghettoized urban system that allocated housing areas in relation to ethnic affiliation, the construction of border settlements (populated by unskilled black labour) in neighbourhoods next to cities to feed the industrial demands of the white minority, and a disparate infrastructural and poor service delivery system.

The electoral victory of the National Party in 1948 resulted in the integration of the black people into city life. This was attributed to industrialization, where black people were required to work in the industries (South African History Online, 2018). The black workers occupied the positions that were vacated by the white people, due to them leaving lowly rated and physical, manual jobs. Indeed, white people were majorly found in well-paid and highly skilled labour in the country at that period. The rural-urban surge that occasioned these labour opportunities for black workers was expansive. The need for accommodation created the necessity to allocate pieces of land to black people outside the cities, which later became ghettos (South African History Online, 2018).

Hurd et al. (cited in Urbanization, 2003) noted that, historically, the process of urbanization experienced three major stages:

> The first is identified as extending from the time when people first began to live in towns up until the 18th century. During this stage few urban areas had more than 100,000 people. The second stage is the rapid growth in the size and number of cities contingent upon the process of industrialization. The third stage is metropolitanization which involves the centralization of people and wealth and of society's political, economic and cultural institutions...other writers would refer to a fourth stage of deurbanization via the growth of suburbs, migration to rural areas, alternative communities and planned 'new towns.'

Urban centres comprise of people from cosmopolitan backgrounds, competing for the available resources, infrastructures and opportunities. Persistent rises in the urban population are driven by the belief that urban life affords migrants the opportunities to improve their livelihood, live a modern life, access sophisticated infrastructures and be gainfully employed. Urbanization in post-1994 South Africa is the migration of people from the rural areas and foreign countries into South African cities. This is characterized by informal occupations of land and housing units and erection of structures outside cities and towns. Within the immediate post-apartheid era, more than 5.5 million people moved into cities between 1996 and 2001 (News24, 2008). According to the Department of Environmental Affairs (2007b), in South Africa,

> Urbanization and population growth have contributed to the rapid expansion and sprawl of human settlements. South African cities are characterized by low-density urban sprawl, where residential areas are apart from places of employment, shopping, and public amenities. Urban development continues to amplify the fragmented nature of our cities through the expansion of peripheral formal and informal settlements. Cities become fragmented into discrete cells of development intersected by road systems, and isolated according to land use, population, and income.

Ruhiiga reveals the policy gaps in the South African urban policy architecture and categorized it thus: "the low priority accorded to population change in the urbanization process, planning outcomes out of tune with policy objectives, failure to reform the urban land market and continuing growth of informal settlements on the urban edge" (Ruhiiga, 2014: 610).

A former Safety and Security Minister, Charles Nqakula, once commented that the sporadic movement of South Africans from the rural zones into the cities resulted in,

> The mushrooming of almost 3 000 informal settlements...The majority of those internal migrants went to urban areas. The consequence is that Gauteng has 639 informal settlements. It is followed by KwaZulu-Natal (618) and the Eastern Cape (416) ... both cross border and internal migrants establish themselves in informal settlements. Most of them have no jobs and live in squalor, while others are drawn into crime to make a living. (News24, 2008)

Urbanization has widened the scope and width of the informal sector due to the integration of unskilled labour, drawn from the rural zones and foreign countries, into the urban business life. Most of the migrants from rural areas, and many refugees from foreign countries, mostly uneducated and unskilled, became engaged in the informal sector and reside in informal settlements. In Africa, the informal sector generates about 93% of all new jobs and 61% of urban employment.

As noted by the African Development Bank (AFDB),

> Since incomes from the informal sector are by their very nature low and intermittent, most migrants naturally seek for shelters or become tenants of slum landlords. As a consequence, many African cities have to deal not only with slum proliferation but also with increasing insecurity and crime. (AFDB, 2012)

The informal settlements, otherwise tagged "informal housing, shanty towns, shack-lands, squatter camps, *favelas*, slums" (Huchzermeyer, 2008: 1), are noted for disparate modes of governance. Thus, "weak institutions have contributed to poor urban enforcement, resulting in dysfunctional land and housing markets, which in turn has caused mushrooming of informal settlements" (AFDB, 2012). Shack dwellers are vulnerable and constitute easy mobilization for violence and other societal ills. "Shack dwellers are exposed to hardship, insecurity and hazards from living in squalid and overcrowded conditions on un-serviced and sometimes unsuitable land. They believe they deserve better, which fuels their growing discontent and violent protests" (Turok, 2015).

The informal settlements have played host to different kinds of crime and violence. For instance, Durban South comprises of largely illegal occupation and one of the respondents raised alarm over the level of insecurity in the area. The crime and manifestation of other social ills (car-snatching, assassination, prostitution, use of hard drugs, theft and armed robbery) have been spread to the cities. This upsurge in urban population engenders poverty and unemployment in the affected cities. It also continues to outgrow national populations; this is a trend that increases shack and illegal settlements, and aggravates the stiff competition for resources and other elements of livelihood in the cities. This calls for the imperativeness of targeted policy action around the use and management of land in urban areas to forestall a more equitable and sustainable use of land.

There is exhaustive literature reiterating the fact that land reform has not positively impacted on the livelihood of the population, especially those living in rural areas (Aliber, 2007). In many instances, agricultural production has declined, and farm income and profits have dropped below the remuneration previously paid to farm workers, before the emergent of new land/farm beneficiaries. In South Africa, living in the city, even if it is in informal settlements, provides more employment opportunities and access to public amenities. Many of shack dwellers have more employment opportunities than people living in rural areas. However, the livelihood of shack dwellers is not better than that of the rural population, who sometimes enjoy job security unlike those in the urban centres. Yet, mobility from the cities to the rural areas remains very low. Only one respondent is averse to the urban life. He bluntly stated,

> I am a village man, I live in the rural area, that's who I am, and that's where I will die. I do not care of what is done in Johannesburg or Pretoria, I do not care what is shown on the television, I care about the community. There is an urgent need to decolonise our people, to decolonise their thinking, to decolonize our education system…to decolonize the mind-set of the youths in the rural areas towards exploiting the opportunities of farming available in the rural areas.

However, emerging farmers in the rural areas have been worse hit by the restricted opportunities for productive agriculture, due to the unavailability of support systems. Another participant commented thus,

> It is not all commercial land that are productive. Large percentage of the land they have, arable land, are not utilized and cultivated. The black man given land have no water system, no infrastructures to till the land. Some of the farms sold were already dilapidating and the government did not offer supports to revamp the farm. Subsidies that were given to white farmers during apartheid to boost their production have been abolished by the ruling party, African National Congress (ANC), thereby short-changing the black emerging workers. It is as if they were set up to fail. Thus, commercial land in the rural areas have failed to maintain the number of farm labour working the farm, while expansion of the farm and farm labour have been unattainable. The result has been large migration of hitherto farm workers in the rural areas to the urban centres in search for other employment opportunities.

Although Aliber (2007) notes the efforts of stakeholders to link small-scale farmers to the market, the experiences of a minority group, the Khomani San of the Southern Kalahari, reveal a contrary reality. The Khomani San, predominantly farmers on their 'new farm homes' (they received 36 hectares of land through the government's restitution aspect of the land reform), decried the lack of linkages between the hinterland where they are located and agricultural markets for their farm products (Francis, Francis, & Akinola, 2016). They revealed cases of monumental loss of farm products due to the non-availability of storage and transportation facilities, which has sometimes motivated the reduction in farm activities, and agricultural divestment in the area. According to a respondent,

> The key should be about how to expand the opportunities in the villages and not just about rural dwellers always expecting to receive large or small parcel of land. Empowering people in the rural areas to develop what they need is a first step towards making people stay in the rural areas.

Achieving this has become complex due to the dwindling agricultural fortune of rural dwellers and the opportunities created by industrialization in the cities.

During apartheid, South Africa was characterized by a migrant labour system because of the industrial and economic prospects of the resource (mining) sector of the economy. However, the post-apartheid era has witnessed a tremendous slump of the resource sector, giving rise to labour migration to the informal sector, transportation and security industries and hospitality. Despite the shift, the city continues to attract more employment than rural zones. As noted by the State of Cities Report,

> Cities, and more specifically large cities, are the mainstays of most countries' economies...They offer the largest concentration of customers and provide the biggest markets in the country. They provide the key distribution functions in most national and regional economies and the global economy. The highest concentrations of education facilities are found in the cities...Cities are the engines of the national economy... (Todes et al., 2008: 12)

Another study concludes that surges in the growth of urban centres have been,

> Underpinned by both economic growths within these areas and conditions in rural areas: extensive displacement from farms; the failure of land reform policies; and by further decline in the agrarian base of the rural

> areas of former homelands. Thus, circular migration is a common form of movement in this context. (Todes et al., 2008: 16)

Globalization, and its resulting trans-boundary migration, especially from the Southern African sub-region and economic stability, as well as industrial growth from the 1990s, has attracted new sets of migrants, both legal and illegal, into South Africa (Department of Environmental Affairs, 2007b). A very important motivation for the surge is that cities are seen as "affordable entry points into city economies where migrants can obtain useful information, skills and job contacts" (Turok, 2015). Furthermore, modernization, through the establishment of industries, universities, hospitals, stadia, airports and malls have attracted more people into the urban centres, has played its part in the urban surge. These establishments have become the supplier of labour to people from the rural settlements and foreign countries. Educational systems, highly respected in Africa, have drawn large numbers of foreigners and have put more pressures on the already densely populated cities, like Johannesburg, Pretoria and Durban (Tella, 2018). Competition between the local population and the foreign nationals for depleting infrastructures, meagre resources and dwindling demands for labour in the cities explains the spate of violent xenophobia in the country in 2008, 2015 and 2018 (Akinola, 2018b).

Urbanization-Land Reform Convergence

Land is not 'just' an economic resource or commodity to South Africans (Akinola & Wissink, 2019). In the South African context, land in rural areas continues to represent a "sense of security, identity and history and a preferred place for retirement" (Posel, 2003: 1). The importance of land to the local population explains the continued agitation for land use and ownership by the black population who suffered land dispossession during apartheid. Apartheid land policies further compound the disparities in the South Africa rural-urban landscape by creating the segregated cities and towns that presently define the South Africa landscape. The sophisticated areas inhabited by the whites became the cities, while those segregated for the blacks—characterized by poverty—are the townships and hinterlands (Mandisa, 2015). Despite government's rhetoric of redressing the skewed land ownership and inequality, post-apartheid South Africa still maintains this spatial planning, arrangement and ownership pattern. According to the Department of Environmental Affairs (2007b),

> This sprawl is often exacerbated by land invasions, as long-standing residents living in backyard dwellings of existing townships, as well as newcomers to the city, occupy open land on the outskirts in hope of securing housing in the future. Illegal land encroachment is attributable to growing impatience with the land reform process, especially in urban areas.

As manifested in Nairobi (Kenya), a city known for illegal occupation and overcrowding, housing structures have been erected on government land. In such arrangements, there are complex landlord-tenant relations, whereby the landlords (not land owner) and residents (perhaps the landlord or residents) have no tenure security, and are thereby in a vulnerable situation (Odeny, 2013: 7). Indeed, tenure security is germane to the decongestion of the city and formalization of informal settlements. In urban areas, where land has gone through many ownerships, it becomes too complex to determine the actual owner of such land; hence, there are difficulties in successful restitution programmes of land reform in the urban centres. If there are no lodging of land claims, there are no restitution to be made.

Land reform is riddled with diverse challenges and limitations. Larger percentages of transferred land have not been utilized by the new black owners, who have voiced out their incapacity—resulting from lack of farm resources—to productively convert the land to successful farmland. The transfer recipients who have been given new farms have shown readiness to relinguish the farm and engage new vocations.

There are many abandoned medium-range and small farms in the rural areas due to land being unproductive and the absence of government support; thus, farmers and farm workers in the rural areas moved to the city in search of better livelihood. Some rural dwellers who have benefited from land redistribution and restitution in the rural areas abandoned their land, due to lack of other associate supports, and joined the rural-urban migration train. John Kane-Berman, at the South African Institute of Race Relations, posits that "the view in the ANC that land is the answer to poverty, inequality, and unemployment has no basis in reality. Ordinary people have long since voted against this idea with their feet by moving to town" (Campbell, 2016).

The ANC, dependent on a rural, black constituency, that sees land reform as a mechanism for mass mobilization of the black majority, have had to accept the land 'expropriation without compensation' policy option. How this will solve the problem of poor service delivery and housing in the city remains unclear. Land reform has excessively focused on redistributing land and land restitution, and neglected tenure security and the equitable distribution of government housing facilities, which are vital motivations for land reform. Commenting on the policy gap in the urbanization-land reform nexus, Cousins (2016) notes that the existing "policy focuses only on rural land, but urbanisation means that there are many other needs and opportunities, such as food production on the edges of cities", causing food insecurity and rising costs of agricultural products and housing facilities.

The government interventionist strategy for providing houses for the underprivileged, under the Reconstruction and Development Programme (RDP), are wrought by ineffectiveness and corruption. Although more than a million houses have been constructed through the government's funded housing and land reform initiatives, there are still strong agitations for the erection of many more millions of such houses (better houses indeed). According to a respondent, many of the RDP houses falls short of expectations. Another respondent queried who the occupiers of the houses were, and what were the 'unannounced' criteria for occupation. Many people who have applied for the RDP houses are yet to be allocated homes. There were also assertions that the houses have become a political tool, and another avenue to compensate close associates of the political class, just as experienced in the land redistribution and restitution schemes.

In South Africa, the nature of agriculture, which constitutes the mainstay of the rural population, is very dualistic. It comprises of a highly developed and predominantly large-scale commercial sector, under the ownership and control of white farmers, on privately owned land, and in contrast there are many small-scale and highly subsistence-oriented black farmers on communally held parcels of land. Stakeholders in the land-agriculture projects do not seem clear on what to promote: a few commercial farms or large numbers of small-scale farms.

Apparently, food scarcity and rising food prices have started to effect South Africans, both in rural and urban centres. Section 2.4.2 of the Constitution made it clear that national land reform scheme remains the fundamental and driving force of a programme of rural development. This has called into question the imperative of using land reform as instrument for galvanizing the rural economy, and increasing land productivity by empowering the rural population who wish to farm. The majority of these people are found in the rural areas, whereby some have started migrating (due to a lack of land for farming or an absence of farm infrastructures or necessary support for land productivity) to the urban centres, adding to the population logjam of cities. Cousins (2016) consistently argues that,

> Current policy frameworks are muddled and the strategic thrust of the programme is unclear, partly because it is not seen as contributing to a wider process of agrarian reform. Policy focuses on rural farm land, but urban centres required a more pragmatic land policy that guarantees effective food production for its teeming population. land reform has been captured by elites: a small number of 'emerging' black capitalist farmers and traditional leaders, but also commercial farmers, consultants and agribusiness corporates.

Cousins (2016) made reference to Section 5(6) of the Constitution, which empowers the state to secure the land rights of black South Africans, who majorly reside in the rural zones. This is germane and critical towards achieving one of the key objectives of land reform, which is to secure the rights of black South Africans—in rural and urban centres—to access, use and own land. Attaining this lofty objective is important "to connect land rights to production, employment and livelihoods" (Cousins, 2016).

The magnitude of land dispossession of the indigenous South African population, by foreign settlers (Dutch and British), was greater than its Africa counterparts, while demands for racial equality were vehemently and violently resisted by the apartheid regime until the early 1990s. The high levels of poverty and skewed land arrangement are attributed to the apartheid legacy. Deininger argues that "countries that had a more egalitarian distribution of land tended to be characterised by higher levels of economic growth" (cited in Lahiff, n.d: 11). More than 13 million black South Africans, the majority of them impoverished, were restricted to the hinterland, and consistently experienced denials of land rights (Lahiff, n.d).

At the advent of majority rule in 1994, about 1.06 million households, comprising of 7.7 million people who resided in informal settlements were predominantly struggling economically. The black populated zones were devoid of infrastructural development and characterized by excessive infant mortality, malnutrition, illiteracy and low per-capital income, unlike the urban centres that boasted modernization and improved livelihoods for the whites (Lahiff, n.d.: 2). Although South Africa is categorized as a middle-income or upper-middle-income country, based on its impressive macro-economic performance and per capita gross domestic product (GDP), widespread poverty is a recurring central feature of South African life. According to Lahiff, high rates of poverty and unemployment in South Africa are "stubbornly impervious to policy prescriptions" (Lahiff, n.d.: 5). The uniqueness of South African poverty and rural-urban reality differ from other African countries in three ways:

> Among the rural poor, income generated directly from agricultural activities and food consumed from own farm production are minor components of household resources (estimated at 10% to 20% of the total); many households continuously rotate between rural and urban base; and rural society is closely linked to the social and health problems of urban areas. (OECD 2006: 25)

The phases of rapid urbanization in the country catalyzed informal development. During apartheid, land dispossession and forced removals saw the labour tenant system exchanged for a contract labour system (Setswe, 2010). Additionally, from 1960 to 1982, about 3.5 million black South Africans were violently removed by the state and relocated to homelands. About 700,000 more people were removed from urban areas which had been declared 'white'. After dismantling the repressive apartheid laws, that encouraged overcrowding in cities, the emerging political elites saw democracy and land reform as instruments to redress the overpopulation that have characterized the urban centre (Setswe, 2010). A respondent affirmed that, "colonialism, with its lopsided development, concentrated infrastructural development in the urban centres which housed the 'whites' and other black elites involved in the expropriation of African resources".

In 2007, the Department of Environmental Affairs (2007a) revealed that more than 28% (13 million) of the local population resided in the former homeland zones, which was associated with complex or contested land rights and chaotic land governance arrangement. Aside from the disorderly land governance structures, rural-urban migration has led to the growth of informal settlements noted for poverty, crime, poor service delivery and absence of security of tenure (Department of Environmental Affairs, 2007a).

Many of the migrants became farm labourers, and their families were exposed to inhuman lifestyles, tenure insecurity, lack of infrastructures and social amenities, and hostilities from farm employers, who have suffered dwindling agricultural returns due to the uncertainties in the economy and land policies. Christo van der Rheede, leader of the AHi Business Chamber, maintains that the 'shifting' policy in the land sector,

> Discourages foreign investment on the one hand and promotes monopolising on the part of the state on the other hand…Existing farmers are ideally positioned to expand the value chain for agricultural products, but they are confronted by contradictory statements about land policies, unsafe circumstances, crime and increasing input costs which discourages them even more. (Smith, 2015)

The uncertainty that characterized the land policy, especially with the advancement made by the state to review the Constitution towards accommodating land expropriation without compensation, the fate of agriculture and agro-investment in the country is bleak.

Conclusion: Decongesting South African Cities

The strategy to curtail the rural-urban movement should be seen in two ways: discouraging it and addressing the urban ills. South African cities are already overcrowded without a concerted plan for its decongestion; thus, government should not only focus on decongesting the cities but engage in pragmatic policy options to curtail the rising movement from the rural zones to the urban areas. The urbanization question is critical and cannot be divorced from both land and agrarian reforms. Reinforcing this view, a respondent noted,

> Land reform in South Africa is very complex, both in the draft of the policy and its implementation. There have also been concerns about its nature and reality. In terms of driving agrarian reform, alleviating poverty and igniting rural development and combating rural-urban migration, the prevalent land policy has no foundation to achieve these objectives. Policy on land needs to be decolonized. The present arrangement reinforced the template adopted during colonialism, and continue to enhance the inequality in land relations in the country.

The government needs to develop a robust plan of action to rid the city of too much people and the social ills associated with urbanization in South Africa.

Public institutions in the urban centres have the responsibilities to respond to the demands of the population influx recorded in South African cities. Stakeholders may also have to consider the upgrading, development and formalization of informal settlements. A robust plan of development and expansion of the informal settlement, with the construction of habitable houses, the provision of social infrastructures and effective service delivery, will decongest the city. A well-targeted investment in human development by the government will create some opportunities for people—rural dwellers or an urban labour force—to identify their choices about staying in the city or in the hinterland.

Indeed, South Africa is not in want of the resources to implement a successful and sustainable land reform programme. Also, the country does not also lack the human capacity to draft and manage an effective reform scheme. However, the missing links are the lack of the political will, the depoliticization of land reform, and the discipline and commitment required for achieving an enduring land reform programme that will increase the livelihood of the rural poor. Ruhiiga (2014) highlights the place of radicalization of urban policy, planning and practise. He concludes,

> Planning for urbanization requires an understanding of the demographic changes taking place within the city itself and the regional context of rural-urban migration. It calls for an urban policy that facilitates orderly development along a pre-determined spatial trajectory that should inform the actual practice of growth. (Ruhiiga, 2014: 610)

Respondents decried the policy gap in urban policy. Stakeholders in the rural development programmes concentrate too much on the agricultural economy, but it is important to also explore the prospects of other sectors of the economy to instigate growth of the rural areas, such as the provision of basic social amenities, roads, transportation, good schools and hospitals, which could improve the quality of livelihood of the rural people.

The government could also provide incentives for the industrialization of the rural areas, while well-thought out incentives could be given to public officials working in public institutions located in the rural areas.

This would reduce the lure of cities and promote reverse migration: an urban-rural movement. Furthermore, the location of universities in rural areas, such as the University of Zululand's KwaDlangezwa establishment, and the expansion of airports, such as King Shaka Airport, which have brought 'life' into the surrounding landscape, are somehow transforming the rural-urban migration and leading to the movement of people from the urban centres to the rural areas. However, it is instructive to note that this form of migration is majorly for a short period of time, unlike the rural-urban migration that tends to be driven permanently.

Across the country, the existing land policy frameworks are disarrayed and the main thrust of the programme is complex, partly due to its inability to contribute to a broader process of agrarian reform and its sensitivity to the historical antecedent of South Africa. Instead of using land as the 'only' instrument of addressing rural poverty, there is a need for rethinking such a view and adopting a comprehensive perspective on rural development, which becomes germane for redressing rural-urban swell.

Provisions of social infrastructures, such as functional clinics or hospitals, good schools (preparatory, primary and high school), good roads and easy access to markets, and, perhaps, the establishment of agro-allied industries, are supplementary mechanisms for the productive use of land in the rural areas. However, if many local populations have access to land used for productive endeavours, with the required associate infrastructural development, the rural-urban surge would be reduced. The CDE (2008: 6) holds that,

> A partnership approach is needed to acquire land in a market-supporting way that meets the real and diverse needs of land hungry, poorly housed, and unemployed people cost-effectively and in the right parts of the country; spreads private ownership of land; and reinforces market processes which are self-sustaining and in themselves redistributive.

The government, at all levels, may explore the opportunities of partnering with non-governmental institutions towards developing a framework of action towards resolving the urban bulge. In conclusion, government and stakeholders in the urbanization-land reform projects have the responsibility to utilize the opportunities presented by land reform for human capacity development, improvement in the livelihood of rural dwellers and the elimination of congestion in South African cities. In contemporary South Africa, land reform has failed to significantly alleviate poverty in the rural areas and urban centres.

References

AFDB. (2012). *Urbanization in Africa*. Available: https://www.afdb.org/en/blogs/afdb-championing-inclusive-growth-across-africa/post/urbanization-in-africa-10143/.

Akinola, A. O. (2016). Human rights, civil society and the contradictions of land reform in South Africa. *Politeia, 35*(2), 52–70.

Akinola, A. O. (2018a). Introduction: Understanding xenophobia in Africa. In A. Akinola (Ed.), *The political economy of xenophobia in Africa*. Cham, Switzerland: Springer International Publishing.

Akinola, A. O. (2018b). South African land reform: An appraisal. *Africa Review, 10*(1), 1–16.

Akinola, A. O., & Wissink, H. (2019). Land reform in Africa: Towards resource utilization and sustainability. In A. O. Akinola & H. Wissink (Eds.), *The trajectory of land reform in post-colonial African States: The quest for sustainable development and utilization*. Cham, Switzerland: Springer International Publishing.

Aliber, M. (2007). *Agricultural employment scenarios*. Pre-workshop Discussion Note, for Employment Growth and Development Initiative, Human Science Research Council, Pretoria, South Africa.

Campbell, J. (2016, June 6). South Africa's land expropriation bill in an era of rapid urbanization. *Newsweek*. Available: http://europe.newsweek.com/south-africas-land-expropriation-bill-467890?rm=eu.

CDE. (2008). *CDE executive summary: Land reform in South Africa getting back on track*. Johannesburg: The Centre for Development and Enterprise. Available: http://www.urbanlandmark.org.za/downloads/LandReform_South_Africa.pdf.

Cousins, B. (2016). *Land reform in South Africa is in trouble. Can it be saved?* Available: https://www.nelsonmandela.org/uploads/files/Land_reform_in_South_Africa_is_in_trouble._Can_it_be_saved.pdf.

Department of Environmental Affairs. (2007a). *State of the environment: Land reform*. Pretoria, South Africa: Department of Environmental Affairs. Available: http://soer.deat.gov.za/197.html.

Department of Environmental Affairs. (2007b). *State of the environment*. Pretoria, South Africa: Department of Environmental Affairs. Available: http://soer.deat.gov.za/492/_3444.html.

ESCAP. (2013). *Urbanization trends in Asia and the Pacific*. Available: http://www.unescapsdd.org/files/documents/SPPS-Factsheet-urbanization-v5.pdf.

Francis, S., Francis M., & Akinola, A. (2016). The edge of the periphery: Situating the ≠Khomani San of the Southern Kalahari in the political economy of Southern Africa, *African Identities, 14*(4), 370–383.

Huchzermeyer, M. (2008, July 3–4). *Settlement informality: The importance of understanding change, formality and land and the informal economy*. Paper presented at the Groupement de Recherche sur Development International (GRDI) Workshop on Informality, Centre for Urban and Built Environment Studies (CUBES), University of the Witwatersrand, South Africa.

Lahiff, E. (n.d.). *Redistributive land reform and poverty reduction in South Africa*. Bellville, South Africa: Institute for Poverty, Land, and Agrarian Studies (PLAAS). Available: http://www.plaas.org.za/sites/default/files/publications-pdf/South_Africa_Lahiff.pdf.

Mandisa, D. (2015). *Urban land ownership*. Southern Africa Bishop Conference Briefing Paper 397. Available: http://www.cplo.org.za/wp-content/uploads/2015/02/BP-397-Urban-Land-Ownership-Nov-2015.pdf.

News24. (2008, August 25). Urbanization 'a big Problem'. *News24*. Available: http://www.news24.com/SouthAfrica/News/Urbanisation-a-big-problem-20080825.

Odeny, M. (2013, April 8–11). *Improving access to land and strengthening women's land rights in Africa*. Paper prepared for presentation at the Annual World Bank Conference on Land and Poverty, The World Bank, Washington DC. Available: http://web.law.columbia.edu/sites/default/files/microsites/gender-sexuality/odeny_improving_access_to_land_in_africa.pdf.

OECD. (2006). OECD review of agricultural policies: South Africa. *Organization for Economic Co-operation and Development*.

Plaatjies, N. (2015). *Rural infrastructure development: The solution for urbanization?* Available: http://www.sabc.co.za/news/a/2d0f2f0049f65b6aa0c3eba53d9712f0/Rural-infrastructure-development:-the-solution-for-urbanization.

Posel, D. (2003, June 4–7). *Have migration patterns in post-apartheid South Africa changed?* Paper Presented at the Conference on African Migration in Comparative Perspective, Johannesburg, South Africa.

Ruhiiga, T. M. (2014). Urbanisation in South Africa: A critical review of policy, planning and practice. *Supplement on Population Issues in South Africa, 28*(1), 610–622.

Setswe, G. (2010, April 8). *Township communities and urbanisation in South Africa township communities and urbanisation in South Africa*. Discussion Guide for the 4th AMREP World Health Day Workshop Session on "Current Challenges in Urbanisation & Health", Burnet Institute, Monash University and Compass. Available: https://pdfs.semanticscholar.org/bb8f/7818cacab72fd08e6ae452ebc5f311df95bc.pdf.

Smith, C. (2015, February 13). Zuma lost GPS signal on land ownership—Business. *Fin24*. Available: http://www.fin24.com/Economy/Zuma-lost-GPS-signal-on-land-ownership-business-20150213.

South African History Online. (2018). *Grade 11—Apartheid South Africa 1940s to 1960s*. Available: https://www.sahistory.org.za/article/grade-11-apartheid-south-africa-1940s-1960s.

Tella, O. (2018). South African higher education: The paradox of soft power and xenophobia. In A. O. Akinola (Ed.), *The political economy of xenophobia in Africa*. Cham, Switzerland: Springer International Publishing.

Todes, A., Kok, P., Wentzel, M., Zyl, J., & Cross, C. (2008, June). *Contemporary South African urbanisation dynamics*. Paper for UNU-WIDER Conference: Beyond the Tipping Point. African Development in an Urban World, Cape Town, South Africa.

Turok, I. (2015). *Informal settlements: Poverty traps or ladders to work?* Available: http://www.econ3x3.org/article/informal-settlements-poverty-traps-or-ladders-work.

Urbanization. (2003). *McGraw-Hill dictionary of scientific & technical terms* (6th ed.) Available: http://encyclopedia2.thefreedictionary.com/urbanization.

CHAPTER 14

Land Reform and the Quest for Women's Land Rights in South Africa: A Case of KwaZulu-Natal Province

Modupe A. Daramola

Introduction

The issue of land and land reform has constituted a problematic and contentious discourse in South African during and after apartheid, and the post-apartheid dispensation continues to be defined by the struggle against land inequality (Akinola, 2018). Contemporary South Africa continues to experience land inequality, conflict and hunger, which is a derivative of the history of land dispossession during apartheid. Moyo (2007) maintains that "land distribution inequalities in Africa vary in their broad character depending on the degree of colonial history, foreign ownership and internal class and ethno-regional differential. Settler land expropriation varied in Africa". The government, through land restitution, redistribution and tenure security, aimed at using land reform as a potent instrument to combat structural violence, widening inequality and poverty (DLA, 1997). Despite the reform agenda, the absence of effective

M. A. Daramola (✉)
University of KwaZulu-Natal, Pietermaritzburg, South Africa

A. O. Akinola et al. (eds.), *The New Political Economy of Land Reform in South Africa*,
https://doi.org/10.1007/978-3-030-51129-6_14

land management and gender construction in land allocations has deepened land inequality. This has restricted the capacity building of women, engendered land unproductivity and aggravated poverty in South African households.

Due to the land policy failure, the South African polity has experienced an explosion of land issues culminating in the proposed 'land expropriation without compensation', which was borne out of the contradictions inherent in South Africa land reform programmes. One of the problematic issues that poses great challenges to the economy of the country is the unresolved question about the place of women in the current land policy. Thus, this chapter focuses on the link between women's rights and land reform in South Africa, with particular emphasis on the province of KwaZulu-Natal. This study is instructive because South Africa is a constitutional democracy, which makes provisions for the property rights of women within the broader framework of human rights.

The concept of human rights became popular in the country due to its defence of women's land rights and opposition to the discrimination of women (Swingler, 2015). Despite all the efforts of the government to institutionalize gender parity through the empowerment of legal institutions for women's rights, the equality of women in terms of access to property and ownership is not yet attained in the country. Of particular concern is women in the rural areas who have faced denials of land rights. In KwaZulu-Natal, rural women continue to experience cultural obstacles against gender equality. This is compounded by the patriarchal nature of the society, the lack of enforcement agencies for upholding women's rights, ignorance among rural women and illiteracy.

Land Reform

Land reform is a pressing issue in many countries of the world today. As an action programme, land reform seems new to many people, but the effect of reform in the land sector affects more than three-quarters of the global population that have undergone major land reform since World War II (Horowitz, 1999). The conditions that have given rise to demands for reform have existed for decades, if not centuries. Peasant discontent and precedents for reform have existed since the dawn of civilization. Only the techniques of reform and the will for action can be said to be new.

The term land reform is viewed differently by different groups. Some view it as mild reforms like measures for improvement of landlord-tenant relations or provision of better agricultural credit facilities (Barlowe, 1978). To others, it means the process of breaking-up of large land-holdings with the expropriation of ownership rights. Some also see it as land redistribution and an opportunity for landless people to acquire land. According to Boyce, Rosset and Stanton (2005), land reform is "the real-location of rights to establish a more equitable distribution of farmland – can be a powerful strategy for promoting both economic development and environmental quality". Furthermore, Barlowe (1978) believes that almost any programme that leads to a change, that is presumed to be for the better, in the manner in which land is held or used, might be described as land reform.

Recently land reform programmes, more specifically those under the market-based approach which came to the forefront internationally during the 1990s, have tended to focus more on land acquisition and less on the requisite settlement support that accompanies it. In many instances, land acquisition is a highly charged political process, with the emphasis on changing landownership patterns and less on what occurs thereafter (Tilley, 2007). As revealed by Tilley,

> A number of different motivations prompting land reforms and their desired outcomes are evident across a range of countries. In turn, each variant of land reform has adopted a particular approach to the provision of settlement support, whether purposefully or by default. (Tilley, 2007: 30)

Historically, land reform meant a reform of the tenure system or redistribution of landownership rights. The concept has been broadened in recognition of the strategic role of land and agriculture in development. Land reform has therefore become synonymous with agrarian reform or a rapid improvement of the agrarian structure, which comprises of the land tenure system; the pattern of cultivation and farm organization; the scale of farm operation; the terms of tenancy; and the institutions of rural credit, marketing and education. It also deals with the state of technology, or with any combination of these factors, as shown by modern reform movements, regardless of the political or ideological orientation of the reformers.

Land reform became popular and was assumed as a powerful tool because of its mass appeal and general effectiveness in redistributing the basis for wealth. The benefits are to stimulate programmes of economic development. However, past experiences of land reform across the globe suggest that it has often had little effect in promoting its specific goal. For example, the land redistribution programmes were carried out in Rumania and some other eastern European countries, after World War I, helped to gratify the land hunger of the peasants but resulted in less, rather than more, agricultural production.

Land reforms vary in their treatment of those whose land rights are redistributed to others. For instance, during the Chinese revolution land was confiscated without compensation. Whereas, in Guatemala, under the 1954 land reform that was aborted quickly by a CIA-backed coup, large landowners were compensated at a fraction of the market value of the land (Tilley, 2007). China, Japan, South Korea and Taiwan implemented highly egalitarian land reforms after World War II. In these societies, land reform not only helped to reduce rural poverty and unleash agricultural growth, but also helped to lay the social foundation for rapid industrialization. Under the household responsibility system, individual families in China have the right to till the land, but not to buy or sell it.

In the former Soviet bloc countries of Central and Eastern Europe, land was generally nationalized and production was, over time, collectivized—a notable exception being Poland, where land remained in the hands of small, family farmers. The distribution of agricultural inputs and outputs and the nature and extent of support provided was also tightly controlled by centralized bureaucracies. Other examples of countries where there is high level of centralization and state involvement are Mexico, Cuba and Nicaragua, where communal or collective institutions play a prominent, but not exclusive, role. Land reforms in these countries, and their resultant support mechanisms, are thereby centred on state, collective and co-operative institutional arrangements (Tilley, 2007).

In South Africa, land reform is defined as the redistribution of landed property, a change in prevailing tenure system or an extension of land rights. Land reform is a purposive change in the way in which agricultural land is held or owned, the methods of cultivation that are employed or the relation of agriculture to the rest of the economy. It is one of the most important and contentious issues facing South Africa in the post-apartheid era, and thus, "land reform in South Africa had long been a source of conflict and the history of conquest and dispossession and of forced removals" (Gumede, 2004: 58).

Understanding the Three Elements of Land Reform in South Africa

As specified in the 1997 White Paper on land reform, South Africa's land reform programme involves three key elements, which are land redistribution, land restitution and land tenure.

Land Restitution

The Restitution of Land Rights Act 22 of 1994 was the first transformation law promulgated by the new government of South Africa. The impetus for land restitution came from those in the rural communities who had lost their land during the apartheid era. The scope of land restitution was expanded also to include urban claims for property lost apartheid (Hall, 2004a, b). The legal basis for land restitution is provided by the 1993 Interim Constitution, Section 25(7) of the 1996 Constitution and the Restitution of Land Rights Act. This gave people and communities who had been dispossessed of land after 19 June 1913, as a result of racially discriminatory laws or practices, the right to restitution of that property or to fair compensation. Therefore,

> The aim of the Restitution programme thus became to restore land to those who had been unfairly disposed since 1913. Restitution is to address the loss of land Rights that resulted from homeland consolidation, forced removals from "black spots" the Group Area Acts, and related laws that designated land on a racial basis as well as losses suffered by former labour tenant beneficial occupiers of land, and residents affected by betterment planning in the former homelands. (Hall, 2004a: 656)

The Restitution of Land Rights Act 22 was promulgated in 1994 in terms of the Interim Constitution of the Republic of South Africa Act 200 of 1993 for that purpose. The Act also established a Commission on the Restitution of Land Rights in 1995 under a Chief Land Claims Commissioner and seven Regional Land Claims Commissioners representing the nine provinces, with the mandate to assist claimants in submitting their land claims, receive and acknowledge all claims lodged, and advise claimants on the progress of their land claims.

The Restitution Act was amended in 1997 to bring it in line with the 1996 Constitution, shifting the approach from a judicial one to an administrative one in 1999. Rather than having to go through the Commission on Restitution of Land Rights, claimants were allowed direct access to the Land Claims Court and the Minister of Land Affairs was given greater powers to settle claims through negotiation. Although there were those amendments, some scholars, like Lahiff (2008) and Cousins (2015), have criticized the slow pace of handling claims. Cousins (2015: 4) maintains that "land restitution continued to grind slowly on hampered by a small budget, capacity problems and inadequate funds for post-settlement".

In 1995, both the Land Claims Commission and the Land Claims Court were established, as provided for by Section 4 of the Restitution Act and Section 123 of the Interim Constitution (Republic of South Africa, 1996). The objective of the Land Claim Commission is aimed at dealing with the administration of land claims and to compensate the present owners and appease the claimants by providing access to land. The Land Claims Court specializes in dealing with disputes that are not solved by the land claims commission and arise out of laws that underpin South Africa's land reform initiatives (South Africa History Online, 2004). Thus, the Land Claim Commission screens all land claims, identifies those that are qualified in line with the Constitution and the Restitution Act and attempts to solve these claims by administrative or by mediation procedures. Presenting an overview of claims, a report notes that,

> The target period for restitution claims were lodged by 31 December 1998, deadline was set to be 2005 but the deadline was then extended to the year 2011 because of lack of funds amongst other obstacles as the main cause. Government mid-term review report shows that by 2011 South Africa transferred over 6.8-million hectares of land to people dispossessed under apartheid, which represents 27% of the government's target of transferring 24.5-million hectares by 2014. (South Africa History Online, 2004)

The White Paper on South African Land Policy of 1997 favoured a market-based approach, in which the concept of willing buyer, willing seller', which depended on voluntary market transactions, had become the cornerstone of policy (DLA, 1997). Land dispossession under white minority rule was achieved through racially discriminative legislation and violence. It was imperative for the new democratic government to strike a balance between nation-building and addressing the land issue (South Africa History Online, 2004). To achieve this, there are specific criteria or qualifications for which the claimant/s must satisfy in order to lodge the claim (DLA, 1997):

1. Must be a person dispossessed of a right to his or her land after 19 June 1913, as a result of past, racially discriminatory laws or practices.
2. Is it a deceased estate disposed of a right in land after 19 June 1913, as a result of past racially discriminatory laws and practices?
3. Must be a direct descendant of a person referred to in paragraph (a) who died before lodging a claim and has no ascendant.
4. An individual, community or part of community dispossessed of a right in land after 19 June 1913, as a result of past discriminatory laws and practices.
5. The claim for such restitution was lodged not later than 31 December 1998.

According to the South African White Paper (DLA, 1997), the key issues facing land restitution are how to:

1. Ensure that the rural and urban claimants who were dispossessed of land after 1913 receive restitution in the form of land or other appropriate and acceptable remedies.
2. Ensure that appropriate administrative and financial arrangements are developed and implemented to respond to the thousands of claims within the time limits set.
3. Respond to claims in urban areas where land has been redeveloped and changed hands since the original removal of the claimants.
4. Ensure the constructive participation of all role players—the Commission, the Land Claims Court, current land owners, national, provincial and local government and the claimants themselves.

In January 2013, the N'wandlamhlarhi Community Property Association was handed more than 13,184 hectares of land (South Africa History Online, 2004). This was after a six-year land claim battle between the owners of Mala Game Lodge in Mpumalanga and the Department of Rural Development and Land Reform, acting on their behalf, was settled for a record amount of a little over R1 billion. This remains the biggest land claim in the history of South Africa.

Furthermore, the government intended to redistribute 30% of land to black people by 2014. However, the Land Claims Commission was unable to finalize all land claims and meet this target. The process of land reform has been slow due to the inflation of land prices by white farmers and other landowners on the identified land, and the falling into disuse of expropriated land given to black farmers. Additionally, the process has been slow, particularly during the first years, due to resources' constraints which have contributed to the ineffectiveness of the courts to deal with the claims.

Claims arising from any dispossessions prior to 1913 may be accommodated by the Minister in terms of preferential status in the Land Redistribution Programme, providing that claimants are genuine. One of the success stories about land restitution was the KwaXiba community, based in the Umkhambathini Local Municipality of KwaZulu-Natal. The community was awarded 4800 hectares of land and would be responsible for the upkeep of the wild game reserve, as stated in the report, "support programmes such as infrastructural development (game fence, ecotourism facilities etc.), game donation/loaning, skills development and training, access to markets and funding will be facilitated to ensure sustainable businesses". According to Cousin (2015),

> The domestic hunting market was approximately R6.4 billion (€430 million), while the international hunting market was approximately R1.4 billion (€95 million) in 2013. In addition to hunting, game farmers can generate income from the sale of game meat, wildlife products and live game.

Contrary to the view of the majority, land restitution continued to be impeded by restricted funding and other neccesary supports for post-settlement support. It remains to be seen how the proposed expropriation without compensation will accelerate land restitution in the country.

Land Redistribution

The primary focus of land reform has been the redistribution of land through a market-led 'willing buyer, willing seller' approach. From 1995, the implementation of the policy took the form of making available Settlement/Land Acquisition Grants (SLAG) to poor households to enable them to purchase land. According to the Land Reform Policy Discussion Document (Republic of South Africa, 2012), redistribution

> Aimed to address the divide between the 87% of the land, dominated by white commercial farming, and the 13% in the former 'homelands' by way of diversifying the ownership structure of commercial farmland. The sub-programme was minimally successful, redistributing about 7% of land to the landless poor, labour tenants, farm workers and emerging farmers productive for uses, as to improve their livelihoods and quality of life as well as to stimulate growth in the agricultural sector.

Lahiff (2008) maintains that 'redistribution is the most important component of land reform in South Africa'. Initially, land was bought from its owners (willing seller) by the government (willing buyer) and redistributed, in order to maintain public confidence in the land market. The redistributive policy sought to transfer land from wealthy landowners, either to those with no land at all (landless peasants and wage labourers) or to those people with tiny holdings (the poor peasants), and in the process to subdivide large landholdings and estates into smaller farms that these new owners, with limited access to financial resources and capital, can cultivate (Byres, 2004; Cliffe, 2007). This system has worked in various countries in the world, but in South Africa it has proved to be very difficult to implement. This is because many owners do not actually see the land they are purchasing and are not involved in the important decisions made towards the land acquisition.

There is also the issue about inadequate funding from the government. Other African countries have had to approach the redistributive aspect of the reform agenda in diverse forms. In Africa, land redistribution was mostly extensive in Kenya, South Africa, Zimbabwe and Namibia, but also occurred to a lesser extent in Mozambique, Swaziland, Botswana, Tanzania and Zambia. The largest scale of white settler land expropriation occurred in South Africa, where 87% of the land was under the control of the white majority, while the black majority had to be relocated to the less-arable hinterland. After independence in the aforementioned countries, the white settler populations inhabiting the countries tended to decrease, although the proportion of land held by white minorities has not decreased proportionately. Colonial land injustices and current land policies have led to increased differentiation in the control of and access to land.

In Zimbabwe, the pattern of land distribution had its roots in the 1890s, when the racially enforced division of land was formalized in 1930, when the country land was divided roughly equally between the black majority and a white minority of 5% of the total population, which illustrates the great disparity in the pattern of land sharing (Kinsey, 2004). According to Gideon (2019), the Zimbabwean government's land policy, through its posture of nationalism, had promised the return of the land as the historical right of dispossessed people, but regulated the land as a productive space, and thus they failed to resolve historical, societal grievances over land until 2000.

Land redistribution without necessary post-settlement support may definitely compromise the ability of recipients, particularly that of the poor households, to make a living based on the new asset (Tilley, 2007). African redistributive land reforms would be expected to involve restoring lands that are physically controlled by large landholders through the resettlement of displaced peasants, and alienated semi-proletarians, and the enlargement of peasant land areas, using repossessed contiguous lands. Securing the land rights of the poor, mainly by re-allocating them the 'title' to independently hold the landholding, and or by upgrading the tenure conditions under which lands are rented, is also relevant in parts of Africa where land rent and sharecropping have emerged, especially in West Africa. Land reform was 'radicalized' in Zimbabwe (Kinsey, 2004) by:

i. Decongesting overpopulated areas.
ii. Expanding the base of productive agriculture.
iii. Rehabilitating people displaced by war.
iv. Resettling squatters, the destitute and the landless.
v. Promoting more equitable distribution of agricultural land.
vi. De-racializing or expanding indigenous commercial agriculture.

The above objectives are underpinned by the aim of addressing the historical injustices of colonial land expropriation in African countries (by white people) and to assert the right of access by 'indigenes' (black people). Through redistribution in Zimbabwe, of medium sized plots, land reform successfully creates opportunities for those who were disadvantaged (Kinsey, 2004).

In South Africa, according to Deininger (2003), non-governmental organizations (NGOs) have supported the formation of a Landless People's Movement (LPM) that demands extensive land reform. However, the contradictions between the mainly middle class, intellectual leadership of the landless peoples' structures, and the trans-class and nationalist nature of the interest in land have become evident in the slow maturation of a nationwide, radical, land reform, advocacy agenda. Nevertheless, the LPM's demand for land redistribution, using an explicit threat to boycott the ANC in elections, has had the effect of bringing greater urgency to the government's land reform initiatives. In reality,

> Land reform is a government programme which is intended to redistribute land in South Africa – in order to address the skewed patterns of land allocation. The case of South Africa illustrates that land reform is one of a number of ways to increase access to land and productive assets for the poor. (Deininger, 2003: 150)

In 2000, the South African government decided to review and change the redistribution and tenure process to a more decentralized and area-based planning process. The idea for the review was to have local, integrated development plans in 47 districts. The hope was for greater community participation and more redistribution to take place, but there were also various concerns and challenges with this system (Hall, 2008).

The Land Redistribution Programme enables eligible individuals and groups to obtain a Settlement/Land Acquisition Grant to a maximum of R15,000, per household, for the purchase of land directly from willing sellers, including the state. The government planned to redistribute 30% of land to black people by 2014. The process of land reform has been slow due to the inflating of prices by white farmers and landowners on identified land on the one hand, and the falling into disuse of expropriated land given to black farmers on the other. Additionally, the process has been slow, particularly during the first years, due to resource constraints which contributed to the ineffectiveness of the courts to deal with the claims. Gumede (2004: 52) believes that "the slow pace so far of redistribution is flaring up conflict between agriculture and government, and among farmers, officials and farm workers".

Land Tenure

The most complex area of land reform in South Africa is land tenure reform. It aims to bring all people occupying land under a unitary, legally validated system of landholding. The South African tenure system aimed at addressing the state of land administration in the communal areas of the former homelands and coloured reserves. Secondly, it focuses on strengthening the security of the tenure of farm dwellers living on commercial farms, and devise secure forms of land tenure, help resolve tenure disputes and provide alternatives for people who are displaced in the process. Its purpose is to develop tenure reform and land rights policies, procedures and products. Land tenure reforms have redefined the status of the right to land among owners and non-owners, and introduced new systems of land administrations (Republic of South Africa, 2012).

In Africa, land tenure reform requires institutional reforms that can defend the poor against potential land losses, as well as accommodate those excluded (which are mostly women, the minorities and the settlers) from increasingly scarce arable lands. Such tenure reforms would also need to be able to prevent and resolve conflicts over competing claims to land rights and ensure the fair administration of land rights and land use regulations. What the land tenure reforms require would include the ability to transact (rent and sell) and mortgage peasant lands, especially in the absence of measures to prevent land alienation and concentration, political contentiousness and feasibility. The roles of African states in promoting equitable access to land and control of land through tenure reforms has had the opposite effect of promoting increased land concentration. The existing African legal frameworks and institutions for managing land allocation, as well as land use or dispute resolution, tend to protect the interests of those with larger land rights, including property rights derived from past expropriation, rather than to protect the interests of the vulnerable and landless majority.

Legal Framework of Women's Rights in South Africa

Human rights are conceived as the undeniable fundamental rights to which individuals (males and females) are naturally entitled because they are human beings (Akinola, 2016). They are rights that are enjoyable by every human, being irrespective of gender, race, ethnic affiliation, social status or any other consideration. According to NELFT (2019), "human rights are the basic rights and freedoms that belong to every person in the world, from birth until death. They apply regardless of where you are from, what you believe or how you choose to live your life". These rights can never be taken away, although they can sometimes be restricted if certain conditions are violated, for instance, if a person breaks the law, or in the interests of national security. These basic rights are based on shared values, like dignity, fairness, equality, respect and independence. These values are defined, highlighted and protected by law. In South Africa, human rights are protected by the South Africa Constitution.

The end of World War II, the establishment of the United Nations, marked the beginning of the modern human rights' movement. South Africa did not participate in the drafting of the International Bill of Rights because of their international isolation during the apartheid system. The International Covenant on Economic, Social and Cultural Rights (ICESCR) and other organizations are part of the instruments proscribing discrimination on the grounds of sex and promoting equal protection before the law. The ICESCR is ratified by 48 out of 53 African states (Banda, 2006) and thus, human rights have achieved universal acceptance. Good governance and democracy are seen as preconditions for the receipt of aid, and this has made most states ratify human rights instruments as a means of accessing aid. Though, it is questionable if the ratification of international human rights instruments to some is a matter of expediency rather than commitment.

Throughout history, women have been subjected to unequal treatment from legal codes within various societies and cultures (Sasha, 2003). Thus, at the global level, the Universal Declaration of Human Rights was adopted in 1948, which provides for gender equality (UN, 2003: 4). South Africa became a signatory to the global framework for promoting gender balance in different spheres of endeavours. However, cases of hostility to women's attainment of their property rights continue to define land arrangement in the country. To redress the bias in sociopolitical norms and macroeconomic policies that favour males at the expense of females, South Africa joined other countries, to make provision for women's rights in the Constitution (Republic of South Africa, 1996). Specifically, Section 9 opposes the "unfair discrimination solely on the grounds of race, colour, ethnic or social origin, sex, religion or language" (Republic of South Africa, 1996: 18).

Generally, the legal framework for women's rights became necessary as a result of the patriarchy nature of society and the reality of women's unequal treatment, and women being deprived of their basic human rights. In the South Africa context, the country is one of the few African countries with a high women's rights performance (Republic of South Africa, 1996: 92). Section 181 of the 1996 Constitution establishes many institutions, like the South African Human Rights Commission, for the purpose of combating gender discrimination (Republic of South Africa, 1996: 92). These institutions were established with a view to ensuring the furtherance of the values and rights identified in the Constitution and other legitimate measures (Stevens & Ntlama, 2016; Swingler, 2015).

South Africa has adopted and implemented gender-based laws, but the state has failed in the implementation of those rights in respect to land rights. Capturing the true picture in South Africa, Gumisai (2005) maintains that,

> Men have gone to the moon and back, yet women are still at the same place they were- that is, trying to sensitive the world to the unwarranted and unacceptable marginalization of women, which deprives them of their human rights.

Theoretical Framework: Liberal Feminism

Liberal feminism holds that females have the right to access societal resources and properties like their male counterparts. Feminist theory provides a deeper grasp of the place of women in South African land reform. This justifies the claim of women for gender equality in the land sector in KwaZulu-Natal province of South Africa. The theoretical framework is the foundation from which all knowledge is constructed for a research study. It presents the selected theory (or theories) that underpins thinking and shapes the perspectives with regard to how to understand the subject under study (Grant & Osanloo, 2014). It involves the study of the roles, rights, privileges, interests and the concerns of women in the society. It is an extension to feminism which locates the rightful place of women in the society. There have been wrong perceptions about women for ages and this has negatively affected the female world by limiting their rights and privileges. This has become the motivation for the attainment of rights and the entitlement of women within the community.

Feminist theory focuses on the extension of feminism into theoretical or philosophical discourse. The basic aim of this theory is to understand gender inequality, gender politics and on the promotion of women's rights and interest. Feminism theory is therefore necessary to understand the nature of gender inequality, and gender role in the South African land sector. The theory emphasizes autonomy and respect for the dignity of women (Enslin, 2003). It opposes the denial of the land rights of women based on any traditional, religious or social consideration.

The importance of land in poverty alleviation, growth, social status, and economic and human development has heightened the need for women to be granted the rights to use and own land in the country. It is believed that liberal feminism, like liberal political theory in general, is sometimes criticized for overemphasizing equality and the promotion of autonomy at the expense of valuing diversity. This has caused liberal feminism to be viewed as a threat to cultural diversity.

According to Enslin (2003), however, cultural diversity has its place in sociopolitical discourse, like land issues, but it is important to encourage the alteration of practices that could harm the interests of women in general. Shah (2010) holds that,

> Women's equal rights and influence in the key decisions that shape their lives and those of children must be enhanced in three distinct arenas: the household, the workplace and the political sphere. A change for the better in any one of these realms influences women's equality in the others, and has a profound and positive impact on child's well-being and development. Gender equality is not only morally right, it is pivotal to human progress and sustainable development.

Generally, liberalism holds that "individual sovereignty is a fundamental value, and that the just state ensures freedom for citizens" (Akinola & Tella, 2013: 105). It is vital to note that liberal feminism is an aspect of liberalism.

Women's Land Rights in KwaZulu-Natal

The Constitution of South Africa clearly presents the foundation upon which the property rights of all people are formed. This is the legal instrument that dictates equal rights for all, irrespective of race, ethnic affiliation, class and gender. This is also the case in many countries of the world. The right to property, which captures land rights, is specifically enshrined under Section 25 of the Constitution of the Republic of South Africa, 1996 (South Africa Constitution, 1996). It was emphatically stated in the Constitution that nobody may be deprived of any property except in terms of law of general application. This aligns with human rights, which talks on the rights every person is entitled to by being a human being. Furthermore, no law in the country should operate in contrary to the provision and intent of the constitutional removal of gender restrictions to land rights. The supremacy of the Constitution is not in doubt but a lack of effective monitoring and implementation has created avenues for its abuse.

Despite the provision of women's rights in the Constitution, the respondents in the study attest to the fact that men still dominate over women in both rural and urban centres. They particularly stressed the enormous control that men have over women in the rural areas, in every respect, citing women's restrictive access to land as an example. They reiterated the weakness of women pertaining to power relations in the community. A respondent queried the usefulness of the Constitution, when women are even afraid of taking their husbands to court in cases of conflict over access to family resources, like land. Women reporting men, even to community leaders, is seen as an affront to customary practice.

Section 25 of the 1996 Constitution commits the government to land reform that provides for land distribution on an equitable basis and creates access to all the historically dispossessed. One respondent queried if women are not part of the historically disposed. With all the legal instruments (both local and international) made for the attainment of women's land right in South Africa, enjoying these rights remains a fallacy in many parts of KwaZulu-Natal.

In communities around Pietermaritzburg, women are largely restricted in the exercise of their land rights, while those around the KwaDlangezwa area showed some improvement in terms of women's land rights. In Durban, respondents testified to women's land rights, but in Durban suburbs, a respondent claimed to have only gained access to land through a male member of her family. This contradicts the perspective of feminist theory, which advocates the attainment of women's rights in all spheres of endeavours. This is in line with the work of Kapama (2017), wherein he also maintains that out of all the rights given to women globally, the right to land and property is one of the most significant of all, particularly on the African continent. This is because a larger proportion of women live in rural areas and their livelihood is closely tied to land.

A respondent from the KwaDlangezwa area opined that the problem she has with the reality of land reform is its failure to enforce women's land rights. She said,

> The constitution says one thing on one hand and people are allowed to do what they like. In the constitution, there is equality of all gender and all are given the rights to societal properties are guaranteed by property rights.

She said further,

> You cannot have a system that says men benefit more in the society than women do in the property right. It is inconsistent with the constitution that talks about equal right for all. The patrilineage system is still very strong in the local communities. The system is an old one, which predates the constitution; so, many are still attached to the traditional system where men are far more superior to women. And women are not allowed to own properties, except when such ownership is in the name of the husband. Men determine when their daughters can even marry, in some cases, who they can marry or not. Sometimes, they allow women to own land as long as they remain single, and once married, the property is retrieved.

Another respondent was quick to interrupt thus,

> Why is it wrong for a woman to own a land and has all the title deed without any link to the husband? Since we there is gender equality in our constitution. It is like the constitution is saying something differently entirely from what we practice in most villages in KwaZulu- Natal area. This equality right is not applicable in many of the suburbs in the province. That is the fact.

This contradicts the perspective of feminist theory, which advocates equal rights for all, irrespective of gender.

Another respondent added that, in some areas of KwaZulu-Natal, women do not own land. According to him,

> They only allocate some portions for women and you are not the owner you are just to use for specific years because the land belongs to the chief. If you know that something is not your own, because land is an asset, you won't invest in it because you are not sure for how long you will be allowed to use the land. So people prefer to find better option in

> urban area and leave the rural area because of the issue of security as well the number doesn't matter since it is not yours. People need land for more than subsistence farming that is why government should help the underprivileged.

Another respondent contradicted the written law that made it appear as if everybody enjoys the same freedom in South Africa, and that 'our land belongs to all':

> In the village, nobody has land to do large-scale farming. You only have a small piece of land to build your house and a place to have your garden. No big land to use as far as I know. That's why men continue to hold unto the limited land that is available. So what is the important or outcome result of the legal framework backing women land rights. In situation where a family got land through the redistribution, if the land given to the family is small, the man tends to take it all. Women are thereby constantly denied their rights to own any part of the land.

A respondent commented on the legal framework that supports women land right in Zimbabwe. She opined that the Constitution of Zimbabwe is similar to that of South Africa as it also contains a declaration of women's rights. These sets out the fundamental rights of Zimbabweans (males and females) to own properties, but in the same constitution, women's land rights are discriminated against on some basis, like customs and marriage, which only affects women. This contradicts the perspective of human rights which advocates the protection of women's interests.

The denial of rights in relation to property is true across African countries. A respondent spoke about her village in KwaZulu-Natal where the chief takes control of the entire land meant for the community and distributes it at his own discretion. This discretion was guided by traditions where family land is allocated to men and put in the custody of the head of the family who are men. Even in cases where the family head is a woman, the eldest men in the family take possession of the land. Women are not emboldened to challenge men in traditional African societies. Whoever dares to question these customs is termed as being rude. As revealed by a respondent,

> because they said we are only to follow our husband to farm and not make any demand or land. For the singles and widows, no one supports their

> right to land ownership in my community. When even the married only get access to land because of their husband.

Thus, women's rights have not been effectively implemented in South Africa, especially in rural areas, because the state's institutions are not really involved in the implementation of women's rights as it is written in the Constitution.

Another respondent from Edendale said she does not understand the land rights given to women in some part of the country. In those communities that believe they are obeying the law by giving women land, these women cannot transfer this land nor sell it. She said that the women who have possession of land should be "able to do anything you like to whatever it is yours. It means the land is still not theirs if they cannot use, sell and exploit whatever it is on the land". She narrated her experience that when her mother died, the land was taken from them by the community, with the assistance of her brother and the children were asked to go and they were given land from their father. They could not inherit the land of their mother. They were therefore left landless despite all efforts to claim back their mother's land.

The Constitution of South Africa supports women's land rights, but the findings of this study reveal that denials of land rights to women persist. As shown by respondents' accounts, many women are deprived of land in many parts of KwaZulu-Natal. The few who have land only use it as tenants, while very few women really have ownership of the land. It is important to know that this practice differs from one community to the other within KwaZulu-Natal, which is predominantly a Zulu community. Every community operates its own customary laws, based on cultural norms, and not necessarily a universal African culture, and may ignore the constitutional provisions on women's land rights, particularly in the rural areas. Government seems not to understand that making a law without implementing it, is meaningless, as people tend to stick with societal practices in place of constitutionalism. Securing land rights can boost the economy of any nation, especially when there are no legal barriers underpinning the productivity of women and their contribution to the economy of their land by having access to land and landownership. This is in line with what capability theory advocates: the well-being of everyone.

There is still ignorance among rural women. During the course of this research, it was gathered that some women are not aware of many legal instruments (international and national) for the promotion of women's rights. Some are aware but do not have enough understanding of how it operates. It is very easy to manipulate these women and deny them their land rights in such circumstances. How will they fight for their rights if they do not even know they exist? Thus, women's rights have not been effectively implemented in South Africa, especially in rural areas, because the state's institutions are not really involved in the implementation of women's rights as it is written in the Constitution.

Conclusions

This work has discussed land reform and women's right in general. It examined earlier works that were written on this research topic and then discussed the key terms in the research. It provided a broad understanding of land, land reform and human rights, especially women's rights. Land is an important factor of production that encompasses so many things. Its economic value is inestimable. Land, a basic source of livelihood, acts as source of employment for women. It is the key agricultural input and it is a major determinant of women farmers' access to other productive resources and services. Therefore, for land to play its primary role in national and regional development in South Africa, there needs to be focused attention on how women have access to land, particularly concerning land rights' delivery and the efficiency of the laws, the structures and institutions for land governance.

Women's rights and assess to land is of great importance in South Africa for an economic growth. Land reform in South Africa is introduced to correct past colonial injustices and since this injustice was not shown to men alone but also towards women, who may have even felt the injustice more than men. Based on their struggle to be liberated, they should also enjoy the same rights as men. Gender inequality should not be in place.

Various international and regional instruments, such as the CEDAW 1979 Convention on the elimination of all forms of discrimination against women and its Optional Protocol in 2000, the 1995 Beijing Declaration and Platform of Action (BDPA), the Protocol to the African Charter on Human and People's Rights in 2003 and the Solemn Declaration on Gender Equality in 2004, have provided for the protection, respect and promotion of women's property rights in Africa, including land rights. Yet, in the rural areas of South Africa, KwaZulu-Natal, women are still being denied this basic right to own land, which is a property right that is clearly written in the Constitution of South Africa.

Some of the rural women in KwaZulu-Natal still depend on men for land access and ownership. This has a negative impact on the country's economy and it is a breach of women's rights, because women's right to land is a critical factor for their economic well-being and empowerment, as well as social status. Land is also a social asset, crucial for cultural identity, political power and increased livelihood. Thus, the denial thereof affects the identity, status and livelihood of women negatively. It also restricts their levels of political participation.

References

Akinola, A. O. (2016). Human rights, civil society and the contradictions of land reform in South Africa. *Politeia, 35*(2), 52–70.

Akinola, A. O. (2018). South African land reform: An appraisal. *Africa Review, 10*(1), 1–16.

Akinola, A. O., & Tella, O. (2013). Cultural adherence and the nexus between women empowerment and millennium Development goals in Africa. *Global Advanced Research Journal of Arts and Humanities, 2*(6), 103–110.

Banda, F. (2006). Women, law and human rights in South Africa. *Journal of Southern Africa Studies, 32*(1), 13–27.

Barlowe, R. (1978). *Land economics*. Englewood, NJ: Prentice Hall.

Boyce, K. B., Rosset, P., & Stanton, E. (2005). *Land reform and sustainable development*. Amherst: University of Massachusetts.

Byres, T. J. (2004). Introduction contextualizing and interrogating the GKI case for redistributive land reform. *Journal of Agrarian Change*, 4(1–2), 1–16.

Cousins, B. (2015). "Land reform in South Africa is sinking. Can it be saved?" *Nelson Mandela foundation: Living the legacy: Council for the advancement of South Africa constitution*. Available https://www.nelsonmandela.org/uploads/files/Land__law_and_leadership_-_paper_2.pdf.

Cliffe, L. (2007). Land reform in South Africa. *Review of African Political Economy, 27*(84), 273–286.

Deininger, K. (2003). *Land policies for growth and poverty reduction*. Oxford: Oxford University Press.

Department of Land Affairs (DLA). (1997). *White Paper on South Africa land policy*. Pretoria: Department of Land Affairs. Available http://www.gov.za/files/whitepaperlandreform.pdf.

Enslin, P. (2003). Liberal feminism, diversity and education. *Theory and Research in Education, 1*(1), 73–87.

Gideon, C. (2019). Land reform and the Calculus for Power in Zimbabwe's Democratic Transition. In A. O. Akinola & H. Wissink (Eds.), *Trajectory of Land Reform in Post-Colonial African States*, Cham: Springer International Publishing.

Grant, C., & Osanloo, A. (2014). Understanding, selecting, and integrating a theoretical framework in dissertation research. *Connecting Education, Practice and Research, 4*(2), 12–26.

Gumede, V. (2004). Land reform in post-apartheid South Africa: Should South Africa Zimbabwe's footsteps? *International Journal of African Renaissance Studies- Multi-Inter—and Transdisplinarity, 9*(1), 50–68.

Gumisai, M. (2005, June). African women battle for equality. *African Renewal.* Available https://www.un.org/africarenewal/magazine/july-2005/african-women-battle-equality.

Hall, R. (2004a). Land restitution in South Africa: Rights, developing, and the restrained state. *Canadian Journal of African States, 38*(3), 651–671.

Hall, R. (2004b). A Political economy of Land reform in South Africa. *Review of African Political Economy, 31*(100), 213–227.

Hall, R. (2008). State, market and community: The potential and limits of participatory land reform planning in South Africa, *PLAAS Working paper 7* (pp. 1–43), Available at https://media.africaportal.org/documents/WP7.pdf.

Horowitz, A. W. (1999). Time paths of land reform: A theoretical model of Reform dynamics. *American Economic Association, 83*(4), 1003–1010.

Kapama, F. (2017). *Securing Women's Rights to Land and Property.* Available https://dailynews.co.tz.

Kinsey, B. H. (2004). Zimbabwe's land reform program: Underinvestment in post-conflict transformation. *World Development, 32*(10), 1669–1692.

Lahiff, E. (2008). Land reform in South Africa: A status report 2008. *Programme for Land and Agrarian Studies, Research Report, 38,* 1–49.

Moyo, S. (2007). The land question in Southern Africa: A comparative review. In Ntsebeza & Hall (Eds.), *The land question in South Africa: The challenge of transformation and redistribution.* Cape Town: HSRC Press.

NELFT. (2019). *NHS foundation trust: Human rights acts.* Available https://www.nelft.nhs.uk/human-rights-act.

Republic of South Africa. (1996). *The Constitution of the Republic of South Africa, 1996.* Available http://www.justice.gov.za/legislation/constitution/SAConstitution-web-eng.pdf.

Republic of South Africa. (2012). *Land Reform Policy Discussion Document*, June 2012. Pretoria: Government Printer.

Sasha, A. (2003). Women's Rights. *Global Issues*, March 14. Available http://www.globalissues.org/article/166/womens-rights.

South Africa History Online. (2004). *Land restitution in South Africa since 1994*. Available https://www.sahistory.org.za/article/land-restitution-south-africa-1994.

Stevens, C., & Ntlama, N. (2016). An overview of South Africa's institutional framework in promoting women's right to development. *Law, Democracy and Development, 20*, 46–68.

Swingler, H. (2015, 25 August). What the constitution promises women. University of Cape Town, *Monday Monthly*. Available https://www.news.uct.ac.za/edition/-edition/2015-08-25-edition-06/-article/2015-08-25-what-the-constitution-promises-women.

Tilley, S. (2007). *International comparative study of strategies for settlement support provision to land reform beneficiary*. Programme for Land and Agrarian Studies, Bellville: University of the Western Cape.

United Nation (UN). (2003). *Human Rights in the Administration of Justice: A Manual on Human Rights for Judges, Prosecutors and Lawyers*. New York and Geneva: United Nations.

Index

A. O. Akinola et al. (eds.), *The New Political Economy of Land Reform in South Africa*,
https://doi.org/10.1007/978-3-030-51129-6

M

N

P

The manufacturer's authorised representative in the EU is Springer Nature Customer Service Centre GmbH, Europaplatz 3, 69115 Heidelberg, Germany. If you have any concerns regarding our products, please contact ProductSafety@springernature.com

Printed and bound by CPI Group (UK) Ltd, Croydon, CR0 4YY
30/09/2026
02225696-0001